Event Management in Sport, Recreation, and Tourism

Now in a fully revised and updated fourth edition, *Event Management in Sport, Recreation, and Tourism* provides a comprehensive theoretical and practical framework for planning and managing events at all levels, from smaller local events to mega-events.

Focusing on the role of event manager and their diverse facilitation responsibilities through each phase of the event planning process, the book is designed to encourage critical thinking, to help the reader to become an adaptable and capable manager ready to cope with the constantly evolving challenges of the contemporary events landscape. The book begins with an updated chapter on the types of knowledge in event management, posing questions that help readers to understand their current knowledge, to decide what they need to pursue, and to advance their knowledge strategies. Containing a rich array of international, real-world case studies, data, and practical examples, from traditional and niche sport, recreation, and tourism contexts, this fourth edition is enhanced by a completely new chapter on practical advances in environmental sustainability that provides an overview of research as well as strategies for moving forward. The book goes further than any other event management textbook in placing social, ethical, and environmental responsibilities at the centre of the event planning process.

Event Management in Sport, Recreation, and Tourism is an essential reading for any student or practitioner working in event management, sport management, leisure management, outdoor recreation, or tourism.

Cheryl Mallen is Associate Professor in the Department of Sport Management at Brock University, Canada. Her research involves knowledge, event management, and environmental sustainability. She is well published, with articles in the *Journal of Sport Management*, *Sport Management Review*, and *European Sport Management Quarterly*, as well as other journal outlets.

Lorne J. Adams is Associate Professor (Retired) in the Department of Kinesiology at Brock University, Canada. He is the recipient of four teaching awards, including the prestigious 3M Teaching Fellowship. He has been a coach and served as Athletic Director for 10 years.

Event Management in Sport, Recreation, and Tourism

Theoretical and Practical Dimensions

Fourth Edition

Edited by

Cheryl Mallen and Lorne J. Adams

Routledge
Taylor & Francis Group
LONDON AND NEW YORK

Designed cover image: Ouchman/Getty images

Fourth edition published 2024
by Routledge
4 Park Square, Milton Park, Abingdon, Oxon, OX14 4RN

and by Routledge
605 Third Avenue, New York, NY 10158

Routledge is an imprint of the Taylor & Francis Group, an informa business

© 2024 selection and editorial matter, Cheryl Mallen and Lorne J. Adams; individual chapters, the contributors

The right of Cheryl Mallen and Lorne J. Adams to be identified as the authors of the editorial material, and of the authors for their individual chapters, has been asserted in accordance with sections 77 and 78 of the Copyright, Designs and Patents Act 1988.

All rights reserved. No part of this book may be reprinted or reproduced or utilised in any form or by any electronic, mechanical, or other means, now known or hereafter invented, including photocopying and recording, or in any information storage or retrieval system, without permission in writing from the publishers.

Trademark notice: Product or corporate names may be trademarks or registered trademarks, and are used only for identification and explanation without intent to infringe.

First edition published by Routledge 2008

Second edition published by Routledge 2013

Third edition published by Routledge 2017

British Library Cataloguing-in-Publication Data
A catalogue record for this book is available from the British Library

Library of Congress Cataloguing-in-Publication Data
Names: Mallen, Cheryl, editor. | Adams, Lorne James, editor.
Title: Event management in sport, recreation and tourism : theoretical and practical dimensions / edited by Cheryl Mallen and Lorne J. Adams.
Description: 4th edition. | New York : Routledge, 2024. | "First edition published by Routledge 2008. Third edition published by Routledge 2017"--t.p. verso. | Includes bibliographical references and index. |
Identifiers: LCCN 2023038344 | ISBN 9781032488486 (hbk) | ISBN 9781032488479 (pbk) | ISBN 9781003391098 (ebk)
Subjects: LCSH: Special events--Management. | Sports administration. | Recreation--Management. | Tourism--Management.
Classification: LCC GT3405 .E9 2024 | DDC 796.06/9--dc23/eng/20231030
LC record available at https://lccn.loc.gov/2023038344

ISBN: 978-1-032-48848-6 (hbk)
ISBN: 978-1-032-48847-9 (pbk)
ISBN: 978-1-003-39109-8 (ebk)

DOI: 10.4324/9781003391098

Typeset in Optima
by Deanta Global Publishing Services, Chennai, India

Contents

List of Contributors		*xiii*
Preface to the Fourth Edition		*xv*
Acknowledgements		*xvii*

1 Hosting traditional and niche events in sport, recreation, and tourism: Knowledge required for success in practice   **1**
Cheryl Mallen

Pursue perspicacity	2
Nurture your flexibility effect	2
Understand niche and traditional events	4
Niche events	4
Traditional events	9
Build your bank of knowledge for hosting niche and/or	
traditional events	12
Common knowledge	13
Advancement knowledge	13
Plan to advance your common and advancement knowledge	15
Conclusion: So, what do you need to know to build for	
success in sport, recreation, and tourism event management?	20
Chapter questions	21
References	22

2 Building fundamental knowledge to be a facilitator of events   **24**
Amy Cunningham and Joanne MacLean

Facilitation by Amy Cunningham	25
What is facilitation?	25

Facilitating communication requirements	27
Facilitating group communication requirements: the case of group rhythm and facilitation	30
Facilitating knowledge transfer	33
Facilitating event structures for governance by Joanne MacLean	34
Event structures	35
Theoretical dimensions of event structures	36
Principles in event structures	39
Application of theory and principles in event structures	41
Conclusions	42
Chapter Questions	43
References	43

3 The development phase of the event planning model — 45
Maureen Connolly and Lorne J. Adams

Facilitating the development of event goals and objectives	45
Examples of event goals and objectives	46
Facilitating event policy development	47
Facilitating policy congruence	49
Assignment A – Staff and volunteer training program	50
Assignment B – Event contracts	50
Assignment C – Event permits and liability insurance	51
Assignment D – The event communication system	51
Example: Policy becomes praxis	51
Assignment E – The event communication system	52
The challenge of facilitating policy statements into practice	55
Facilitating event volunteer management *by Lorne Adams*	55
A volunteer management program	56
Conclusions	64
Chapter questions	64
References	65

4 The event operational planning phase of the event planning model — 67
Cheryl Mallen

Mechanism 1: The cultivation of the operational planning network	67
Application of contingency theory	70

Application of complexity theory	70
Application of dissipative structures	70
Application of agency theory	71
Application of the theory of marginal gains	72
Mechanism 2: Generating written operational plans	72
The written event operational plan: Establishing a design format	73
Logical operational planning	73
Sequential operational planning	74
Detailed operational planning	75
Assignment A: Level 3 planning	76
Mechanism 3: The inclusion of contingency and emergency plans	76
Assignment B: Contingency issues	79
Mechanism 4: Update and test the communication system	80
Assignment C: Develop a diagram of the communication structure	81
Mechanism 5: Establish meeting agendas	81
Assignment D: Meeting agenda development	83
Mechanism 6: Integrating the operational plans between event components	83
Assignment E: Integration of operational plans	84
Mechanism 7: Prepare for event issues and political 'games' with a guiding ethical statement	84
Mechanism 8: Preparing for the activation of the operational plans	86
Mechanism 9: Practice to develop your operational planning skills	86
Conclusions	88
Chapter questions	88
References	89
Appendix A: Case study – An event volunteer management operational plan	91
Case assignment	91
Appendix B: Case study – Segments of operational plan for event transportation	97
Appendix C: Case study - Sections of operational plan on the hospitality component	105

5 Issues and management strategies in event operational planning 115
Nicole Greco and Cheryl Mallen

Defining issues management	115
Knowledge in issues management	115
Best practices	116
Events as legacies	117
Event issues and management strategies	117
Timing issues	118
Accountability/authority issues	119
Knowledge management issues	120
Funding issues	121
Relationship issues	122
Turnover of staff/volunteer's issues	124
Case assignments	124
What can event managers do about arising event issues?	128
Conclusions	129
Chapter questions	129
References	130
Appendix: A research strategy for determining event issues and strategies	133
A modified Delphi research technique	133
The interview and questionnaire framework	134
The Delphi participants	134
Data analysis	135

6 The event implementation, monitoring, and management phase of the event planning model 136
Lorne J. Adams

Implementation: executing the plan	136
Disseminating implementation requirements and hosting production meetings	137
Monitoring the dynamic and fluid operational environment	139
Managing operational plan implementation	140
Overcome foreseeable failure when managing deviations from the plan	141
Predetermine the decision-making team and process	143
Programmed and non-programmed decisions	144

Inherent implementation, monitoring, and management issues in operational network practice	144
Issue: operational plan detail and implementation performance	145
Issue: implementation knowledge and performance	146
Issue: Deviations from the plan	147
Issue: Implementation conflict	147
Issue: Implementation communication	152
Conclusions	152
Chapter questions	153
References	153

7 The event evaluation and renewal phase of the event planning model — 155
Scott Forrester and Lorne J. Adams

Background knowledge for the event manager	155
What is an evaluation?	155
Why is evaluation necessary?	156
What are the key evaluation questions to ask?	158
What are the other areas of consideration when designing an evaluation?	159
What is the role of theory in evaluating events	169
What are the general steps for conducting evaluations and making decisions?	170
The Three Horizons for event renewal and growth over time	171
Conclusions	172
Chapter questions	173
References	173

8 Safeguarding the natural environment in event management — 175
Greg Dingle, Chris Chard, and Matt Dolf

What is environmental sustainability?	175
Why is environmental sustainability important in event management?	177
Environmental change, vulnerability, and the need for resilience and adaptation for sport, recreation, and tourism events	178

Roles and responsibilities for environmental sustainability in
  event management 180
The triple top line and the triple bottom line 183
Life cycle assessment 184
Carbon footprint 186
Ecological footprint 186
Assignment A: Understanding event-related, environmentally
  focused organizations 187
Assignment B: Event decision-making for environmental
  sustainability 188
Assignment C: Ace Corporation Triathlon Group (ACTG)
  sustainability ownership and accountability 189
Assignment D: Using a carbon footprint to minimize
  accommodation impact 190
Conclusions 191
Chapter questions 192
References 192

9 Environmental sustainability in sport, recreation, and tourism: "You ain't seen nothing yet" 199

Cheryl Mallen, Justine Schwende, Efthalie (Elia) Chatzigianni

Calls to enact environmental sustainability 200
Sport, recreation, and tourism environmental sustainability in
  practice 201
    Events and network relationships that aid in
      environmental sustainability 201
    Events and environmental awareness programs 202
    Event actions toward carbon neutrality to improve air quality 203
Event facilities and environmental sustainability 205
  Event facilities and renewable energy 205
  Event facilities generating waste mitigation and efficiencies 206
  Event facilities and water safeguards 207
Events and other environmental strategies 208
Research in event sport, recreation, and tourism environmental
  sustainability 208
Moving forward in event environmental sustainability 211
  Apply appreciative theory for a mindset that seeks solutions 211

Contents

	Embed environmental actions	212
	Generate leadership to guide the way forward	212
	Conclusions	214
	Chapter questions	214
	References	215

10 Event bidding — 223
Cheryl Mallen

	What is a feasibility study?	223
	What is a candidature document?	224
	What is a bid questionnaire?	224
	What is a bid dossier?	226
	What is a bid tour?	228
	What are the critical factors in a successful bid?	229
	What is one critical factor for bid success?	234
	Conclusions	236
	Chapter questions	237
	References	237

11 Politics in event bidding and hosting — 239
Trish Chant-Sehl

	What is meant by the "politics of events?"	239
	Politics in the decision to bid or not to bid	241
	Politics in the event bid phase – the committee	242
	Politics in the event bid phase – the proposal	244
	Politics in the event bid phase – the decision-makers	247
	Politics in the event bid transition and review phase	248
	Politics in the event hosting phase	250
	Overcoming politics in event bidding	251
	A key factor in managing event politics – consistent communication messaging	252
	A key factor in managing event politics – establishing core values	252
	Conclusions	254
	Chapter questions	254
	References	254

12 Facilitating quality in event management   256
Craig Hyatt and Chris Chard

Can an event manager meet all requirements for quality? 256
What is quality? 257
Quality is defined as ruggedness and longevity in the
    manufacturing industry 257
Definitions for quality in the service industry 257
Expanded meanings of quality 258
    Quality is conformance to specifications 258
    Quality is excellence 259
    Quality is value 259
    Quality is meeting and/or exceeding customers' expectations 260
    Aesthetic quality 260
    Functional quality 261
    Technical quality 261
A lack of guidance for quality in event management 262
Issues in creating quality statements and defining quality in
    event management 264
    Limited control over inputs influences quality 264
    Financial constraints influence quality 265
    Issues in stakeholder expectations as quality perceptions 266
    Contingency plans influence quality 267
Assignment 1: Evaluate sample quality statements 268
    Quality statement for Rally in the Valley 269
    Quality statement for Nantou Balloon Fest 270
    Quality statement for Rocking on the River 270
Assignment 2: Generate your quality statement for the work of
    an event manager 271
Conclusions 272
Chapter questions 273
References 273

13 Conclusions   275
Lorne J. Adams

Index   *281*

Contributors

Trish Chant-Sehl is Director of University Advancement at McMaster University, Hamilton, Ontario, Canada.

Efthalie (Elia) Chatzigianni is Associate Professor in the Department of Sport Management and Organization at the University of Peloponnese, Greece.

Chris Chard is Associate Professor in the Department of Sport Management at Brock University, St. Catharines, Ontario, Canada.

Maureen Connolly is Professor in the Department of Kinesiology at Brock University, St. Catharines, Ontario, Canada.

Amy Cunningham is a musician and recording artist at Independent, Vancouver, British Columbia, Canada.

Greg Dingle is Lecturer in Sport Management at the Centre for Sport and Social Impact in the Department of Management and Marketing at La Trobe Business School, La Trobe University, Bundoora, Australia.

Matt Dolf is Director of the Office of Wellbeing Strategy at the University of British Columbia, Vancouver, British Columbia.

Scott Forrester is Associate Professor in the Department of Recreation and Leisure Studies at Brock University, St. Catharines, Ontario, Canada.

Nicole Greco is a graduate of the MA Program in the Department of Sport Management at Brock University, St. Catharines, Ontario, Canada.

Contributors

Craig Hyatt is Associate Professor in the Department of Sport Management at Brock University, St. Catharines, Ontario, Canada.

Joanne MacLean is Dean in the Faculty of Health Sciences at the University of the Fraser Valley, Abbotsford, British Columbia, Canada.

Scott McRoberts is the Athletic Director at the University of Guelph, Ontario, Canada.

Preface to the Fourth Edition

Objectives

- To focus on a readership that includes second- and third-year higher education students in the fields of sport, recreation, sport tourism, and/or program management.
- To provide a combination of theoretical foundations, practical principles, and examples that specifically relate to event operational planning and management.
- To encourage students and practitioners to act as critical interpreters of the requirements for event environmental management. The text will avoid providing a series of checklists as this does not reflect the fluidity of environmental management or foster critical thinking.
- To provide theoretical information and show how theory integrates with the practical elements of the subject in a manner that assists students to be event managers.
- To present an operational planning model for event environmental management, including the bidding phase; the development phase; the logistical phase; the implementation, monitoring, and management phase; and the evaluation and renewal phase.
- To avoid the general approach of other textbooks in the field of event management which tend to have a formulaic application and to concentrate only on the operational planning aspects.

An overview of the focus of this text

This text focuses on sport, recreation, and tourism event management and emphasizes the complex role of an event manager as a facilitator throughout the event planning phases.

Preface to the Fourth Edition

Other textbooks provide one chapter on each of the multiple areas of events (including one chapter on marketing, one on selling sponsorship, one on law and liability, etc.) or they have offered a "to-do list" for creating an event. There are a multitude of courses and textbooks on event and facility management in the areas of marketing, law, and human resource management. However, none of these textbooks in the marketplace concentrate specifically on the theoretical foundations and practical principles of event operational planning, or provide examples. The contemporary sport, recreation, and tourism manager needs a text that concentrates on the application of theory to practice, specifically in event management.

Event elements within the framework of this text

An event manager has a complex role in the staging of an event that necessitates managing a multitude of activities within a changing event environment. In performing this role, both depth and breadth of knowledge are necessary across multiple areas of focus. These areas of focus include the four phases of the planning model:

1 the development phase
2 the logistical phase
3 the implementation, monitoring and management phase
4 the evaluation and renewal phase

Additionally, knowledge is needed in areas such as bidding, environmental sustainability, and the management of the politics associated with events, along with staff and volunteer management. Furthermore, an event manager's training needs to be diverse and extend beyond the focus of this text. Examples of additional areas within the realm of event management are financial management, marketing, sponsorship, facility management, and law. Each of these areas of expertise can be applied to the organizing and production of an event, and each is sufficiently important to warrant a full text on their topics. There are multiple texts on the market that focus on these additional areas of event management – but not on the role of the event manager as a facilitator during operational planning. Therefore, this text aims to concentrate on that gap in the literature.

Acknowledgements

Cheryl Mallen would like to acknowledge her wonderful family for a lifetime of support and encouragement. Love to you all!

Lorne J. Adams would like to acknowledge Liana for her support and patience with this project. Thanks also to my co-editor, Cheryl, who has redefined the meaning of deadlines and turnaround time. I am dedicating this edition to Bruce Wormald, a dear friend, who always believed in me and supported me even when I doubted myself.

1

Hosting traditional and niche events in sport, recreation, and tourism

Knowledge required for success in practice

Cheryl Mallen

Event management is a vital topic because of the relevance of sport, recreation, and tourism events to a "country's, culture, community, and economy" (Hussein & Mohamed, 2013, p. 39). Developing your knowledge is critical for meeting the challenge of getting into – and working successfully within – the event management industry. This means going beyond gaining and understanding "information" on what something means, toward advancing your "knowledge" to an ability of *how* to do it (Victer, 2020). In event management, your career may depend on your knowledge of *how* to plan.

In this chapter, the focus is on operational planning for any of the multiple components of an event. These components include, for example: event accreditation, accommodation, ceremonies (including opening, closing, and awards), financial management, food & beverage management, human resource management, governance (including a working knowledge of organizational event structures, strategic alliances, policies, and the impact of globalization), law and its application (including negotiations, contract development, licencing, and understanding/enacting laws for events concerning eliminating discrimination), the professional management of participants, officials, the media and public relations strategies, medical services, security, ticketing, transportation, venue management, warehousing, social responsibility, along with effective event environmental sustainability. It is

> ***Perspicacity:*** the development of your knowledge that leads to personal quick insights and understandings for efficient and effective decisions and actions, including the management of any event issues. Such insights and understandings help make you competent in the event management industry.
>
> In other words, you have instincts concerning the best decisions for an event based on your knowledge – developed through a combination of coursework and practical experience at events and in life.

Figure 1.1 Perspicacity defined

the position of the author of this chapter that planning skills are needed for a plethora of positions in the sport, recreation, and tourism industries.

Whatever component(s) of event management you choose as a focus, it is imperative that you plan your pursuit of knowledge in a manner that leads to *perspicacity*. In combination with perspicacity, you need to nurture your *flexibility effect*, understand *niche and traditional events*, and develop *common and advancement knowledge*. Let's examine each of these concepts.

Pursue perspicacity

The question arises: what are you trying to obtain through your education and efforts in gaining work experience? It is the position of the author that, overall, you are trying to obtain knowledge that leads to *perspicacity*. This *perspicacity* involves the development of quick insights and understandings that support actions that make you competent in the sport, recreation, and/or tourism industry. In event management, this competence stems from an ability to make decisions, to plan, to implement planned activities, and to manage arising issues when hosting events. Your perspicacity can make you an efficient and effective event manager (Figure 1.1).

To obtain perspicacity in event management, you are encouraged to nurture your flexibility effect, gain understandings of the different types of events (including niche and traditional events), and continuously build your bank of common and advancement knowledge. Let's now move to discuss these topics.

Nurture your flexibility effect

You are working to become an asset for the event industry. One way to continuously build on your abilities is to develop and apply your individual perspectives, opinions, approaches, experiences, ideas, and options, which can help create knowledge differentiation, or what has been termed one's "*flexibility effect*[s]" (Connor & Prahalad, 2002). This means that the impact of your personality, your motivations, perceptions, understandings of change and its impacts, along with your communication, socialization, and interpretation skills, and specific learning (such as understandings of emerging technologies in event management or the application of strategies for effective environmental sustainability) are critical in developing your competitive advantage. This advantage is produced as building your abilities in multiple areas improves your insights and understandings, which will help you to use your knowledge effectively, or develop new knowledge for the event industry. Your *flexibility effect* is based on your individual viewpoint(s), which are foundational to developing instincts concerning decisions and actions. Your *flexibility effect* is therefore, an important element in your pursuit of knowledge that leads to *perspicacity*.

An example of a *flexibility effect* involves an individual who has developed excellent socialization skills. They can apply their skills to the dissemination of event instructions to staff/volunteers in a manner that is motivating to others, and to making staff/volunteers comfortable in bringing arising issues to their attention throughout the hosting of an event. Additionally, their socialization skills involve an ability to listen to staff/volunteer feedback, and to developed instincts concerning the management of a variety of individual personalities involved in an event. Another example involves an individual who has experience with another culture (from travel and family experiences). They can use their understandings of cultural differences to effectively manage the variety of people that may be involved in an event.

To advance your *flexibility effect*, one must accept, nurture, and build on your differentiated ideas, communication style, personal interpretations of knowledge, understandings of other points of view, while being open to considering a range of responses necessary in event management. Such differentiation can impact decisions – and help you to communicate decisions – positioning you and your specific *flexibility effect* as a competitive advantage (Figure 1.2).

Your knowledge, perspicacity, and flexibility effect can be applied to either niche or traditional events. We now move the discussion to an outline of the characteristics of both types of events.

> ***Flexibility effect:*** involves nurturing your personal perspectives, opinions, approaches, experiences, ideas, and options to create knowledge differentiation, or one's "flexibility effect[s]." Differentiated ideas, interpretations of knowledge, responses, and ability to communicate event operational plans helps you to develop instincts based on your individual viewpoint and provides a potential competitive advantage.
>
> In other words, it is important to nurture your position on topics and strategies – as well as to learn from others – in the process of building your knowledge and advancing your ability to use such knowledge to any effect in the industry.

Figure 1.2 Flexibility effect defined

Understand niche and traditional events

Consider the potential number of events that are hosted every year – and the number of associated event managers. In many countries throughout the world, there are event managers hosting tourism-focused festivals/shows, conferences, and banquets. Additionally, local recreational sport events abound. Further, competitive sport events encompass the local, regional, provincial/state, national, and international levels, and many are hosted to promote tourism. These events include a plethora of leagues, circuits, or tours for a variety of age groups and abilities. Add to this the number of niche events (or novel, next generation events) being invented and the number of event managers required increases concomitantly.

The exact number of sport, recreation, and tourism event managers needed for the events held annually worldwide is unknown. Calculations are difficult due to the complex conditions of the event industry. However, a general estimation is that millions of events are staged, and each one needs a well informed, prepared, knowledgeable, and experienced event manager. There is, thus, a demand for those who are building their knowledge for perspicacity (and applying their flexibility effect) for the field of event management.

Now, let's examine the two event typologies – niche events and traditional events. Both have specific characteristics. We begin with the ever-growing field of niche events.

Niche events

A niche event is forged through innovations that either alter or renew an event, or generate a completely new event for a particular audience or group of participants. Anyone can design and host niche events by setting new directions and offering creative event opportunities. It takes inventiveness and skill to plan the components of an event. Many niche events are hybrid events. This means that niche events can be created on the basis of recognizable activities from other events, such as sporting events, that are then altered to produce the new generation of the event.

Niche events are springing up throughout the world in unconventional forms. There are multiple manners in which to make the event unique; examples abound, including:

Examples of niche events as tourism destinations: Scandinavian iceberg and northern lights sightseeing events; South African slum jeep tours; Niagara-on-the-Lake, Canada, ghost tours of historical homes; Nik Wallenda high wire tight rope walks between skyscrapers, held in key cities around the world; along with the ever evolving cultural or heritage festivals and celebration events springing up within communities.

Examples of niche events generated to market a particular product: Red Bull (an energy drink company) created their "crashed ice" series of events whereby competitors wear ice hockey equipment, including skates and helmets, and race down a man-made undulating course made of ice. Competitors must skate downhill, jump, navigate fast turns, and beat other competitors on the racecourse, as well as the clock and time from other races. Red Bull has also hosted their Stratos event, or a free fall space dive, among other events.

Examples of niche events using unique venues: events have been held in castles (or in castle grounds), on a ship that is anchored or floating past patrons on shore; and in the sky. It is predicted that more niche events will be held in the sky with an increased use of drones and rockets.

Examples of niche recreational or competitive sport events that have been designed by changing the playing surface: volleyball has been played on a variety of courts such outdoors in winter for "snow volleyball" and on a platform in a body of water during the summer months for "water volleyball," or "bossaball," in which a type of volleyball is played on an inflatable bouncy floor. Additionally, niche basketball events have been played on a series of conjoined trampolines instead of a traditional basketball court. Meanwhile, snowmobile racing has moved to the summer months and races have been held on grass. Niche skiing and snowboarding events have been conducted around the world on hills of sand instead of mountains of snow. Niche bike events include bike polo played on cement instead of on horses and grass. The Antarctic ice marathon uses trails of ice. Further, examples include Association football (soccer in North America) that is played on sand instead of grass, and "teqball," with a curved pingpong-type table where the feet and body are used to get the ball back and forth between team members. A final example includes underwater hockey played in a pool.

Examples of niche events generated by adapting the player format to design a niche event: examples include basketball 3-on-3 formats, and cricket that is played indoors with six players on each side.

Examples of changing the rules to design a niche event: examples include the World Outdoor (Ice) Hockey Championship that uses adapted rules to award a goal for each penalty to avoid having a participant sit out in the cold to serve the penalty; or "snowkiting" in which the rules allow the snowboard to be attached to a kite that aids participants to traverse up and down hills. Also, pickleball uses a tennis net but changes the rules of tennis to allow the use of a ping pong-style racket and plastic ball with adaptive rules.

Examples of niche events created by extending and/or combining sporting activities: this has included an adapted rhythmic gymnastics team event for men that combines dance and tumbling routines. There is an Asian-developed version of volleyball that involves a lower net and three players per side with no hands allowed. Players kick and head the ball back and forth over the net, and can leap, twist, and flip, using martial arts and gymnastics moves, to return the ball back over the net. The T-Rex race held in Japan involves a running race on the beach with each contestant in an inflatable T-Rex costume. Additionally, there is cycleball, which uses a bicycle to move a ball around an indoor court. A final example includes a version of chessboxing for a combined brains and brawn event that involves switching between rounds of boxing and playing chess.

Examples of niche events focused on a particular skill: this type of niche event includes the golf long ball/drive and hole-in-one contests; baseball home run derbies; basketball dunking contests; ice hockey shooting skills competitions; and rugby skills challenges involving catching, passing, kicking, and overall agility.

Characteristics of niche events

There are three key characteristics of niche events. The first is that the event is created and adapted for a particular sport, recreation, or tourism audience. The second is that there does not have to be a governing body that has established time-honoured rules and regulations, although an organizing body may exist that can provide rules and regulations for the event being held at a particular time – with the option to change the rules in the future. The third characteristic is that the event may exhibit recognizable components (such as elements from a sport) or may be fully unconventional in its form.

A niche event can be continuously adapted for a particular audience. The event can be adapted at any time to incorporate innovative designs or meet the changing needs of the participants, tourists/spectators, or marketing requirements. Adaptations can be made to any individual element of the event, or the entire event can be adapted at any given time. Niche events involve the freedom to design an event with the use of conventional or unconventional components or activities. This type of event, thus, can be adapted to another generation of the event at any time for a particular audience. Whatever the focus, an individual event, a circuit of events, or a league at the local, regional, national, or international level, the possibility remains for full scale changes to the niche event at any time based on the needs of the audience and the planning ability of the event manager.

One of the reasons a niche event can adapt to a particular audience quickly is that it does not have a governing body establishing rules and regulations that have been devised over time and must be followed every time the event is hosted. The rules and regulations established are not expected to be passed down from generation to generation or from event to event – they can be brand new! There is always the potential for adapting the rules and regulations due to the influences of culture or of the incorporation of new equipment technology, or for adapting for a particular age group, type of abilities, or the creative genius of the event manager.

Niche events exist in multiple forms, as the use of innovative designs and formats generates new sport, recreational, and/or tourism events. In this realm of new development, the question arises: why have niche events been advancing in our times?

Cheryl Mallen

Why are niche events on the rise?

The author of this chapter proposes that niche events stem from an outgrowth of our need to learn about, and to practice for, the changes that we face in society and in our institutions. Change is not new, as there has been a demand for developing the skills necessary for managing evolutionary change over millennia that includes survival contingent on individual or group adaptability. Our contemporary time of change has been noted as including an environment of complexity and unpredictability and we must, thus, learn to adapt to this environment (Choo & Bontis, 2002; Curado & Bontis, 2006; Lee & Shek, 2022). Niche events in sport, recreation, and tourism provide opportunities to practice for such change.

In the process of learning to accommodate change, a concept has surfaced that was coined by Limerick, Cunnington, and Crowther (1998) as "*collaborative individualism*" (p. 103). This concept involves a group or a collective of responsible individuals being "held together by common cultures, shared world meanings, and values" (Limerick et al., p. 128). This collective encourages the development of a mindset that one must embrace being an individual who is able to collaborate with others and who must innovate to survive. Each of these elements must be embraced simultaneously, and all members within the collective must have a voice. At the grassroots level, *collaborative individualism* occurs as groups use innovative design to create niche events. Bound together by common threads from an event's culture, meaning, and value, groups can create, share, and nurture adapted meanings and values to create niche events. These niche events can be described as design experiments. As these individuals retain and develop their personal voice, they are encouraged to collaborate to develop innovations for managing our contemporary environment. Niche events offer an opportunity to experiment with *collaborative individualism*. These experimentations offer an opportunity to test what will work on a larger scale and with different participants or audiences. Further, niche events provide experiences that help one develop a mindset for adaptations and innovations, along with practical experience in change management. Learning about such events is part of your base of knowledge for the event industry. Anyone can design and host a niche event.

An example of "*collaborative individualism*" could be an individual who enjoys volleyball, but who does not want to be restrained by traditional regulations. So, they gather other like-minded individuals and collaborate on the development of a niche volleyball event (i.e., one in which you are only allowed to use your head and shoulders during play). This group exhibits the shared desire to play volleyball outside the bounds of tradition – but they are not eliminated from playing traditional volleyball with others.

Use creativity to design and host a niche event

What niche events have you heard of or witnessed? What niche event could you develop? Niche events continue to emerge and are expanding the array of sport, recreation, and tourism events being produced annually. You can start a local trend that could expand into a worldwide phenomenon. Begin by testing a niche event at a small local venue, recruit others willing to participate, and gain event management experience along the way. Consider adaptations or innovations that could be made within an event that has occurred in the past, and let them give rise to a novel or niche event. This niche event does not have to be a wholesale innovation. It can involve basic, simple adaptations, or it can generate a completely innovative event for a particular audience. Remember, someone designed each niche event and had the courage to host such an event. Some event managers have established and advanced their careers through this avenue. Can you design a niche event that could potentially be implemented in the future? If so, what would you do to generate an innovation? Or, perhaps, you would prefer to work on a traditional event.

Traditional events

Traditional events are also thriving worldwide. Traditional events generally have two key characteristics. The first characteristic is that there is a governing body. This body establishes and enforces standardized rules and regulations to be followed during the production of the event, and sanctions participants or events that do not follow the rules. This governing body can be structured as an organization, association, or federation that governs the event. Their rules and regulations specify elements, such as constitutive rules on the competition area dimensions and equipment; the regulative rules or policies that dictate participants age, weight, gender, status, nationality, dress, number of participants, and acceptable actions for participation; and auxiliary rules based on eligibility or ineligibility, the use of new technology, etc.

Examples encompass governing bodies for traditional multi-sport events that extend from the local recreational community event, such as age-based activities, to large-scale competitions that promote tourism markets, such as the Indigenous Games, African Games, Asian Games, and Commonwealth Games, along with the Olympic and Paralympic Games. Additionally, single sport events have governing bodies, for example the Cricket World Cup, Rugby World Cup, Tour de France Cycling, and Wimbledon Tennis. Some of the governing bodies hold influence within a particular country, such as with box lacrosse in Canada; high kick and leg wrestling competitions in the Arctic; hurling and Gaelic football in Ireland; rodeo and jai alai in the United States; sumo wrestling in Japan; and ringball and jukskei in South Africa.

The various governing bodies can have influence at any of a multitude of levels from the local to the regional, provincial/state, national, or international levels. This means, for example, that the governing body can influence events held at the recreational level – so a community recreational activity can be hosted in a manner that exhibits the same rules and regulations as formal high-level competitive events. These activities encompass a wide range from archery to yachting.

The second characteristic of a traditional event is that the activity is recognizable and time-honoured. Adaptations can be made to the activity, including the need to adapt for the age of the participant population or due to the impact of new technologies. A traditional event may undergo adaptations or transformations over time, however these transformations do not give rise to an entirely new event. Change is limited. There is universality in the implementation that is repeated and traditional. From generation to generation the event is conducted and practiced following the rules and regulations, including the traditions, customs, and routines for a consistent, mature, respected, and recognizable event. The general rules for a traditional event are followed even as the focus changes from a recreational activity to a high level of competition and/or a tourism event.

An example of a recognizable and time-honoured traditional event is Association football (or soccer in North America). This sport can be played on a range of levels, from a local recreational level to elite competition, with a generally consistent use of rules and regulations at any level making the event time-honoured and recognizable. If played in a single game, league, or circuit format, the rules and regulations for the events are standardized by the bodies that govern. Multiple bodies govern football/soccer throughout the local, regional, provincial, or state, national, and international levels throughout the world. Some bodies adapt the rules for their purposes, such as age levels, however the event itself resembles the football/soccer that is played worldwide. Even when it is not a formal local recreational activity – just a makeshift activity with a homemade ball and makeshift fields – the players can attempt to emulate the characteristics of the traditional event.

Niche events can evolve into traditional events

Niche events can evolve into a traditional event. Examples can be found in the 2024 Summer Olympic Games in Paris list of competitions. Some of the events include niche events that have now moved to traditional forms and have been included in the competition schedule at the highest level of competition – including sport climbing, skateboarding, and breaking (or break dancing).

The triathlon is another example of a niche sport that has become a traditional event. This tri-activity sport event combines three events. The events have been adapted depending on where the event is held around the world and who designed the event. Many of the events use a combination of swimming, cycling, and running or walking. The combination of sporting activities for this niche event grew from a local to an international phenomenon. Consistent event categories were used in many of the events. For instance, the Ironman Triathlon, such as the event held in Hawaii, USA, and others held around the world, implements regulations for the event combination of swimming, cycling, and running that are practiced in a consistent manner year after year. The triathlon event was eventually accepted into the group of sports to be staged at the Olympic Summer Games. This acceptance meant that Games participants were selected from a series of triathlon events conducted with standardized rules and regulations. In addition, there was recognition of the event as a triathlon at every level from local to internationally staged events when these three event combinations were used. It was at this point that the triathlon entered the realm of a traditional event.

Even as the triathlon has evolved into a traditional event, it continues to develop as a niche event. The niche triathlon event has been spurred on by continuing to adapt the multi-activity event elements. This includes adapting to use two sport activities, such as walking and cycling, or adjusting to allow a team of three members to compete, each completing one of the activities. This continual use of adaptations to the triathlon keeps the event in the realm of niche events. This means that the triathlon can be categorized as a traditional event while remaining, sometimes, a niche event.

Further examples of events that were born as niche events and evolved to become traditional events can be found in the sport of skiing/snowboarding. Events such as mogul competitions, the half-pipe, ski cross, and ski dancing began as niche events – and then these events transformed into traditional events. Volleyball is a further example of a traditional event that generated a niche element. Beach volleyball has now become a traditional event. Today, many events with niche roots have been included in major traditional events and now have standardized traditional rules and regulations.

The demand for event managers for niche and traditional events requires the development of the knowledge (including perspicacity) that supports the hosting of a successful event.

Build your bank of knowledge for hosting niche and/or traditional events

Getz and Page (2016) stated that "increasingly it will be necessary to 'custom-design' highly targeted event experiences, and this has to be based on greater knowledge" (p. 620). This knowledge includes *common knowledge* and *advancement knowledge*. Both types of knowledge are needed and can increase your abilities and the success of an organization (Gupta et al., 2022) – and in this case, this knowledge can aid in your success as an event manager (Figure 1.3).

> ***Common Knowledge:*** stems from your general understandings of topics. Common knowledge can be obtained by reading, completing research, taking classes, gaining experiences in the industry, having a mentor, etc. It is the foundation upon which you make judgements. This type of knowledge is needed in the pursuit of *perspicacity* for competence in the event management industry.
>
> Common knowledge in event management encompasses, for example, general understandings of event industry organizations, the events hosted, the role of the event manager and the working context, the communication systems, decision-making processes, encultured knowledge (general understandings of a variety of cultures in our global world), enbrained knowledge (general ability to think through the requirements for hosting an event – a niche or traditional event), and basic understandings of the impact of emerging technology on events.

Figure 1.3 Common knowledge defined

Common knowledge

Common knowledge involves general understandings. This type of event management knowledge can be verbalized, recorded, and shared through interactions (Abbas et al., 2022; Spender, 2002). These knowledge-sharing interactions can include, for example, taking classes that relate to the various event components outlined at the beginning of this chapter, reading related research, participating in experiential activities in the field where you can observe actions and participate in the industry (without high levels of responsibility), and by having conversations with individuals in any area of focus in event management. Both classroom instructors, along with individuals within the industry, can describe, teach, and guide the acquisition of and development of your common knowledge. Each interaction helps to contextualize, interpret, and conceive of options for use when you are working within the industry.

Common knowledge is, thus, explicit, and provides a foundation that is necessary for your participation in the event management industry. This is because your common knowledge is built on your existing knowledge. The expansion of your base of knowledge is used to make decisions as well as to judge the value of new knowledge (or new ways to conduct events), and facilitates the integration of one's currently held knowledge with new knowledge. This common knowledge becomes "the platform for everything else. It lies deep and brings together, in contextualised thought and action" (Spender, 2002, p. 157). For example, an understanding of ethics helps you to develop a guiding ethical statement that you can use in decision-making when in the event industry. Building *common knowledge* generates cognitive understandings and positions you with basic competence in the field. The more varied your common knowledge, the greater the foundational base of event management knowledge you develop.

Advancement knowledge

In contrast, developing *advancement knowledge* can really set you apart in the industry. This is because *advancement knowledge* is in-depth knowledge that can lead to a high level of competence in the event industry – *it is implicit*. *Advancement knowledge* encompasses a variety of forms – and takes them from common basic understandings of the form to in-depth understandings. One form involves *enbrained knowledge*, or an ability to mentally think through the requirements for planning an event without a template. This type of knowledge means you have planning skills that allow you to go beyond the strategies previously used to organize event activities and to apply your knowledge based on the specific event type, the facility used, and the available resources, including the staff and volunteers, financing, and available technology. The planning level is logical, sequential, and importantly, detailed. Meanwhile, *encultured knowledge* can be advancement knowledge if you have developed beyond basic understandings of the various world cultures and of how to build individuals into an effective working team. This in-depth knowledge enables you to effectively work with people from other cultures by understanding their needs and cultural impacts. Another type of knowledge involves novel elements being integrated into event management. An example includes emerging technologies that use artificial intelligence (AI) to determine "the best staffing, logistics, and budget for the event; monitor changes to the budget and scheduled activities" (Hussein & Mohamed, 2013, p. 30) (Figure 1.4).

Moving beyond common knowledge to advancement knowledge involves obtaining personal experience(s), as it is not usually expressed (Abbas et al., 2022). This lack of expression is because the knowledge can be tacit (held in one's mind), can stem from experienced instincts, and can be hard for one to describe. It may, however, be shared by spending time with those that have such knowledge and learning about best practices (Abbas et al., 2022).

Pursuing experiences with high levels of responsibility in the industry supports the development of advancement knowledge.

Advancement Knowledge: This is in-depth knowledge acquired from experiences that include high levels of responsibility in the industry. It can be tacit (held in your mind) as it is developed through your personal experiences. It is critical to your *perspicacity* for competence in the industry.

Advancement knowledge in event management encompasses, for example, *intimate* knowledge on hosting events, including managing arising political issues and associated pressures, understanding the intricacies of working with those from various cultures; having the ability to develop excellent logical, sequential, and very detailed operational plans that staff/volunteers can follow with few arising questions or issues; along with having instincts for successfully managing the changes that can occur in events.

Figure 1.4 Advancement knowledge defined

Plan to advance your common and advancement knowledge

You can develop a plan to aid in attaining knowledge to advance your common and advancement knowledge for the event industry. A format is now offered that encourages you to: (a) recognize the common and advancement knowledge that you have concerning the event industry, (b) outline what additional knowledge you need to attain, and (c) to plan how you can acquire the knowledge necessary for success in the event industry.

Complete the ten key questions posed below that are designed to help you prepare a strategy to advance your overall *perspicacity* for the event management industry. The questions are made for you to consider the development of your *flexibility effect*, your *common*, and your *advancement knowledge*, and your understandings of *niche and traditional events* in the event industry, along with your skills in managing staff and volunteers. The questions may not be able to be completed in one sitting; the answers need to be developed over time – as is your knowledge.

1. *Select an event where you'd like to be the event manager (consider any event level from a local to the international level).*
   Event selected: _____
2. *What do you know about the history of your selected event?*
   Record specifically what you know about the history of the event.
   (a) Then, rate your level of common knowledge on the history of the event:

   Very little knowledge 1...2...3...4...5...6...7...8...9...10 High level of knowledge
   Your rating: _____

   (b) Record at least five points outlining what you need to know about the history of the event (consider understandings about the participants, participation trends, previous issues with equipment, etc.).
   (c) Establish your personal plan for acquiring the additional common knowledge about the history of the event.
3. *Determine your "enbrained knowledge" or ability to think through the requirements and develop written operational plans for hosting an event.*
   (a) Rate your overall level of common knowledge for thinking through the requirements of an event component and generating logical,

sequential, and detailed operational plans, as well as communicating the plans to staff/volunteers.

Very little knowledge 1…2…3…4…5…6…7…8…9…10 High level of knowledge

Your rating: _____

(b) Rate your level of common knowledge of planning during the specific phases of events, including:

(bi) The *event development phase* (including, for example, establishing the event governance structure, policy development, writing contacts for services, starting the hiring process for staff/volunteers, securing a facility, equipment, and television and online services)

Very little knowledge 1…2…3…4…5…6…7…8…9…10 High level of knowledge

Your rating: _____

(bii) The *event logistical planning phase* (including, for example, writing operational plans, fostering contacts and networking, communicating with, and training, staff and volunteers for their specific roles, coordinating activities between components, establishing meeting agendas, hosting meetings, as well as developing contingency and emergency plans).

Very little knowledge 1…2…3…4…5…6…7…8…9…10 High level of knowledge

Your rating: _____

(biii) The *event implementation, monitoring, and management phase* (including, for example, executing an event operational plan into practice, implementing the event communication system to ensure all interactions are coordinated for an efficient event, decision-making, managing the media, sponsors, and arising event issues).

Very little knowledge 1…2…3…4…5…6…7…8…9…10 High level of knowledge

Your rating: _____

(biv) The *event evaluation and renewal phase* (including, for example, obtaining feedback on an event (during the event and post event) from staff and volunteers, recognizing staff/volunteers, as well as generating and disseminating recommendations for future events)

Very little knowledge 1…2…3…4…5…6…7…8…9…10 High level of knowledge

Your rating: _____

(bv) Create a written overview of your top priorities concerning what you need to know about event operational planning for hosting an event prior to applying for an event position.

(bxi) Establish a plan to gain the required common knowledge to understand event operational planning for hosting an event (for example, what courses should you take, people to talk to, readings). Also, how can your advancement knowledge (or instincts) be advanced with practical experiences?).

4. *Determine your knowledge on planning for a wider body of components that make up an event:*
   (a) Rate your common knowledge on two (2) components from the following list of event components (not a component already used in an answer above): event accommodation, accreditation, security, ceremonies (including opening, closing, or awards), food & beverage management, media and public relations management, security, ticketing, transportation, venue management, or warehousing).

   (ai) 1st component selected: _____
   Very little knowledge 1…2…3…4…5…6…7…8…9…10 High level of knowledge
   Your rating: _____

   (aii) 2nd component selected: _____
   Very little knowledge 1…2…3…4…5…6…7…8…9…10 High level of knowledge
   Your rating: _____

   (b) Create a written overview of your top five priorities concerning what you need to know concerning planning for each of the event components selected.

   (c) Establish a plan to gain the common knowledge required to understand the planning requirements for the selected components (for instance, obtain and review previous operational plans); and improve your advancement knowledge with practical experiences.

5. *What "encultured" knowledge do you have? In event management this includes your understandings of, and being able to effectively work with, people from a variety of cultures, and facilitating effective team work.*

(a) Rate your common knowledge of other cultures in our globalized work environment.

   (ai) List a country and rate your understanding of their culture: _____

   Weak knowledge   1...2...3...4...5...6...7...8...9...10   strong knowledge
   Your rating: _____

   (aii) List another country and rate your understandings of their culture: _____
   Weak knowledge   1...2...3...4...5...6...7...8...9...10   strong knowledge
   Your rating: _____

   (aiii) Rate your ability to maintain harmonious working relations at all levels in a multicultural environment.
   Weak ability 1...2...3...4...5...6...7...8...9...10 strong ability
   Your rating: _____

(b) Outline a plan that offers the opportunity to learn about different cultures and manage a variety of types of personalities that may work at events. Also, what experiences can you obtain to move beyond common knowledge to further your understandings of the intimate nuances of a culture?

6. *What do you know about how emerging technologies are impacting events or will impact events in the future?*

   (a) Record three (3) emerging technologies that are applicable to event management.

   (b) Next, indicate how each of these emerging technologies may impact an event manager in their role into the future.

   (c) Rate your knowledge on being prepared to adapt to emerging technologies in event management:
   Very little knowledge 1...2...3...4...5...6...7...8...9...10 High level of knowledge
   Your rating: _____

   (d) Create a written overview indicating two (2) emerging technologies and what you need to know about them and how they could impact the event manager in the future?

   (e) Establish a plan to further your knowledge on emerging technologies in event management practice

7. *How can your flexibility effect be used as an advantage? This includes accepting, nurturing, and building on your differentiated ideas, communication style, personal interpretations of knowledge, and understandings of other points of views while being open to consider a range of responses to actions necessary in event management.*
    (a) List your personal areas of interest in event management (list 1–3 components).
    (b) Next, list your personal attributes that can be advantageous in event management (Consider your hobbies, technological interests, cultural background, personal skills, etc.).
    (c) Outline what you can do to understand and then nurture your combined event management areas of interest and personal flexibility effect attributes to position you as an asset in the industry.
8. *Outline courses you can take over the duration of your degree that are applicable to event management and can aid in your understanding of events. Consider courses with a focus on areas such as:*
    - communications
    - diversity and inclusion
    - ethics
    - finance and economics
    - human resource management
    - innovation and entrepreneurship
    - leadership
    - legal transactions and contracts
    - marketing
    - media management
    - negotiations
    - organizational behaviour
    - policy
    - power and politics
    - public relations
    - sales and promotion
    - social responsibility
    - sponsorship
    - strategic alliances
9. *List key experiences you can obtain in the industry (such as volunteer opportunities, internships, and mentorships) that will aid you to develop your knowledge concerning event management. What level of*

responsibility will you have within these experiences and how can you increase your level of responsibility? Also, will you pursue experiences as an inhouse worker or virtual worker – or both?
10. *Outline your experience working with staff and/or volunteers, including your ability to foster contacts and motivate people, along with your mediation and negotiation skills.* How can you gain experience in this area?

Overall, the questions are presented for you to consider your current state of knowledge and how you can further your knowledge to be successful in the event industry. Use your answers to the questions above to guide you to further reading (such as reading research on the field) and to determine the experiential opportunities you need to pursue to develop your understandings of best practices. These experiential opportunities vary from 1-day events to longer internships, and mentorships. Build your field experiences until you acquire ones that provide you with rising levels of responsibility and event management experience for any of the components of an event that you may want to pursue. No one course or experience can fully prepare you for the event industry. You need a combination of courses and a variety of industry experiences with rising levels of responsibility. Further, you need to constantly expand the questions above to challenge your personal understandings and further advance knowledge. For instance, when discussing any theory within a course, apply it to event management. Ask yourself how the characteristics of the theory can be applied to guide an event manager. Remember that you are pursuing *perspicacity* – to have quick insights and understandings for efficient and effective decisions and actions while in the industry – or to be a competent event manager. This takes effort and time – hopefully, you will keep advancing in perspicacity over your entire career.

Conclusion: So, what do you need to know to build for success in sport, recreation, and tourism event management?

The author of this chapter promotes the position that you are trying to obtain *perspicacity* – or being competent with the development of quick insights and understandings for efficient and effective decisions and actions when in the event industry. As part of pursuing *perspicacity*, you can nurture your *flexibility effect* for an advantage. This includes encouraging your personal perspectives, opinions, approaches, experiences, ideas, and options to create knowledge differentiation, or one's *flexibility effect[s]* as a potential competitive advantage. Also, consider your individualized perspectives, etc., as well as speciality areas that are needed for the industry that you can develop with your *flexibility effect*. For example, developing expertise in ensuring environmental sustainability within every step of an event or the integration of emerging technologies within events. Further, an understanding of *niche and traditional events* can open your options as to where you want to be in the event industry – including developing your own niche event. The combination of traditional and niche events in the fields of sport, recreation, and tourism is changing and expanding – and each event requires a competent event manager.

Today's competent event managers have skills that advance beyond using previous event operational plans or pre-established lists that dictate the replication of actions used to stage previous events. Contemporary event managers need to be able to manage the complexity of events and plan by thinking through and self-determining the requirements of staging traditional or niche events. This demands knowledge of, coupled with experience in, event management.

Be ready to be successful in the sport, recreation, and tourism event industry! Develop understandings of what you know about the event industry today, what you need to know for your future, and how you can obtain such knowledge. There are plenty of avenues to pursue in the event management industry, and knowledge in this growing field is multi-directional, challenging, and rewarding.

Event management knowledge does not arrive in an instant – it is developed over time. It is a complex industry, so give yourself time to develop. Keep plugging away by diving in and planning to advance your readiness and become an asset for the industry. Completing the questions posed within the chapter above should get you started when generating your plan for improving your overall *perspicacity* for the event industry.

May you successfully advance your preparedness and be able to host events that inspire well into our collective future!

Chapter questions

1. Define the terms *perspicacity*, *flexibility effect*, and *collaborative individualism*.
2. State the two characteristics of *traditional events* and the three characteristics of *niche events*.

3. Describe three *niche events* and explain the characteristics that make them niche events and not *traditional events*. What would be necessary for them to become *traditional events*?
4. Explain why *niche events* are growing in our times. Next, outline your personal perspectives concerning why niche events are growing.
5. State the differences between *common and advancement knowledge* and outline two examples of how to obtain each type of knowledge.
6. Outline what *encultured knowledge* and *enbrained knowledge* entail – for common and advancement knowledge.
7. Start completing the ten questions posed in the chapter that encourage you to understand your state of knowledge for event management and to develop a plan for acquiring the necessary knowledge to work in the event industry.

References

Abbas, Y., Martinetti, A., Rajabalinejad, M., Schuberth, F., & Dongen, L. (2022). Facilitating digital collaboration through knowledge management: A case study. *Knowledge Management Research & Practice, 20*(6), 979–813. https://doi.org/10.1080/14778238.2022.2029597

Choo, W., & Bontis, N. (Eds.). (2002). *The strategic management of intellectual capital and organizational knowledge*. Oxford University Press. ISBN 019513866X

Conner, K., & Prahalad, C. K. (2002). A resource-based theory of the firm: Knowledge versus opportunism. In W. C. Choo & N. Bontis (Eds.), *The strategic management of intellectual capital and organizational knowledge* (pp. 103–131). Oxford University. ISBN 019513866X

Curado, C., & Bontis, N. (2006). The knowledge-based view of the firm and it's theoretical precursor. *International Journal of Learning and Intellectual Capital, 3*(3), 367–381. https://doi.org/10.1504/IJLIC.2006.011747

Getz, D., & Page, S. (2016). Progress and prospects for event tourism research. *Tourism Management, 52*, 593–631.

Gupta, A., Singh, R., Kamble, S., & Mishra, R. (2022). Knowledge management in industry 4.0 environment for a sustainable competitive advantage: A strategic framework. *Knowledge Management Research & Practice, 20*(6), 878–892. https://doi.org/10.1080/14778238.2022.2144512

Hussein, A., & Mohamed, R. (2013). Feasibility study for developing an event prioritizing system using CMS's. *International Journal of Intelligent Systems and Application in Engineering, 11*(1s), 30–45. ISNN: 2147-6799

Lee, R., & Shek, V. (2022). *Retaining knowledge: Human and intellectual capital*. Routledge. ISBN 10.4324/0781003112150-4

Limerick, D., Cunnington, B., & Crowther, F. (1998). *Managing the new organization: Collaboration and sustainability in the post-corporate world* (2nd ed.). Business and Professional Publishing. ISBN 10:1865089958

Spender, J. (2002). Knowledge management, uncertainty, and the emergent theory of the firm. In C. Choo & N. Bontis (Eds.), *The strategic management of intellectual capital and organizational knowledge* (pp. 149–162). Oxford University Press. ISBN 019513866X

Victer, R. (2020). Connectivity knowledge and the degree of structural formalization: A contribution to a contingency theory of organizational capability. *Journal of Organization Design, 9*(7). http://doi.org/10.1186/s41469-020-0068-3

2 Building fundamental knowledge to be a facilitator of events

Amy Cunningham and Joanne MacLean

The development of expertise as a facilitator is needed at all levels of events – from small local events to large international sport, recreation, and tourism events. This expertise takes time to develop with practice, reflection, and metacognition – or an understanding of your intellectual capacity (Cravens et al., 2022), your ability to self-regulate your behaviour, and your talent for adapting your behaviour based on reflecting on outcomes (Fleur et al., 2021). Unfortunately, due to the dynamic event environment and complexity of facilitation skills, it is unlikely that experts can transfer this knowledge to you using didactic methods (Ritchie et al., 2020). You need to develop your facilitation skills – first, by understanding what they are, and then, second, by gaining such skills through personal experience. This includes navigating the complex event collaboration requirements with one's intellectual and interpersonal skills for individual "people management," "group management," and "knowledge management" that are applied to meet event requirements (Cravens et al., 2022; Love et al., 2021). Anyone interested in sport, recreation, or tourism event management should continuously work on advancing their understandings of – and gaining experience in – facilitation.

This chapter introduces the key role of an event manager as a facilitator throughout an event. A definition of facilitation is provided below, and then an overview of the role of the facilitator is offered. This is followed by the theory of facilitation and its application. Key aspects of event facilitation are discussed, including communication requirements, governance practices, and tips to keep in mind for best practices.

Facilitation by Amy Cunningham

One of the most exciting aspects of event management is the requirement of producing a team effort. The event needs a facilitator to guide the process of *sharing knowledge* between members. In addition, the event manager is responsible for *facilitating* event processes. These are the processes that are found within the collaborative effort of planning, implementing, and evaluating an event, where all members of the group need to feel that they are a part of the team effort. Facilitation is, thus, a part of action learning that can be practiced (Abbott & Winterburn, 2022).

The role of the event manager as a facilitator is, thus, one whereby they must have skills in "assessing people, processes and outcomes, and creating infrastructure for program monitorship" (Ritchie et al., 2020, p. 1). This facilitation role will be discussed in more depth below, but first let us take a step back and investigate the meaning of facilitation itself. The concept of facilitation is crucial to the role an event manager must play, and the theoretical framework from which we will draw our understandings concerning facilitation will be provided.

What is facilitation?

A facilitator builds an independent group of workers and uses their "practice-based form of interpersonal expertise that supports group members to do their best thinking" (Cravens et al., 2022, n.p.). In other words, as Bens (2000) outlined, facilitation is "a way of providing leadership without taking the reins" (p. 7) while the group goes through their routine practices, problem solving to meet requirements, and generating improvement where required to host an event (Perry et al., 2019). Moving from being a novice to being an expert in event facilitation requires facilitation experience. This is because facilitation skills involve a type of knowledge that is hard to articulate and share – it is more of an art of motivating and managing people, and accomplishing activities. Further, it involves conducting reflective practice (Schön, 1983; 1987) to continuously improve.

Facilitation theory assumes that learning will occur with the aid of one who facilitates the process of learning as opposed to one who simply provides knowledge to a group (Laird, 1985; Lambert & Glacken, 2005). Within this theory of facilitation, it is believed that since change is constant, the greatest facilitators are those who have learned how to learn and can lead others in self-directed learning and critical thinking (Lambert & Glacken, 2005; Peel, 2000). This style of leadership encourages the development of empowered learners and contributors to group processes, in which the creation and dissemination of knowledge are dependent on all members of the group.

To be an effective facilitator, according to this theory, certain assumptions must be met. According to Bens (2000), believers in facilitation theory and practice assume that:

> People are intelligent, capable and want to do the right thing.
> Groups can make better decisions than any one person can make alone.
> Everyone's opinion is of equal value, regardless of rank or position.
> People are committed to the ideas and plans that they have helped to create.
> Participants can and will act responsibly in assuming true accountability for their decisions.
> Groups can manage their own conflicts, behaviours, and relationships if they are given the right tools and training. The *process*, if well designed and honestly applied, can be trusted to achieve results (p. 8).

Now that we have a general understanding of what is meant by the theory of facilitation, the role of an event manager acting as a facilitator can be explored.

Throughout the production of an event, as a facilitator, your job is to *get others to assume responsibility and to take the lead*. Rogers and Friedberg (1994) expressed this facilitation leadership role as the following:

> A leader is best
> When people barely know that he exists,
> Not so good when people obey and acclaim him,
> Worst when they despise him.
> Fail to honour people; they fail to honour you
> But of a good leader, who talks little,
> When his work is done, his aim fulfilled,
> They will all say, "We did this ourselves." (p. 21).

A facilitator becomes the director of the performance, where each participant plays a central role (Vidal, 2004). By the end of this performance, with

Building fundamental knowledge

the creation of group synergy, which should be one of the main goals of true facilitation, the participants will have had "the pleasure of working creatively and collectively to achieve some goals" (Vidal, 2004, p. 394). Overall, facilitators aim to make specific processes easier during all phases of the event.

There are many specific skills, experiences, and knowledges that the event manager must possess to facilitate an event (Peel, 2000; Thomas, 2004). This array of skills includes knowledge that involves intuition about the processes which they are guiding, to help them "act on their feet" and make quick decisions with regard to the needs of a group or process (Peel, 2000); the event manager must also be adept at change management (Ritchie et al., 2020). By making these processes easier, specific tasks will be completed, goals will be met, and the team will feel a pleasurable synergy after a job well done (Vidal, 2004).

A good facilitator empowers the group and the individuals within it to rise to their own potential and have the confidence to be an equal player on the team so that no one becomes dependent on a "teacher." Everyone is shown to be their own developer of knowledge in a shared learning environment, and the strengths of the individuals within the collective can be drawn out and their benefits maximized within the overall process (Peel, 2000). Review Figure 2.1 for an overview of the difference between teaching and facilitating.

Figure 2.2 offers a comprehensive outline of some of the specific roles that a facilitator would play during the event managing process.

> Describe the difference between *teaching* and *facilitating*.
> Determine the *advantages* and *disadvantages* of teaching compared to facilitating.

Figure 2.1 Questioning the difference between teaching and facilitating

Facilitating communication requirements

A facilitator must manage many different areas during an event. This requires a "diverse range of knowledge and skills" (Ritchie et al., 2020, p. 1). We will now discuss one specific area – the critical communication requirements that underscore the work of a facilitator. Greenberg (2002) explains that "communication is the process through which people send information to others and receive information from them" (p. 217). This process can be a difficult one to facilitate, as it is made up of numerous interactions between various members of a team, all of whom bring their individual personalities, knowledge,

> A facilitator
>
> Helps the group define specific goals and objective.
>
> Provides processes that assist members to use their time efficiently to make good decisions; helps group members understand these processes.
>
> Guides group discussion to keep things on track.
>
> Keeps accurate notes that reflect the ideas of the group members.
>
> Supports members in assessing their current skills and the building of new ones.
>
> Uses consensus to help the group make decisions that take all members' opinions into account.
>
> Supports members in managing their own interpersonal dynamics.
>
> Helps the group communicate effectively.
>
> Helps the group access resources.
>
> Creates a positive environment in which members can grow and work together toward attaining group goals.
>
> Fosters leadership in others by sharing leadership responsibilities.
>
> Supports and empowers others to facilitate.
>
> (Bens, 2000; Peel, 2000; Vidal, 2004)

Figure 2.2 The event manager as a facilitator

skills, and communication styles to the table. It is, thus, critical in the development of the event network. The process also includes the dissemination and understanding of event policies, both for staff and volunteer practices, as well as guidelines for participation.

Communication is a key role of the event manager as facilitator. They must make sure that communication lines are open, that members of the team feel that they are being supported, and that specific processes and requirements are articulated and managed throughout the overall process (Bens, 2000). These requirements include facilitating understandings of the individual roles at the event, how the work of individuals is part of the integrated whole, as well as presenting ideas for solutions to arising issues. This requires the creation and facilitation of a safe environment in which to communicate and evaluate ideas or solutions, including an environment that values the diversity of team members as adding to the potential strength of knowledge of collaborative activities.

In organizational settings, the communication process can be extremely complex depending on the design of the organization. In many cases, information may need to flow up or down through the "ranks" or be transmitted to certain individuals via other individuals (Greenberg, 2002). The complexity of these links can lead to communication breakdowns and confusion if not managed properly. The wonderful thing about facilitating a group of individuals with whom you are considered a part of the team is that most of the communication in this process will move horizontally. As Greenberg states: "Messages of this type are characterized by efforts at coordinating or attempts to work together" (p. 201). By focusing and guiding group members' communication and decision-making processes in a structured form, a facilitator can reduce the chances of engaging in faulty processes and harness the strengths of the group as they work toward a shared vision. If the proper communication requirements have been articulated and set in place by the facilitator at the onset of the event planning process, the facilitator should fade into the collective, only to be called upon to manage problems and situations as they may arise.

As a facilitator, the event manager is constantly listening, thinking, and reflecting throughout the process as decision-making and problem-solving activities occur between group members. In any group situation, decisions will need to be made, and conflicts will need to be resolved. This means that those closest to implementing the work have input on managing issues. Additionally, they also have a say in managing, for instance, the tradeoffs that happen at events during times of competing objectives (Cravens et al., 2022). A typical tradeoff situation includes the pressures to complete event logistics under time restraints and at the same time trying to ensure the event is enacting pre-determined strategies as safeguards for environmental sustainability. The voices of those enacting the event activities in an environmentally sustainable manner are important in solving this dual task. While the overall process of task completion is equally the responsibility of each member of the group, it is the role of an effective facilitator to guide the group to a synergy that is borne of effective communication (Vidal, 2004). In this regard, historically a facilitator would act as a neutral party who reminds the group of their aims, guides the group's communication requirements, sets specific strategies at the onset of the process, and interjects as necessary to guide the group back into synchronicity as needed (Laird, 1985; Rogers & Friedberg, 1994).

Another communication task for facilitators of events involves ensuring staff and volunteers understand that issues and problems are to be handled with ethically based decision-making. Ethical decisions, and associated actions or behaviours, are generally based on what you accept as "moral rules, principles, obligations, agreements, and values and norms" (McNamee & Fleming, 2007, p. 426). Decisions based on ethical reasoning are not mandated or imposed but are grounded in individual and/or group perspectives. While sport, recreation, and tourism events must still follow the law, ethical reasoning can differ from event to event based on the selected features that underscore decisions.

An adaption of the International Association of Facilitators' Statement of Values and Code of Ethics – as applied to event management – is presented for your consideration as an ethical guide. This code is based on five elements, and you are encouraged to reflect on these elements for each of your decision options. The elements comprise:

1 That an event facilitator ensures the decision makers *understand the event expectations and desired event outcomes*. This feature involves *valuing the group as an entity that is guided to work together toward its common goal(s)*. Consequently, an event manager needs to value and facilitate a process to establish clear communications and consensus concerning event expectations and outcomes.
2 That an event facilitator ensures a process that promotes *open, honest communications* and, importantly, seeks to minimize *conflicts of interest*. An event manager, therefore, is responsible for the process used for event communication.
3 That an event facilitator promotes *excellent group autonomy* – this includes *respect for the event processes and people* (including the boards of directors, staff, volunteers, participants, media, sponsors, etc.). This respect involves areas such as *safety, equity, trust, collegiality*, and *confidentiality*. Further, this feature can also include the concepts of integrity and inter-dependence, as well as transparency in disclosures.
4 That an event facilitator ensures that *all event processes, methods, and tools are designed to directly meet the event goals*.
5 That an event facilitator *supports processes that develop the knowledge of those involved in the event, as well as stewarding the process to develop further event knowledge*. This includes ensuring the opportunity for professional development through event management participation (Figure 2.3).

We now explore the concept of facilitating communication further by considering a specific case.

Facilitating group communication requirements: the case of group rhythm and facilitation

According to the seminal work by Drucker (1946), "an institution is like a 'tune'; it is not constituted by individual sounds but by the relations between them" (p. 26).

Building fundamental knowledge

An event can exhibit institutional characteristics, and requires the facilitation of the relations between the many individuals involved to create a coordinated tune.

> Be a supportive communicator.
> Focus on the problem instead of the person.
> Match words with body language and encourage group members to do the same.
> Encourage the group to acknowledge each other's ideas.
> Keep the conversation going.
> Encourage open feedback.
> Encourage the use of simple language.
> Paraphrase to clarify; repeat what people say to assure them they are being heard and to make sure the group has understood and is clear.
> Walk the talk (don't say one thing and do the other) and watch for this behaviour in group members.
> Be a good listener and encourage the group to do the same; consider the use of a "talking stick" to ensure that everyone has a chance to speak and be heard.
> Stay neutral and avoid sharing your personal opinion unless it is requested; focus on your *process* role of communication.
> Ask questions; this will invite participation, help to gather information, test assumptions, and get to the root causes of problems.
> Synthesize ideas; encourage group members to comment and build upon each other's ideas.
> Stay on track; set time guidelines for each discussion.
> Summarize clearly.
> (Bens, 2000; Greenberg, 2002)

Figure 2.3 Facilitation tips

Lulu Leathley, from Vancouver, British Columbia, Canada, is an individual who specializes in facilitating group rhythms (group drumming circles). She promotes the importance of facilitated communication in group processes. The teachings of Leathley position the facilitator's role as beginning with the act of being a conductor. In music, the goal is to reach a moment in the facilitation of group music-making where everyone (despite their musical background and experience) feels empowered and collectively reaches a place of group synergy. It is her goal to slowly fade into the background and become a part of the group so that the music created is dependent upon each person and no one becomes dependent on her as a leader. To accomplish this goal, she sets certain communication requirements (both verbal and non-verbal) at the beginning of the group drumming circle. She very clearly articulates the importance of listening to each other, making eye contact, and getting in touch with inner intuitions and rhythms. In other words, she encourages and empowers group members to look inside of themselves for the knowledge that she believes they already possess to create something that is a sum of all parts of the collective. Throughout the facilitation process, she encourages the group to bring their own inner rhythms and strengths forward to contribute to the collective song. She makes sure to keep the rhythm going, despite the ups and downs, and provides ample room and encouragement for feedback. At the completion of a successful event, there is the energy of connection.

In music collaboration, there is an overall feeling that is felt by the musicians when everything culminates in a satisfying "click" (Sawyer, 2006). This synergistic click is challenging to attain, as reaching this goal takes the cooperation and ability of all the group members working together. The facilitator's job is to communicate with the group both verbally and non-verbally in the beginning and then to re-enter and guide the group and *sense* what is needed throughout the process.

Experience in facilitation allows you to become quicker with your intuitive decision-making abilities, and your *flexibility effect* includes personalizing your knowledge, perceptions, and ideas to create an advantage. A facilitator's role, therefore, is to use one's knowledge to foster the event processes. This facilitation includes recognizing when certain group members are overpowering others, when people are not listening to each other, or when the group is approaching a collective musical disaster. In this situation, Leathley responds and reacts to the needs of the group based on her own experience, knowledge, skills, and intuition: *the flexibility effect* she has acquired as a music teacher and facilitator.

If the group has succeeded in coming together and clicking, there is an overwhelming sense of empowerment, pride, and accomplishment as a collective at the conclusion of the event. As mentioned in the previous section, this is the sign that the event facilitator has been effective and successful in their role. Facilitating communication within the group process, then, can be seen as one of the most important roles of the event manager.

A sport, recreation, or tourism event manager facilitates the communication processes. Their experience, knowledge, skills, and intuition contribute to the ability to create a collective synergy in event production.

We have now reviewed the meaning of facilitation and the role of the facilitator, specifically regarding communication process requirements. Now let us consider another important role in facilitation, the transfer of knowledge.

Building fundamental knowledge

Facilitating knowledge transfer

Above, we have discussed the role of the event manager as a facilitator and what that entails during group processes in the organizing of an event. As a facilitator of a collaborative or group effort toward an event, it is your job to make sure knowledge is transferred and built upon between group members. This transfer helps to ensure that the best and most informed decisions are made in the pursuit of task completion, drawing on the collective knowledge of the group. But how does the facilitator go about ensuring that his/her own knowledge is being transferred to inform the field as a whole?

The sharing of knowledge with others invites and assumes that other facilitators will in return share their knowledge, and as a result the knowledge apex will broaden and expand. This has very positive outcomes if we are to assume that the goal of sharing and receiving new knowledge is to continuously work toward honing our effectiveness and expertise as facilitators. This means that the facilitator must establish a safe environment for discussing knowledge, including strategies for managing event activities. Knowledge transfer is a long, steady continuous process that needs to be completed over the entire time of the event, including all four phases.

Within a practical setting, let us revisit Lulu Leathley's facilitation of rhythm-based events. As a facilitator within a network of other facilitators, Leathley engages in many specific knowledge transfer strategies which enable her to inform her field, contribute to the expansion of the knowledge pool, and broaden her own knowledge base. Some of these strategies include:

> Building relationships and sharing dialogue about experiences with other facilitators,
> Attending rhythm facilitation conferences,
> Continuously attending training sessions with other facilitators with varying levels of experience,
> Joining discussion groups and posting information on various websites,
> Becoming an active member in the rhythm facilitator's guild,
> Assisting others to develop facilitation skills by lending talents and experiences to mentorship programs.

In these activities, there is a climate of cooperation and support that aids in the important transfer of knowledge. As a result of this enthusiasm and support, the community of facilitators continues to grow, and individuals develop their *perspicacity* (quick advanced insights and understandings) based on the knowledge that is shared. There are many ways in which an event manager may facilitate this knowledge transfer, and above we have examined various examples within one case. We have also outlined the specifics of facilitation, the role of the event manager as a facilitator, the importance of communication requirements, and the methods by which they may be facilitated. Let us now begin a discussion on another area of interest in the development phase of the planning model, the facilitation of structures for governance when staging an event.

Facilitating event structures for governance by Joanne MacLean

Small to large events within sport, recreation, and tourism have levels of magnitude, appeal, and complexity that require well-designed event structures that contribute to successful delivery. Oftentimes, the structure and governance of event management are "silent," somewhat behind-the-scenes compared to the main program of activities that are consumed or watched. However, the elements of effective structure and governance are foundations of success. Successful events simply cannot be achieved without a structure for planning and delivering the event that enables effective communication, decision-making, and appropriate amounts of flexibility among event managers. In order to understand this in further detail, the purposes of the following sections include: defining the concepts related to event structures and good governance of event management; outlining the theoretical dimensions of event structures that will enable the delivery of successful events, without identifying the specifics of that structure; identifying the principles that result in the creation of effective event structures; and applying the theoretical dimensions and principles of event structures identified above to different types of events currently popular in the business of sport, recreation, and tourism.

By following the topics identified above, readers will gain an appreciation for two important fundamental principles about facilitating event structures for event management: first, different kinds of events require different event management structures that provide the appropriate management for the particular event; and second, we believe that event managers are better served learning the *guiding principles* that will enable them to make decisions about the most appropriate and effective structure for the event being planned, as opposed to duplicating the structure from another event. You may label these two fundamental principles *flexibility* and *specificity* regarding event management structures. The following sections will help you understand these and other principles and their application in creating effective event structures.

Event structures

So, what exactly do we mean by the term *event structure*? This term refers to breaking down the tasks associated with delivering the event such that employees or volunteers have specific roles and an understanding of how these roles interrelate. The structure involves individual positions or groups of individuals in committees who control tasks and understand their authority, which decisions they must make, and the reporting relationships between individuals and committees. Typically, event leaders publicize a management structure in the form of a chart with boxes and connecting lines outlining the task areas, with proximity between areas that need to cooperate and/or collaborate, and reporting directions. This management structure can be made complex by the number of areas of focus in an event, which can include, for example:

Accommodation management
Accreditation management
Ceremonies (opening, closing, and awards) management
Communications management
Competition management
Drug testing or doping control
Food and beverages management
Hospitality and protocol services
Human resource management (Volunteers & staff)
Media management
Medical management
Merchandising
Officials management
Participant management
Results management
Security/safety

Spectator services
Transportation and parking services
Ticketing management

Theoretically, the structure of an organization is usually examined from three points of view (Slack & Parent, 2006): the first viewpoint is *formalization* (the degree to which rules and regulations, policies, and individual and committee roles are defined to guide the activities of event managers). The second viewpoint is *complexity* (the scope and number of different individual committees and sub-units required to deliver the event, and the density of the hierarchy of authority involved). The third viewpoint is *centralization* (the degree to which decision-making is controlled by those in charge of the event or delegated to individuals working at the level of committees or individual jobs). The event structure can be designed to be high or low in each formalization, complexity, and centralization, depending on the type of event.

Event structures are developed to aid the governance of an event. Governance refers to exercising the authority to define policy regarding how the event will be run, who does what, and when and how they do it. If an event is to be successful, then the structure created to deliver it must provide for effective transfer of knowledge and effective decision-making. Facilitating event structures means that you have the knowledge necessary to create the most appropriate organizing structure for your event.

In addition to the theory discussed above regarding event structures, there are other important theories that have been developed which aid in understanding effective event structures. The theoretical dimensions of event structures that we have chosen to include in this discussion involve: systems theory, contingency theory, and complexity theory. The following sections will briefly introduce each theory in the context of understanding effective event structures for good governance and successful event management.

Theoretical dimensions of event structures

Event structures vary considerably. For concrete local examples, examine how your educational recreational events are structured. Compare the recreational event structure to a local tourism event and a locally held elite sport championship. Each event can be unique in its structure. The structure dictates the hierarchy, which in turn influences the freedom to act in the process of making, relaying, and implementing decisions and actions when staging an event.

When creating an event, you will need to consider a structure that will lead to the most effective and efficient delivery for staging the event. To achieve this goal, there are several theoretical perspectives that relate information about effective organizations and event structures. The theoretical dimensions or characteristics outlined next are largely complementary, in that parts of each theory may apply in specific ways to an event structure you develop.

Systems theory

Systems theory stresses that event management structures rely on the environment within which they operate for many of the materials that will be required for hosting the event. Materials include a wide variety of items such as people, equipment, technologies, and facilities, to name a few. Systems theory suggests that the event will have three different systems working together: *input systems*, *throughput systems*, and *output systems*. To run an event, you must take in resources (inputs), create the event activities (throughputs), and generate end results for participants or others (outputs). The three systems interrelate and depend on each other for success. A change in one inevitably affects the other parts of the system. Any event you are organizing involves inputs or the acquisition of raw materials (competition facilities) and human resources (volunteers) to organize the event; throughputs might include the application of technology (website designed for managing communication and registration) and information (the number of participants that can be accommodated); and outputs include the enjoyment of participants and the dollars raised for the charity of choice. The overall event system interacts within its component parts and with its environment. Facilitators of events must understand that the application of systems theory identifies the importance of component parts of the organization structure as their dependence on and influence on one another.

Contingency theory

A rational extension to systems theory in understanding the organizing structure and management of an event involves *contingency theory*. It is important to note that *contingency theory* is different than contingency issues that can occur at an event. Contingency issues can be, for instance, when a pipe breaks and the volunteer room gets flooded. *Contingency theory* suggests that the effective structure of an organization is contingent on contextual factors of the environment within which it operates, such as size, competition, strategy, resources, and so on. This contingent structural situation can be explained further with the concept of *dissipative structures*. This concept implies that a structure can be reproduced or repeated if in a steady state (in equilibrium). However, achieving and maintaining this steady state is difficult because structures tend to combine, be pulled apart, and then recombine again.

As an example, the structure of a volunteer meeting established for event accommodation management can be dissipative. This is because the volunteers are assigned and most attend the first meeting – but in subsequent meetings, there are volunteers missing and others have arrived that were not there at the first meeting. This means that the volunteers have been placed within a structure for managing the event accommodation requirements, but this structure has unstable conditions. This type of change is not incremental growth or decline that is predictable but dynamic and non-linear, as it is convened, pulled apart, and then reconvened again at another time, while dependent upon variables that impact volunteer attendance. The event manager, thus, must be open to the conditions of uncertainty and complexity and cannot expect a continuous state of equilibrium whereby every volunteer attends every scheduled meeting. The structure for managing volunteers must be established in a manner that can accommodate change.

This concept re-emphasizes that a structure is contingent upon the environment. As such, the design of the event structure and its units must "fit" with the environment and work well in coordination for the event to succeed. There are multiple conditions that impact the design. For example, in a tourism event, the structure of the organizing system will need to account for the number of participants, the age group, and potentially the cultural mix. Further, the size of registration may be wholly contingent on how many facilities exist, how much time can be acquired within facilities and the services that are available. These factors may be impacted by other events running proximal to yours in timing or location. Such factors are often termed constraints, and facilitators of events need to understand event constraints and contingencies that will lead to optimal organizing structures, decision-making, and leadership.

Overall, event managers should not expect to continue with the same operating structure that was used in a previous event, and need to be open to organizational structural changes based on the concept of dissipative structures and contingency theory. Event managers must, therefore, be able to think through, determine, and facilitate the implementation of the event organizing structure best suited for any event.

Complexity theory

In keeping with systems and contingency theories, *complexity theory* works to identify how organizations optimally adapt to their environments. Using this theory, managers focus on the required complexity of structure that can achieve the mission of the event while retaining the ability to adapt and make strategic decisions quickly. Complexity theory identifies the importance of complex adaptive systems, structures that commonly consist of a small number of relatively simple, partially connected structures. In a recreational charity event example, a simpler structure involving committees for scheduling, facility organization, registration and volunteers that connect to each other via a tournament leaders' committee will be better able to communicate, make effective decisions, and adapt to its environment.

Theories expand our understandings

In academic study, the word theory is used to describe the logical explanation for a phenomenon that has been studied systematically and is thought to expand our understanding. The theories briefly described above provide a foundation for understanding why and how event structures may be optimally designed. How can we facilitate effective structures? What makes an event structure effective and another ineffective? How do event structures come to influence good governance, such that the decision-making, policy development, and efficiency of the event are optimized? Understanding the above theories sheds some light on answering these questions. And from these theories, along with trial and error of what works in practice and the transfer of this knowledge, a variety of principles in event structures have been identified. Let's look at these in further detail.

Principles in event structures

Principles can be likened to rules or understandings that have resulted from theory and practice regarding how and why things work. In developing effective organizing structures for event management, principles are identified that will help event organizers create the optimal structure for the event and environment within which the event is being delivered. Identified below are some of the major principles applying to event structure development.

> *Form follows function:* This principle suggests that the type of structure created to manage the delivery of an event should be predicated on the purpose of the event and the definition of governance roles (for example, developing policy, managing, operating) within the event management design. Copying the event structure from a previously successful event does not necessarily result in a workable structure for another event. For example, using the structure developed to deliver the Rugby World Cup would be ridiculous when delivering a high school basketball tournament because the former event is so much larger and more complex than the latter.
>
> *Operating specialization:* optimal event structures identify the activities required to deliver the event, and cluster similar or like activities together into sub-units to encourage communication and decision-making. By so doing, efficiency is created by maximizing interconnections among managers with responsibilities that impact one another, leading to more autonomous but interconnected work groups.
>
> *Increasing complexity impacts both the planning and time required for planning:* the more complex an organizing structure, the more planning is required to ensure that the structure functions optimally. It stands to reason that this will take more time than with a simple structure. An example of this principle is with the organizing of the Olympic Games. The Olympic Games' operating committee structures are designed six to eight years in advance of the competition at a minimum, and the extent of planning is exceptionally broad.
>
> *Communications efficiency:* planning does not take place in the brain of one person in isolation from others. Therefore, the structure for event management must create links and liaisons for individuals to communicate their activities and decisions, and this communication must be formally arranged to be efficiently enacted. The speed and number of communications in the network can be enhanced depending on the type of event structure created.

Synergistic outcomes: synergy refers to the phenomenon of greater efficiency and outcomes occurring when two or more agents work together than could be achieved had each completed the same tasks in isolation. Event structures that create opportunities for synergistic outcomes are said to be efficiently lean and more effective for task accomplishment (Kilmann et al., 1976). The accruing synergistic outcome results from the idea that the overall accomplishment is more than a simple summation of output, meaning that the whole is greater than the sum of its parts.

Understanding the theories and principles relative to facilitating effective event structures is very important, but knowing how to apply the ideas presented to create actual event structures is perhaps even more critical for the success of the event and its managers. Next we move to a discussion of the application of key characteristics of the above theory.

Application of theory and principles in event structures

The theory and principles outlined earlier in this chapter regarding the development of effective event structures apply to both traditional and niche events. In practice, traditional events may involve more formality of structure than niche events. This is dictated by the governing body and its established policy regarding how the event is to be organized. Systems theory suggests that the environment within which the event is hosted must be considered for both traditional and niche events. The resources required to create the event, the anticipated outcomes of the event, and the event activities will also need to be considered. Contingency theory purports that the importance of fitting the event structure to both its purpose and environment, creating a structure that fits appropriately with the size, resources, and intent of traditional and niche sporting events is paramount. Complexity theory also establishes the importance of matching the event's organizing structure to its environment and purpose, in order to create a structure that matches the strategy and adaptability that might be required in the environment. Being able to adapt to unforeseen problems, pressures, and changes is a fundamental requirement for traditional and niche event structure frameworks. This can be optimized when the structure created for the event is directly linked to its purpose (form follows function). While it might seem precipitous to use another successful event structure when planning a new event, it is a risky proposition. Linking form and function, or creating an event structure that identifies the intent and governance roles that most specifically meet the needs of the actual event, is very important. While this is critically important for traditional sport event structures, it may be even more critical for niche events where the event structure does not have the guidance of a governing body, established policy, or other comparable events. Similarly, creating a clear understanding of the operating specialization for the event and linking the activities of sub-units with common or dependent roles will encourage effective communication and create efficiency. This is the case with both traditional and niche sport events. The complexity of the event structure will surely impact the amount of planning that is required to enable effective communication and decision-making along with the time it will take to make the event a reality. Planning, with the specific intent of ensuring coordination among the parts of the event organizing structure, is an important role for event managers that can have multiple, synergistic outcomes of much greater magnitude than the impact of the work of an individual or committee. Event leaders need to take a role in creating synergy among the parts of the event organizing structure, where the impact will be a positive result in both traditional and niche sport event structures.

Creating event structures that will result in good governance is the goal of understanding and applying the theory and principles discussed above. A structure that is flexible provides for effective levels of communication, decision-making, and exchange of information among the individuals delivering the event. The structure created, while being specifically designed for the purpose of the event, will best serve the needs of event managers, and contribute to overall success. Effective event structures for governance go "hand in glove" with facilitating effective event networks that offer additional groups or constituent organizations relationships and resources to aid in the development of an event, our next topic of interest.

Conclusions

In this chapter, the key role of an event manager as a facilitator was introduced. A definition of facilitation was provided, along with the theory of facilitation. The role of the event manager was outlined as that of a facilitator that guides the event through all aspects of an event. Examples offered outlined facilitating the development of event structure for governance to establish the framework for an event. Further, systems theory, contingency theory, including dissipative structures, and complexity theory were applied to the key role of event facilitation.

Chapter Questions

1. What does one do when they "facilitate" event activities and what are the key areas of focus?
2. What types of knowledge does one need to successfully facilitate?
3. How is facilitation different from teaching personnel involved in an event?
4. An event structure can be examined from three points of view, including formalization, complexity, and centralization. Describe these three points of view.
5. Describe the characteristics of systems theory, contingency theory, and complexity theory and relate these theories to the development of event structures and the role of a facilitator.
6. What is a dissipative structure and how do they apply to event facilitation?
7. Outline how contingency theory differs from a contingency issue.
8. What does the principal "form follows function" imply?
9. What experiences have you had in facilitating group activities? How can you advance your experience in event facilitation?

References

Abbott, C., & Winterburn, K. (2022). *Action learning facilitation: Practitioner insights.* 19(2), 184–187. https://econpapers.repec.org/scripts/redir.pf?u=http%3A%2F%2Fhdl.handle.net%2F10.1080%2F14767333.2022.2130726;h=repec:taf:alresp:v:19:y:2022:i:3:p:301-311

Bens, I. (2000). *Facilitating with ease! A step-by-step guidebook.* Jossey-Bass Publishing.

Cravens, A., Jones, M., Ngai, C., Zarestky, J., & Love, H. (2022). Science facilitation: Navigating the intersection of intellectual expertise in science collaboration. *Humanities & Social Sciences Communications,* 9, 256. https://doi.org/10.1057/s41599-022-01217-1

Drucker, P. (1946). *Concept of the corporation.* John Day Publishing.

Fleur, D., Bredeweg, B., & van den Bos, W. (2021). Metacognition: Ideas and insights from neuro- and educational sciences. *NPJ Science of Learning, 6*(13), 1–10. https://doi.org/10.1038/s41539-021-00089-5

Greenberg, J. (2002). *Managing behaviour in organizations*. Prentice Hall Publishing.

Kilmann, R., Pondy, L., & Slavin, D. (Eds.). (1976). *The management of organization design: Strategies and implementation, Vol. I*. North-Holland Publishing.

Laird, D. (1985). *Approaches to training and development*. Addison-Wesley Publishing.

Lambert, V., & Glacken, M. (2005). Clinical education facilitators: A literature review. *Journal of Clinical Nursing, 14*, 664–673. https://doi.org/10.1111/j.1365-2702.2005.01136.x

Love, H., Cross, J., Fosdick, B., Crooks, K., VandeWoude, S., & Fisher, E. (2021) Interpersonal relationships drive successful team science: An exemplary case-based study. *Humanities & Social Science Communications, 8*(1), 1–10. https://doi.org/10.1057/s41599-021-00789-8

McNamee, J.J. & Fleming, S. (2007). Ethics audits and corporate governance: The case of public sector sport organizations. *Journal of Business Ethics, 73*(4), 425–437.

Peel, D. (2000). The teacher and town planner as facilitator. *Innovations in Education and Training International, 37*(4), 372–380.

Perry, C., Damschroder, L., Hemler, J., Woodson, T., Ono, S., & Cohen, D. (2019). Specifying and comparing implementation strategies across seven large implementation interventions: A practical application of theory. *Implementation Science, 14*(1), 32. https://doi.org/10.1186/s13012-019-0876-4

Ritchie, M., Parker, L., & Kirchner, J. (2020). From novice to expert: A qualitative study of implementation and facilitation skills. *Implementation Science Communications, 1*(25), 1–12. https://doi.org/10.1186/s43058-020-00006-8

Rogers, C., & Friedberg, H. J. (1994). *Freedom to learn*. Macmillan College Publishing.

Sawyer, K. R. (2006). Group creativity: Musical performance and collaboration. *Psychology of Music, 34*(2), 148–165.

Schön, D. A. (1983). *The reflective practitioner: How professionals think in action*. Basic Books Publishing.

Schön, D. A. (1987). *Educating the reflective practitioner*. Basic Books Publishing.

Slack, T., & Parent, M. (2006). *Understanding sport organizations: The application of organization theory* (2nd ed.). Human Kinetics Publishing.

Thomas, G. (2004). A typology of approaches to facilitator education. *Journal of Experiential Education, 27*(2), 123–140.

Vidal, R. (2004). The vision conference: Facilitating creative processes. *Systemic Practice and Action Research, 17*(5), 385–405.

3 The development phase of the event planning model

Maureen Connolly and
Lorne J. Adams

This chapter examines the first phase of a four-phase event planning model, the *Development Phase*. The event manager is a facilitator of event activities throughout all the phases. In the Development Phase, this facilitation role encompasses a plethora of areas. Examples offered in this chapter include event goals and objectives, policy development, contracts, and establishing event volunteer programs. We conclude with a multiphase assignment on facilitating the development of additional elements in this phase including event legacy statements, a staff training program, permits and liability insurance, as well as an effective event communication system.

Facilitating the development of event goals and objectives

An event manager is responsible for facilitating the generation of event goals and objectives. *Goals* are overall statements that clearly outline what you expect to accomplish/achieve for the event. Multiple event goals can be established; for instance, goals can be established for the overall event as well as for each of the multiple components within an event, such as accommodation, accreditation, transportation, food, and beverage components, and so forth.

Objectives need to be established to indicate who, what, when, where, and how each goal statement will be accomplished. The objectives provide the specific directions that guide the activities to make each goal statement become a reality. They can describe what needs to be accomplished, who is responsible, what is expected, when it is to be completed, the products/services needed, as well as the objectives, the financial requirements, and the time frame.

DOI: 10.4324/9781003391098-3

Event Development Phase

The event manager facilitates the development of event structures for governance, event networks, policies, volunteer practices, and participation

Event Evaluation and Renewal Phase

The event manager facilitates the selection of event components to be evaluated, the completion of the evaluation tasks, and the implementation of the evaluation recommendations

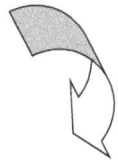

Event Operational Planning Phase

The event manager creates and facilitates the development of written operational plans that are logical, sequential, detailed and integrated, along with contingency plans and the activation of a plan refining process

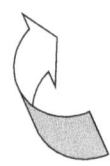

Event Implementation, Monitoring and Management Phase

The event manager facilitates the implementation of the written operational plans, monitors activities looking for deviations, and manages all deviations from the plans

Figure 3.1 An event planning model

Examples of event goals and objectives

Goal: To create a world-class accommodation experience for event guests and participants staying at the ___ Hotel. This includes providing fast and easy check-in and check-out services, having a safe and secure hotel environment, being friendly and helpful to every event guest, and ensuring excellent communication – including signage at the facility (by Jonathan Hanley).

Associated Objectives for the Event:

- Have a satisfaction rating of four stars out of five or higher from every event guest staying at ____ Hotel for the event
- Keep check-in and check-out service time to a maximum of 15 minutes or less
- Ensure that each guest receives prompt, professional, friendly, and courteous service
- Ensure that all guests and staff are treated with the respect and dignity they deserve

Policies are generally needed to ensure that objectives are realized.

The development phase

Facilitating event policy development

As an event manager, you will come face to face with both established policies and the need for developing new policies. Sometimes you will feel constrained or limited by policy and other times you will wish that you had a policy in place to help you deal with one of the contingencies that has arisen from an event you are managing. Such is the life of an event manager. You must negotiate a world that is at once well defined and perhaps restrictive in some matters, but ill-defined and fluid in others. As these issues arise you will need to ask yourself whether existing policy helps with the present situation, or whether it needs to be modified. You might also need to ask whether a new policy needs to be developed, or whether the issue can be dealt with without a formal policy.

The foundations of policy development include four general purposes or types of policies that are germane (Graff, 1997; Howlett, 2019; Post & Preston, 2013). Each policy type is germane to your role as an event manager, and they include:

   Policy as a statement of belief, position, or value.
   Policy as a method of risk management.
   Policy as a rule.
   Policy as an aid to program effectiveness.

Event policy development involves the generation of statements or premises that direct the personnel involved in an event. Policies direct (or guide) expected approaches, actions, accountability, and the consequences of actions for the structure, network, staff, and volunteers in an event. The combination of event policies provides the foundational decision-making framework for all actions and desired outcomes. The goal of policy development is to guide event personnel by providing direction in those key areas: approach, procedures, and actions/protocols.

According to Webster (1985) and Merriam Webster (2023), policy is prudence or wisdom in the management of affairs, sagacity. Sagacity means discernment or the ability to do the right thing in the moment. Since both authors of this chapter work in higher education, they view curricula and policy as analogous allies. The term "curriculum," meaning a set of guiding principles for how a single course unfolds, also applies to how a degree unfolds, or how a program of study unfolds, or how the academic plan of an institution of higher education unfolds. "Curriculum" and "policy" might as well be synonyms. So, we encourage you to apply several guiding questions associated with curricula. Ask:

> What are the intentions?
> What are the assumptions?
> Who or what are the resources, how will they be distributed, and under what authority?
> What are the relationships necessary for things to work, and what is the authority structure for advancing these relationships?
> What has or has not worked and how do I know?
> What or how shall I learn from this and what is the process for adapting to the learning?

These questions can also be used to initiate the development of policies. Answering questions such as those posed above can aid in revealing topics that can be used to develop policies for an event. Overall, policies are necessary to provide the foundational framework of how committee members, and others associated with the event, are to interact in order to be efficient, effective, and ethical. Procedural policies are needed to guide actions during interactions. Protocol policies are necessary to provide rules of behaviour during the interactions. The intertwining of policy between and among these factors increases accountability and fosters corporate responsibility (Waddock & Smith, 2000).

Example of event policy and contracts topics from a student paper:
By Landon Fletcher

- Event health and injury policy
- Scheduling policy
- Alcohol and drug policy
- Ineligible participants policy
- Violence policy
- Policy concerning types of transportation to be available, for disabilities, VIPs, and participants
- Required accreditation for transportation use
- Transportation routes and scheduling policy
- Parking services contract
- Tow truck company contract
- Limo and bus contract

Facilitating policy congruence

When facilitating the development of event policy, consider the concept of congruence. It has been noted that congruence involves "the suitability or appropriateness of the chosen policy given the external and internal operating pressures experienced" (Ghobadian et al., 2001, p. 387). This suitability requires an understanding of whether a policy can realistically be implemented based on the pressures experienced when facilitating an event. To aid in effectively bringing a policy into effect while under pressure, an event manager must facilitate the advance of three equally important elements to achieve policy congruence, including: (i) a well-defined policy, (ii) clearly formulated and articulated strategies for implementation, and (iii) an implementation management strategy (James et al., 1999). All three elements are important as they overlap upon each other and are dependent upon each other for successful policy development and implementation. A well-defined policy involves short and coherent statements that are easy to interpret consistently. The strategies for implementation must include an examination concerning the demand for event coordination. Further, there is generally a need to lower this coordination demand and, at the same time, ensure the event has the capacity to coordinate the policy implementation requirements (Sarma et al., 2008). Further, event policy development and implementation must also consider cultural sensitivity, with authentic attention being paid to relationships with Indigenous peoples and their land rights, as well as ecological and environmental sustainability (Wood, 2002; Truth and Reconciliation Commission of Canada, 2015; Wabie et al., 2021). Additionally, an implementation management strategy involves streamlining policy-driven event processes, the sharing of expertise, transparency in communication, a monitoring system, and training to enact a policy. "Enacting policy" is one of those phrases that looks simple on paper. Simple, but not easy. Regardless of the country, region, and city in which you host your event, failing to engage authentically with cultural values will result in reputational damage to your event and to you, as the manager who did not prepare the event with cultural sensitivity in mind. For example, the timing of an event should consider cultural, ethnic, and/or religious affiliations and observances, such as Ramadan or Passover. It should consider the climate and weather patterns and the cultural value of any sites being used for the event (Game et al., 2018). Policy development and implementation must also consider food and clothing customs and rituals, as well as relational dynamics, language preferences, interpreters and translators, community leaders, Indigenous land practices and treaties, arrival and departure times of delegates, traffic patterns and transportation, communication patterns, among others (Nastasi & Hitchcock, 2016).

There are several elements in the Development Phase of the Planning Model. This next section encourages you to complete a multiphase assignment based on the key premise that you cannot be an excellent event manager if you do not learn to think through the event hosting requirements and ensure they are congruent across all event elements. This thinking through or "pre-event anticipation" sets the stage for you to forecast potential problems or crisis points and have alternatives in place before a cascade effect unfolds. It also sets the stage for moving you into an event manager's frame of mind. The multiphase assignment requires you to apply your knowledge and determine how you will obtain additional knowledge to complete the task, as you think through the requirements specific to the traditional and niche events that need to be organized. Working through an assignment such as this requires you to select an event of your choice and then to generate an overview of the planning items for the Development Phase elements outlined below. In your engagement with the assignment, consider what you have read about cultural sensitivity, environmental sustainability, consultation, and anticipation. You may also choose to delay these assignments until you have completed the chapter. Regardless – if you want to take event management seriously, you will eventually need to practice. Your first policy development and implementation experience should not be at your first event.

Assignment A – Staff and volunteer training program

Design an event staff training program. Consider the goals and objectives; policies; recruitment and interview processes; general event training and details concerning the specific components; communication processes; and retention and recognition activities.

Assignment B – Event contracts

Determine the event contracts. Where would you go to obtain a previous contract and/or to learn about the details required in each contract? Develop a list of contracts needed for your selected event. Then, in point form, provide an overview of the key elements that need to be outlined within each event contract.

Assignment C – Event permits and liability insurance

Think through the requirements for event permits and liability insurance for your selected event. Determine where you would go to obtain each type of permit and liability insurance, and provide an overview of the data required to complete the permit and to obtain the insurance, the cost, and the timeframe needed to complete the paperwork and obtain permit/insurance documents for an event.

Assignment D – The event communication system

Devise an effective event communication system; provide a diagram illustrating who will be able to contact whom and how. Be sure to consider the communication requirements for all members on the event organizational chart, such as the event volunteer management team and the event staff, and how your event staff will communicate with venue staff, volunteers, participants, transportation, accommodation, and emergency services.

Example: Policy becomes praxis

As you read the following example, make a note of which policies need to be made more explicit, and where gaps may appear in written policy. The example makes clear the link to contingency issue management. Once you have completed reading the example, based on your knowledge and thinking through of the issues and how they affected the participants, you should be able to indicate the type and the context of policies that you would need as an event manager.

Further, be sure to consider two additional policy areas that are applicable to every event. These areas include policies based on the specific laws enforced within a country, as well as institutional customs. These laws and customs may change based on different countries' interpretations, and an event manager must be open to incorporating both areas within event policy praxis.

Assignment E – The event communication system

This example is an annual meeting and conference focused on disability experience and involving disabled and non-disabled participants. The conference and AGM included approximately 120 disabled and non-disabled participants, 65 disabled youth, an organizing team of 10–12, a conference services team of four, various support staff and 65 student volunteers. There was also significant liaison with the surrounding city and region.

As far as sport, recreation, or tourism events go, a five-day, 300-person event is hardly extravagant; however, the contingencies were intriguing, to say the least. Chief among these were the heavy construction projects scattered across the area hosting the event, making entrances, exits, way finding and overall access a challenge for non-disabled participants, and a nightmare for disabled participants.

There were obvious explicit rules (i.e., policies). The safety and dignity of all participants was a priority. Disability-identified individuals were consulted on how needs were to be met. No effort was spared to make campus spaces accessible. Planning began 15 months in advance of the event. The unspoken rules were more subtle, of course. Assume that everyone has good intentions; all stakeholders get equal credit; no one argues or fights, instead having mature disagreements; reputational impact is significant; promised activities will unfold as they have been described; all volunteers and support personnel will show up and know what they must do. Deeper subtexts were anxiety over injuries, ignorance of the embodied complexities, fear of saying the wrong thing or being inadvertently offensive, food allergies, getting lost on the way to activities, missing buses and planes, and no shows.

The larger system at work for this event to be successful was an authentic meritocracy; that is, a code of conduct where people do indeed work hard for the good of the event, feel a sense of pride in that work ethic, and are publicly appreciated for that work ethic.

Also significant was a commitment to considering the complexities of people, places, objects, and happenings, and the existential or "lived" dimensions of body, space, time, and relation. When we consider "lived" experience, we mean those taken for granted aspects of bodily life that are so familiar that they become invisible. The event manager must learn to make the familiar strange, thereby bringing "lived" experience to conscious awareness. Within the conference, there were several prominent happenings including an opening ceremony, various receptions, excursions to the surrounding region's tourist sites, a closing banquet, an annual general meeting, conference sessions, keynote and plenary speakers, and an activity and social program for the youth delegates.

One youth delegate activity was sailing. The sailing activity had been organized months ahead of time with the number of kids who needed special seats or partners being discussed, along with the number of boats available and the number of support personnel needed to be present on site. There was one-to-one volunteer support for the delegates, but none of the volunteers had expertise in sailing. The host city provided free bus transportation for the delegates and their volunteers, and medical support and coordinators for the three buses. Directions to the site were in hand. The weather was perfect. We had mistakenly assumed that the weather was our only uncontrollable contingency, and at the outset, it was cooperating. As one contingency after another presented itself, we realized in hindsight that we had not taken seriously enough the "lived through" experiences of body, space, time, and relation. The saga unfolds.

The greater than typical numbers of people using wheelchairs and ambulatory assists meant that boarding the buses took an hour longer than we had planned. Although we had cell phones, there was no phone contact at the destination site so we could not inform them of the late arrival. This is an example of non-disabled people underestimating the time it takes for a disabled person to access and gain entry to a transportation vehicle. Further, the delegates on the buses were experiencing an hour of waiting in a hot space in close quarters with other bodies, so the embodied experience of that hour probably felt much longer and the bodily experience of sweating on vinyl seats with 30 of your close friends was also a less than exhilarating start to the activity.

Finally, the buses departed, and air conditioning and motion dismissed the previous frustrations. Directions to the site were excellent; getting from the site entrance to the boats was more complicated as there was no signage, no familiar humans, and no obvious signs of a sailing activity for disabled youth. Thanks to innovative and observant volunteers, we were able to make our way to the dock where three boats and three sailing support personnel awaited 65 children and youth as the weather developed into the hottest day on record.

Results included dehydration leading to seizures and adverse medication reactions in several delegates (unanticipated body responses); numerous non-event people in the general area volunteered their boats, drinking water, and a variety of play objects (balls, frisbees, kites). This was an unanticipated but welcome experience of a lived relation. Once again, the felt sense of lived time reared its ugly head as waiting for turns felt endless; however, volunteers maximized the waterfront site, thereby using lived space in an innovative and safety-conscious fashion. The coordinators learned from the earlier lived time bus loading adventure and began a phased return to the campus once groups of delegates had completed their recreational sailing and tourism experience. As a planning team, we had woefully underestimated lived time and lived bodies and had overestimated the lived relation preparedness of our sailing program team. Our volunteer and citizen lived space and relation contributions were pleasant surprises.

This one occurrence within a larger event is a dramatic example of how considering lived bodies allowed us to plan, adapt, and evaluate our behaviour. However, it did not allow us to turn back the clock and pretend that all was well and that our planning and policies had been adequate to the challenges of our highly (bodily) contingent population.

It must also be said here that even if our group had not been a group of disabled children and youth, several significant errors occurred long before the sailing day happened. I challenge you now to revisit these earlier posed questions considering the event just described.

> What were the intentions?
> What were the assumptions?
> Who or what were the resources?
> What materials were needed?
> What were the relationships that are necessary for it to work?
> Were there any applicable laws and customs?
> What did not work and how did I know?
> What/how shall I learn from this?
> What can be done better next time?

Now, add to your reconsideration of these questions one final reflective activity: Assume that your overall approach is a contingency-based model with a serious consideration of bodily contingency. Suggest one procedure and one protocol, along with required policies that might have made a difference for the sailing day. Embracing contingency will allow you to anticipate and respond in ways that make your policies coherent and your events memorable for all the best reasons, including actions that promote dignity and respect.

The challenge of facilitating policy statements into practice

One challenge in event management is the facilitation of the generation of policy statements that direct personnel in their expected approaches, actions, accountability, and in their awareness of and reflections on the consequences of actions. Overall, the practice of generating policies is used to guide activities within the structure of an event, including the staff and volunteers. And, as has been mentioned earlier, making the familiar strange is a key anticipation strategy that should also inform event policy development, implementation, and evaluation.

Another important area for consideration in the development phase of the planning model is the management of event volunteers. Review your answers to Assignment A above and then consider the items discussed below on facilitating event volunteer management. What could be added to ensure your Assignment A is complete?

Facilitating event volunteer management

by Lorne Adams

Volunteers are as diverse as the society in which we live, encompassing rich and poor, employed and unemployed, professionals and labourers, moms and dads, young and old, and friends. A volunteer provides their services and talents with no expectation of remuneration in return for their involvement, other than a sense of contributing to the greater good.

Volunteering is the most fundamental act of citizenship and philanthropy in our society.

It involves offering time, energy, and skills of one's own free will. It is an extension of being a good neighbour, transforming a collection of houses into a community, as people become involved in the improvement of their surroundings and choose to help others. By caring and contributing to change, volunteers decrease suffering and disparity, while they gain skills and self-esteem and change their lives. Overall, they mobilize "people to improve lives, communities and society" (Volunteer Canada, 2017, p. 1).

A volunteer management program

Unless you are involved in an already established program you may need to be the driving force behind establishing a volunteer program that will benefit both your event and the volunteer. Starting from scratch may seem a little daunting, but just like the rest of the concepts in this text, some careful planning will go a long way to ensuring everyone's needs are met. Just as you have established values, goals, and objectives for your project, the same thought processes will go into the creation of a successful volunteer program.

Why a volunteer management program should be developed

Quirk (2009) asked questions concerning the need for, and value of, the development of a volunteer management program. In response, there should be some direct service value to your organization. In addition, this service value extends to the individual volunteer, and the opportunity should be available to serve the larger community and to develop personal skills. It is through volunteering that you may make connections or linkages that would not otherwise be possible, or perhaps you simply have an increased profile locally and/or beyond. The management of the volunteers should not be left to chance but should be a well-planned and organized program. To begin this program, a code for volunteer management is needed.

A code for volunteer involvement

An organization called the Canadian Code For Volunteer Involvement (CCFVI) (2017) suggests that the development of a code can outline values, principles, and standards that aid in decision-making. As such, the CCFVI consists of several important elements, including:

> Values for volunteer involvement
> Core statements of the importance and value of volunteer involvement
> Guiding principles for volunteer involvement

The development phase

- Principles detailing the exchange between voluntary organizations and volunteers
- Organization standards for volunteer involvement
- Standards in developing or reviewing how volunteers are currently involved. (p. 5).

Volunteer Canada (2017) also outlined some national standards for volunteer involvement in an audit tool that provides a sound basis for mounting a volunteer program. Johnson (2006) has also provided guidelines for volunteer training that contributes to inclusive practices.

Support for the volunteer management program

A volunteer management program needs to be established with the full support of the organization, including the Board of Directors and the Executive Committee (Quirk, 2009). Obviously, a program cannot be successful if only a small segment is committed to the enterprise. As Penner (2002) has pointed out, there is a certain amount of neophobia – fear of the new – that both individuals and organizations harbour. The amount of stress that change induces is related to the size and impact of the change, the amount of preparation performed for the change, and the level of input from those affected by the change. This means that the introduction of a volunteer program requires that your communication skills are well developed and that you are equipped to be an agent of change. The benefits of your new program will need to be well articulated and should answer questions such as:

What are your short-term goals?
What are your long-term goals?
What benefits will the organization accrue from this volunteer management program?
How much money will be required to support the program?
What human and technological resources will the program require?
Where are volunteers needed?
What specific skills will volunteers need?

As Hager and Brudney (2004) indicate, "Benefits and challenges are two sides of the same coin" (p. 2). Being fully aware of both will aid in gaining support from all sectors in the organization.

While they bring much to the table, "volunteers are not free" (Quirk, 2009, p. 2). This means that there is a need for financial and human resource support for the volunteer management program. It will be your job to determine what resources are needed for the program and you will also need to develop those resources. Even if your organization is small, someone is going to have to provide training and supervision to those volunteers. As more volunteers are needed, the level of supervision, reporting, and accountability also increases. This may mean that someone will have to be assigned those responsibilities and, further, you may need to hire someone to assume that responsibility. Either way, event managers must address that there are direct and indirect costs for the volunteers. There may be some training involved for the person who will supervise volunteers. You may wish to send that person to training workshops or conferences. In addition, a volunteer recognition program is not without cost. As the event manager, you will need to account for these costs. You will need to assess whether those costs provide you with the benefits you hope for and if the funds are not available, fundraising may be necessary.

The volunteer management program structure and processes

Next, you will need to think through how you would like the volunteer management program to function and how each volunteer role fits into the functional processes (Quirk, 2009). The functional processes can be established by asking the questions:

To whom will the volunteers report?
How will volunteers report?

Consideration of the benefits of a volunteer management coordinator could be valuable. Hager and Brudney (2004) looked at the net benefits accrued by an organization in terms of the investment in a paid staff member who assumed volunteer management duties. For years now, their research has shown that the lowest level of net benefits was associated with not having a volunteer coordinator. Conversely, they found that net benefits to the organization increased as paid staff members (1/3 time, 1/3 to 2/3, 2/3 time and above) devoted more time to volunteer management. They were surprised, however, to find that unpaid managers in the volunteer management role had net benefits just as high as those paid volunteer coordinators who spent a substantial amount of time on volunteer management. While they admitted that this phenomenon needed further study, it appears that in some organizations an unpaid volunteer can be just as effective as a paid staff member. They hypothesized that unpaid volunteers have what Susan Ellis (2011) has called "the luxury of focus" (para 3); that is, those volunteers that were not constrained in their duties by other organizational duties and commitments were able to have better focus on the volunteer task at hand. They further explain that unpaid coordinators may have a special rapport with their volunteers, which may improve the experience and performance of the volunteer program. Having the right person in the right place appears to provide substantial benefit to an organization.

Volunteer roles

At this point an assessment can be made as to the specific tasks that volunteers will complete. Again, answering a few questions can aid in the development of this activity, including:

> *Are there tasks that could easily be passed off to a volunteer that would free up staff to do other activities?*
> *How do the volunteers assist us in achieving our mission goals and objectives?*
> *How many volunteers will be needed?*
> *How many different types of volunteers are needed and what specialized skills are required? What type of involvement will we be asking of the volunteers?*

Hager and Brudney (2004) have indicated that volunteers have different interests and ways in which they can contribute. Their research indicated that organizations derive more benefits if they arrange for volunteers to perform a variety of functions within the organization. They concluded that using volunteers in a variety of assignments was positively related to net benefits. Even though the "use (of) volunteers in various assignments incur(s) greater demands on management and greater challenges" (p. 8).

Volunteer recruitment and assignment

The volunteer assignments should fit the specific needs of the organization and the volunteer. To get started, one of the things you can do would be to make a list of all the different types of volunteers your organization will need, and then develop a profile of the individual best suited to that type of job. Think about where you might encounter that type of individual and what would be the best way to get in touch with them. Quirk (2009) recommends identifying "recruiters" who can ask their friends and contacts to volunteer. "The number one way volunteers get involved is from being personally asked" (Quirk, 2009). This is a very powerful statement and reaffirms the need to constantly develop and expand our network. The more people we have in the network, the greater the resource pool from which to draw.

Before we can match profiles though, it is imperative that, for each volunteer assignment, a clear and detailed position description is created. Volunteers need to know specifically what their duties and responsibilities will be and what skills they will need for a particular task. Volunteers should also be provided with a realistic estimate of the amount of time a particular assignment will entail. It is just as unfair to overestimate the level of time commitment as it is to underestimate the level of time commitment. Given, as we have mentioned before, that volunteers tend to be episodic and interested in satisfying their own needs, a realistic statement about what personal benefits might be gained from volunteering should be included. In summary, recruitment messages need to be clear and realistic and should outline the expectations for each assignment.

Another consideration in volunteer recruitment is the level of risk associated with each position. The risk can be to either the organization or to the individual volunteer. Obviously, we want to minimize the risk for all concerned, but we probably cannot eliminate it entirely. This may mean that new policies will have to be developed or that differential levels of screening and supervision will be required depending on the assessment of the level of risk. To that end, CCFVI (2006) recommends that "Screening procedures are delivered consistently with no exceptions made for certain individuals or positions" (p. 20).

As part of the recruitment process, and to attract the best people, a list should be created of where best to post the call for volunteer positions. Some will require the use of broad-based media, while others, depending on the task, may need to be targeted as a "very specialized audience."

As part of the recruitment process, as well as an application form, taking the time to develop meaningful interview questions will help the process immensely. Well thought out questions will allow you as manager to assess what the volunteer has to offer the organization and whether they match the profile you have developed for the position. Also, good interview questions and a well-conducted professional interview allow the potential candidate to assess their own level of fit with the organization and whether their individual needs will be met by this particular assignment. They should also know at this stage that screening is an essential process and that the level of screening is concomitant with the level of risk inherent in the position.

Volunteer training

People volunteer because they have an interest in your event or cause. It is fair to assume that by doing so they want you to succeed, for your event to be a success or your cause to be recognized. It is also fair to assume that they too want to succeed at whatever assignment they have taken on. As the event manager you need to provide them with the tools (resources) and the training required so they and you can succeed. Once the interview and hiring process is complete, the volunteer needs to know about the mission, goals, and objectives of the organization. That is, they need to understand where the organization is going and how it is going to get there. Understanding the *core values* and being given an opportunity to discuss them formally or informally increases commitment and motivation. Informed people are cooperative people, and they may in fact become "advocates" for the organization, increasing your recruitment pool, your recognition in the community, or your reputation.

A *policy and procedure manual* should be provided to each volunteer, or a copy should be made available via the website. Further, volunteers should be given an opportunity to review the manual and there needs to be a mechanism for questions/feedback. In particular, the policies and procedure specific to their assignment should be highlighted.

Additionally, if the event is involved in corporate social responsibility, this needs to be incorporated into the volunteer training activities. It is imperative that all the volunteers involved in the event are involved in instituting the corporate social responsibility activities to help the program succeed. This topic is addressed in full in the imprint (section) below.

Given the type of assignment and level of risk, volunteers should be given adequate training to perform their duties. For some jobs, that can be as simple as an orientation meeting with a small fact sheet referencing specific tasks. These procedural guidelines are relatively simple and should be easy to follow. Other jobs, with elevated risk, may require specialized or even intensive training. This may mean that they are assigned a paid staff as mentor or that they need to attend special training sessions. The goal is to be able to complete their assignment without putting themselves or others at risk.

Volunteers should also be made aware of where their job begins and where their responsibilities end. This is not to curtail the enthusiasm of the individual; understanding the specific boundaries of a task prevents "job creep," communication problems, and potential conflict. Going outside the intended boundaries may also increase the risk to the individual, others, and the organizations. Ongoing supervision and regular performance evaluation should, however, ameliorate the problem. This should also give the volunteer an opportunity to provide feedback and input to the organization. The popularity of reality TV shows like *Undercover Boss* has consistently pointed to the need for an opportunity to connect to the people "on the ground" doing the work and acting as the face, and indeed as the spokespeople, of the company. Training, supervision, and feedback are big elements of satisfaction.

While it is unpleasant and not a desired outcome, there will be situations that require either a reprimand or in some cases outright dismissal. It is imperative that there is a well-delineated policy and procedure in place that clearly outlines what the grounds for dismissal are, and how it will be enacted. These rules and regulations cannot be made up as they are needed, but must be pre-determined. Each volunteer should be made aware of this at the time they are informed of the mission and goals, etc. Should the situation arise, it is imperative that the protocol is invoked, and that the dignity of the individual is respected.

Volunteer retention and autonomy

I am not sure who said it, but some sports figure once said, "It is hard to excel at things you don't enjoy!" This quote is particularly germane to the notion of volunteer retention. How long do you persist at activities you don't enjoy? Given the wide array of activities available to provide us with enjoyment, we either simply quit the activity or don't return to it in favour of something else. Volunteer retention programs need to nurture environments that are conducive to keeping volunteers.

Organizations need to develop a culture that is both welcoming and respectful. As indicated above, many organizations could not get by without volunteers. To treat them as valuable contributing members of the team is to create a symbiotic relationship that allows everyone to flourish. This relationship can be created by simply "managing," or by walking around observing and speaking with people. Your presence, even occasionally, gives status to the work being performed and provides a sense that you are invested and that you care. Opportunities to provide feedback both formally and informally provide a sense of being heard and valued. Input from volunteers can be incorporated into planning and evaluation. If volunteers are equal and contributing members of the team, the likelihood of retaining them is enhanced. Similarly, staff who work frequently and effectively with volunteers should also be recognized for their commitment to creating a positive culture for the organization.

There are many things that might attract volunteers' attention once they have selected your organization. You want to be able to keep them, particularly if there is a large investment of time, money, and training. As Hager and Brudney (2004) have indicated, to enhance retention, organizations should focus on "enriching the volunteer experience" by "recognizing volunteers, providing training and professional development, screening them and matching them to organizational tasks" (p. 1). Hager and Brudney go on to say that volunteers have been widely used to meet organizational needs for services and administration. "Most charities could not get by without their volunteers...Turnover of volunteers can disrupt the operation of the charity, threaten the ability to serve clients and signal that the volunteer experience is not as rewarding as it might be" (p. 12).

Volunteer recognition

As we have indicated earlier, volunteers provide their skills, expertise, and time with no expectation of monetary return. This does not, however, mean that we can abdicate our responsibility to acknowledge and recognize the significant contribution they make. As an event manager, you have an obligation to acknowledge publicly and formally the contribution of volunteers. This can be completed in several ways, such as printed materials, personal letters, in mass media when speaking publicly about the event, and when talking to volunteers in person.

Formal methods of recognition, such as dinners, receptions, certificates, reference letters, and letters of commendation, need to be provided both consistently and in a timely fashion.

Informal methods of recognition also need to be delivered in a timely and appropriate manner. Something as simple as an article of clothing that links the volunteer to the organization and the event goes a long way to creating a culture that increases the likelihood of that person volunteering again.

A trained, motivated volunteer base that you can count on is an invaluable resource for an event manager. Like most other concepts in this text, that type of resource does not just happen. It takes pre-planning and attention to detail. It also calls upon your skills as a manager of people to ensure that volunteers feel that they have made a worthwhile contribution and that their involvement is valued and acknowledged.

Just as important in event management is the staff management program. An assignment now is for you to devise a staff management program for an event that incorporates the elements of structural development, recruitment, training, assignment of tasks, monitoring and management, retention, and recognition.

Conclusions

The initial Development Phase of the event planning model challenges the facilitation skills of an event manager. The critical aspects that need to be facilitated at this stage of an event encompass areas such as the advance of the event goals and objectives, as well as policies, contracts, and the communication system, along with the staff and volunteer management program. Understanding facilitation and advancing one's skill in this area is vital to the success of any event.

Chapter questions

1. Develop an overview of what an event manager does during the Development Phase of an event and the skills required to complete the tasks.
2. What are the four general purposes of policy development?
3. What are the three equally important elements in event policy congruence? Also, how can these elements be accomplished in event management?
4. Describe how an event manager must manage the tensions implicit in contingency, anticipation, authentic consultation, and environmental sustainability.

5. Discuss the impact of volunteers in the field of event management and the need to properly engage with and prepare the volunteers.
6. Describe practices within a volunteer life cycle.
7. Describe a minimum of three strategies outlined in this chapter that are used to reveal areas that require the generation of policy statements that direct personnel involved in an event.
8. What is cultural sensitivity? What is its importance in event planning and policy development?

References

Canadian Code for Volunteer Involvement (CCFVI). (2006). *An audit tool*. https://volunteer.ca

Ellis, S. (2011). Volunteering in for-profit settings: Exploitation or value added? *Energize*. https://www.energizeinc.com/hot-topics/2000/february

Game, E. T., Tallis, H., Olander, L., et al. (2018). Cross-discipline evidence principles for sustainability policy. *National Sustainability, 1*, 452–454. https://doi.org/10.1038/s41893-018-0141-x

Ghobadian, A., Viney, H., & Holt, D. (2001). Seeking congruence in implementing corporate environmental strategy. *International Journal Environmental Technology and Management, 1*, 384–401.

Graff, L. (1997). *Excerpted from by definition: Policies for volunteer management*. Graff and Associates.

Hager, M., & Brudney, J. (2004). *Balancing act: The challenges and benefits of volunteers*. The Urban Institute.

Howlett, M. (2019). *Designing public policies: Principles and instruments* (2nd ed.). Routledge.

James, P., Ghobadian, A., Viney, H., & Lui, J. (1999). Addressing the divergence between environmental strategy formulation and implementation. *Management Decision, 37*, 3338–347. http://dx.doi.org/10.1108/00251749910269384

Johnson, M. (Ed.). (2006). *Disability awareness: Do it right*. Avocado Press.

Merriam Webster Dictionary. https://merriam-webster.com/dictionary/policy.2023

Nastasi, B. K., & Hitchcock, J. H. (2016). *Mixed methods research and culture specific interventions—Program design and evaluation*. Sage.

Penner, L. (2002). Dispositional and organizational influences on sustained volunteerism: An interactionist perspective. *Journal of Social Issues, 58*(3), 447–467.

Post, J. E., & Preston, L. E. (2013). *Private management and public policy-the principle of public responsibility*. Stanford University Press.

Quirk, M. (2009). *Fourteen steps to develop a top-notch volunteer program*. CharityVillage.com. https://charityvillage.com/14_steps_to_developing_a_top_notch_volunteer_program/

Sarma, A., Herbsleb, J., & van der Hoek, A. (2008). Challenges in measuring, understanding, and achieving social-technical congruence. Workshop on Social-Technical Congruence, Leipzig, Germany. Available as Technical Report CMU-ISR-105, Carnegie Mellon University, Institute for Software Research International, Pittsburgh, PA.

Truth and Reconciliation Commission of Canada. (2015). *Final report of the truth and reconciliation commission of Canada. Summary: Honoring the truth; reconciling for the future. Winnipeg.* The Truth and Reconciliation Commission of Canada.

Volunteer Canada. (2017). *Canadian code for volunteer involvement.* https://volunteer.ca/vdemo/ResearchAndResources_DOCS/Volunteer_Canada_Canadian_Code_for_Volunteer_Involvement_2017.pdf

Wabie, J.-L., London, T., & Pegahmagabow, J. (2021). Land-based learning journey. *Journal of Indigenous Social Development, 10*(1), 50–80. https://journalhosting.ucalgary.ca/index.php/jisd/article/view/70389

Waddock, S., & Smith, N. (2000, Winter). Corporate responsibility audits: Doing well by doing good. *Sloan Management Review,* 75–83.

Webster's new collegiate dictionary. (1985). Thomas Allen.

Wood, M. E. (2002). Ecotourism: Principles, practices, and policies for sustainability. UNEP. United Nations Environment Programme. UN Publication.

The event operational planning phase of the event planning model

Cheryl Mallen

The second phase in the event planning model is the *Event Operational Planning Phase*, or the *Logistical Phase*. During this phase the written operational plans for the variety of event components are generated. Examples of event components include accommodation, accreditation, ceremonies, communications, food and beverage services, hospitality services, media management, participant management, security, volunteer management, results and awards, spectator services, and transportation.

Logistical plans are the guiding instructions for hosting an event. This chapter details a series of mechanisms that contribute to operational planning success. Assignments are presented throughout the chapter, and additionally, case studies are outlined in the Appendix. Review the case studies to determine the critical aspects of event operational planning – such as potential arising logistical issues, how much detail is necessary to properly guide others involved in event management, and writing succinctly.

Mechanism 1: The cultivation of the operational planning network

To begin the operational planning process, an event manager facilitates the formation of an operational planning network. The creation and use of this network requires an event manager to have the skills and sensibilities to facilitate the assignment of the best possible people, along with the correct number and combination of individuals with planning expertise, to meet the operational planning requirements for the event. There is no single formula for assigning the network of individuals correctly; each situation is unique.

DOI: 10.4324/9781003391098-4

Event Development Phase

The event manager facilitates the development of event structures for governance, event networks, policies, volunteer practices, and participation

Event Evaluation and Renewal Phase

The event manager facilitates the selection of event components to be evaluated, the completion of the evaluation tasks, and the implementation of the evaluation recommendations

Event Operational Planning Phase

The event manager creates and facilitates the development of written operational plans that are logical, sequential, detailed and integrated, along with contingency plans and the activation of a plan refining process

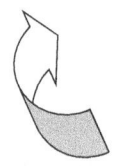

Event Implementation, Monitoring and Management Phase

The event manager facilitates the implementation of the written operational plans, monitors activities looking for deviations, and manages all deviations from the plans

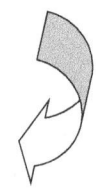

Figure 4.1 An event planning model

However, if individuals are assigned incorrectly, problems that influence the efficiency and effectiveness of the plan may arise. Further, the task of creating operational plans for each component requires an intricate combination of talented planners who can develop the operational plans for their own component as well as coordinate and cooperate with other event component personnel.

A simple exercise will demonstrate the complexity of assigning individuals to tasks. Consider subdividing the members of a class to complete operational plans for eight selected event components (for a traditional or niche event). How would you subdivide the class? What elements would you consider in subdividing the group? There are many ways to assign network members, including: dividing individuals into groups that have similar expertise; creating groups that offer a wide variety of expertise which could broaden the knowledge base; or creating groups that are devised based on whether they work well together. Individuals could be placed in groups based on their personal interest in the component. There is no one right way to subdivide the class that can be applied to every situation. It is important for an event manager to develop an understanding of, and sensitivity to, the elements of assigning individual members of the network based on the context.

Individuals assigned to each event operational planning component make up a node. A node may be further subdivided into constituent nodes. For example, those planning the accommodation component can be subdivided into constituent nodes whereby each is responsible for the accommodation plans of a separate part, such as those for the event participants, another for the officials, and a third node that manages the accommodation for the organizing committee members. Links between constituent nodes foster the interactions required to complete the overall accommodation planning tasks.

The links between nodes (including links within a component and between components) create a network of multilateral intra-organizational alliances. These links determine how members interact to establish plans, manage planning decisions, and manage issues or problems. Each link is part of the structural design, creating a network alliance that can be unique in its application.

The design of the network alliance is crucial to the effectiveness of the development of successful operational plans. What guides the design of each network in the operational planning phase? Wijngaard, deVries, and Nauta (2006) hold that it is the authority and responsibility assigned with the tasks that determine a configuration or structure. This structure establishes the expected behaviours of the event operational network members and the event planners that guide the network design. This means that an event manager needs to be sensitive to the event context to effectively configure the multilateral positions, the role of the members, the power, approvals, subdivisions, and overall autonomy required for event operational planning. A combination of organic structures – through which members have the authority to make decisions concerning their component – as well as hierarchical structures may be needed to suit a particular complex event environment. There is no single predetermined structural design that has been deemed best for operational planning for event components. An event manager needs to be open to different intra-organizational network designs that may be needed for the various event components. Whatever structure is designed for an event, an event manager must monitor its applicability to the event activities and facilitate adaptations if needed.

Theory can be reviewed to gain understandings of the influences that impact the design of a network alliance. For example, the characteristics found within contingency theory, complexity theory, dissipative structures, agency theory, and the theory of marginal gains can be applied to a network design.

Application of contingency theory

Contingency theory indicates that there is no single correct way to structure the alliance linkages between the planning nodes – the event structure selected must be the proper fit for the pursuit of superior performance (Victer, 2020). This fit involves accounting for environmental factors (Safari & Saleh, 2020). This is because characteristics of contingency theory tells us that the search for one correct structure is simply not available in the world, as one system of organization cannot be found that "is superior to all others in all cases" (Owen, 2001, p. 399).

An application of the characteristics of contingency theory during the event operational phase implies that an operational network design that worked for a previous event may not work for any other event. This means that an event manager cannot simply apply a network design that worked for a previous event – the event manager must be able to "think through" the appropriate network design to be created for each event. The structure of each operational planning alliance must be efficiently designed for the specific needs of each event.

Application of complexity theory

Complexity theory indicates that a basic condition of our contemporary environment is that it is in a pivotal state (Doherty & Delener, 2001). This means that the conditions include levels of "uncertainty, diversity and instability" (Stacey, 1996, p. 349). Complexity stems from change and we cannot expect to work in an environment devoid of change. An event manager, thus, must have a mindset that change is normal, and be open to, and prepared for, changing conditions. Further, a stable state is not achievable because the "world is primarily made of dissipative structures" (Keirsey, n. d., para. 9).

Application of dissipative structures

Dissipative structures involve a constant evolving of structures as they are being pulled apart and refitted by several forces, and this means one cannot be expected to be in a state of "equilibrium" (Keirsey, n. d., para. 9). An example involves a classroom of students that comes together once per week. When the class has finished for the week, the students leave the classroom or dissipate. They come together again the next week, but all

The event operational planning phase

may not be the same. Some students may miss this class, others may attend that missed last week, students may generally be in the same seats with a few exceptions. There may be, for whatever reason, a change in the classroom. This means the structure of the class is a dissipative structure that is reproduced or repeated and a fully steady state (or equilibrium) is difficult because structures tend to be continuously pulled apart and then recombined again.

An event manager must efficiently design the operational network alliance to be adaptable to conditions of change. An understanding that change is expected implies that once the network alliance is designed and instituted, the work of the designer is not finished. The network must be managed to cope with new or changing conditions. For instance, if volunteers cannot make it to the scheduled training session, perhaps two sessions are required to aid in accommodating the lives of the volunteers. Change may involve the movement of network members within the nodes, the replacement of some members or the reconfiguration of how the nodes interact. Multilateral intra-organizational network alliances are made over time, and adaptations must also be made continuously to ensure that the design meets the flexibility demands for developing flexible operational plans to stage an event.

Overall, those managing events need a mindset for change, and to prepare for potential change, to accommodate the lives of the volunteers. Managing change can be time consuming. Dissipative structures, however, are a reality and a key reason why event managers must learn to "think through" event requirements and not rely on previous event operational plans.

Application of agency theory

Agency theory pertains to two key issues that are applicable to the operational planning phase. Both issues deal with ensuring the cooperation of planning efforts. The first issue involves times when "the desires or goals of the principal and agent conflict [as] ... it is difficult or expensive for the principal to verify what the agent is actually doing" (Eisenhardt, 1989, p. 5). An application of this issue means that the operational planning network needs to:

> Ensure that all parties understand their expected behaviour while in the operational planning phase;
> Encourage the group to work toward the collective goals and objectives;

    Facilitate efficient group progress; and
    Ensure excellent communication among the network members concerning the operational planning progress.

Completing these elements can aid in verifying the progress being made by the multiple members in the network who are generating the operational plans and ensuring coordination between a variety of planners.

The second issue in agency theory involves "risk sharing that arises when the principal and agent have different attitudes toward risk" (Eisenhardt, 1989, p. 58). An application of this issue means that the network members must manage operating planning risk elements, such as the timing of the completion of operational plans, and be concerned with the impact of critical time periods.

Application of the theory of marginal gains

The theory of marginal gains indicates that small improvements, such as pushing for even 1% improvements, can make a difference over time (Harrell, 2015). An application of this theory to event management in the operational planning phase implies that small improvements in preparing for change, operational planning detail, ensuring the integration of various components into seamless plans, staff and volunteer training, etc., can improve the overall event. An event manager should, thus, constantly seek to promote improvement.

Mechanism 2: Generating written operational plans

The event operational network members are assigned the task of generating the written operational plans that constitute guiding instructions for staging each component within an event. This task compels the members of the operational network to produce the directions for the delivery of the event (Wijngaard et al., 2006). These written operational plans establish the goals and directions for managing all functions of staging the event. Generally, multiple operational plans are created in tandem. All members of an operational network within each node are required to have the expertise needed to meet the scope of responsibility for the planning function. This scope includes designing the written format for the operational plan and creating logical, sequential, detailed, and integrated plans.

The written event operational plan: Establishing a design format

To begin the task of recording the step-by-step instructions for the operational plan, a format is needed to achieve consistency and control (Wijngaard et al., 2006). This format guides how all written operational plans are to be laid out. Multiple formats have been used for sport, recreation, and tourism events. There is no one correct format that can be used. The general rule for selecting a format is to ensure that all requirements of the plan can be expressed. These requirements can include a number of items such as:

- An executive summary
- The timing of each planned activity
- A detailed list of planned tasks
- The authority for each planned element
- Event diagrams illustrating activity sites and the placement of key event items

Any format selected must account for the complexity and fluidity of event operational planning along with the requirements of what must be recorded within a specific plan to ensure that the elements are communicated in an easy-to-use manner. See examples of design formats in the operational plans provided in the Appendices at the end of this chapter.

Logical operational planning

Operational planning includes the deliberate creation of suppositions, assumptions, and conclusions for the development of a coherent and logical step-by-step written list of reasoned event activities to stage a successful event. During the creation of the written operational event plans, all members of the operational planning network must learn to determine and record the individual activities or tasks necessary to complete their event component. This activity requires a "thinking through" process that is not a simple activity. This is because concentration on each element within the component, and the delineation of each logical step, along with the recording of the steps, is a complex and time-consuming task.

Why is a list or template to follow for operational planning not provided

Many events that have previously been held have information that can be reviewed, such as lists or outlines of event activities. This reference information may provide guidance for developing logical operational plans for an event. However, the reference information is contextually specific and does not take into consideration the unique nuances that may exist within other events. The information is tied to the structure of the operational network, and the components and detailed actions that were designed for that event.

Reference information is valuable only for gaining common knowledge about an event. The reference material does not replace an event manager's responsibility to "think through" each activity and develop advanced knowledge of the specific facility and activities of the current event. There are no shortcuts to the thinking through process for excellent event-specific operational plans.

Sequential operational planning

Each operational plan needs to itemize the event tasks in an ordered and reasoned sequence. The most common method used to achieve this end involves using the concept of time. For example, an operational plan can be subdivided to record all of the tasks that must be completed within 3, 6, or 12 months prior to an event, as well as the activities during the week prior to the event and a minute-by-minute list of tasks for each day of the event. As a parallel activity, separate sequential plans can be created to outline the specific items needed from the venue (such as rod and drape, tables, chairs), including the time and site at which they are required.

To help in the development of sequential operational plans, the concept of *weaving* is used. Weaving involves conceptually thinking through the requirements for each specific element of an event one at a time. For example, a network member can conceive of and record the tasks necessary to complete the media management operational plans by conceptually weaving the potential requirements of one media member from the moment of arrival at the event parking lot to their departure. This weaving process is followed repeatedly to develop the multiple logical and sequential steps that must be recorded in the operational plan. A planner can *weave forwards* or *weave backwards*.

Weaving forwards involves recording elements as they will happen, in a progressive, unfolding process. In contrast, weaving backwards requires conceptually thinking of the end product and then backtracking to determine the step-by-step activities that were completed.

It does not matter if a planner conceptually thinks through the planning requirements by weaving forwards or backwards. The aim is to develop a process that assists in determining the sequential steps to stage the event.

Detailed operational planning

The amount of detail required in an operational plan differs from event to event and can be a difficult decision for an event manager. The plans need to be written in a clear format to ensure that other members in the network can read, understand, and be guided to complete the tasks as outlined. The plan must provide clarity, limit emerging questions, and reduce the potential for improper interpretations concerning the actions needed to produce the event. A detailed account of each task is necessary, but the difficulty lies in determining the appropriate threshold for detail. How much detail is required?

There are three threshold levels of detail in operational planning. Each level requires a different amount of detail in the written record concerning each event task. The three levels are referred to as level 1, level 2, and level 3 planning. The higher the threshold level, the greater the detail provided within the operational plan.

> *Level 1 planning* provides the lowest level of planning detail. A level 1 plan uses a minimal level of detail to explain each task. Level 1 planning is open to questions concerning the clarity of the event tasks and does not provide a detailed step-by-step list of directions to avoid misinterpretations should others enact the plan. Consequently, level 1 planning is open to the interpretations of those implementing the plans, and these interpretations may alter the planned activities.
>
> *Level 2 planning* requires a higher or medium amount of planning detail. This level of planning provides general clarity and offers more detailed step-by-step directions to enact the plan. Level 2 planning answers the majority of the questions one would have if implementing the plan. However, the plan is still open to some interpretations that may alter the planned activities.

Level 3 planning demands the highest level of detail. The level 3 plan provides clear instructions and includes the intimate requirements to complete the tasks. Level 3 planning is open to a limited number of questions and potential plan deviations, as minute details for the completion of each task have been provided.

An event manager must facilitate an understanding of the sensitivities of the detail required for a particular event. There is a subtle difference between providing instructions and offering too much detail to the point where the network members do not read the plans. For example, select a familiar task and consider at which point you could be given too much detailed instruction that would inhibit your ability to complete the task.

Review the case studies in the appendices at the back of this chapter to review the detail stated and determine the arising questions and detail required should you have to implement the plan.

Practice and develop your planning skills with the following assignment:

Assignment A: Level 3 planning

Develop a level 3 operational plan to aid a primary sponsor (from a company of your choice) that will be making a presentation at your chosen event (pre-event or post-event). How will you prepare to manage this participant prior to the event (i.e. provide travel and parking information) and on the day of the event (i.e. who will meet/greet them)? Think through the operational planning requirements. See Appendix for a 3-column chart format to get your started.

Mechanism 3: The inclusion of contingency and emergency plans

Events are susceptible to *contingency* and *emergency issues* – and event managers must be cognisant of potential issues and their impacts on an event. Contingency issues cause deviations from the event operational plan. Event managers facilitate the development of continency and emergency plans to manage issues efficiently and effectively. The outcome is back-up plans.

Contingency issues differ from an application of contingency theory that is focused on the event structure established in the pursuit of excellence in

The event operational planning phase

Level 1 planning detail	Level 2 planning detail	Level 3 planning detail
Anthem singer booked, arrives, and completes their technical check; readies for performance	**1-week prior to event:** Volunteer Z briefing • Date: ___ Time: ___ Site: ___ • Briefed on their role with anthem singer by _____ • Parking lot attendant to call when singer arrives **Event day:** Anthem singer arrives in 'green' room Anthem singer technical check: • Time: • Site: _____ • Singer escorted to staging area for technical check by: _____ • Wireless microphone available	**3-months prior to event:** Anthem Singer • Contract signed • Directions and parking pass sent via email by volunteer Z • Singer confirms items received **1-week prior to event:** Volunteer Z briefing • Date: ___ Time: ___ Site: ___ • Briefed on their role with anthem singer by _____ • Provided written briefing notes Parking attendant briefing – given instructions/cell number (in writing and verbal overview) to call volunteer Z upon arrival of anthem singer Anthem Singer confirms: • Bilingual anthem, max. 2 min. length • Introduction statement/reviewed/confirmed (in writing) Public Address Announcer • Anthem singer introduction confirmed **Event day:** Anthem singer arrives via personal car by 15:30 (3:30pm): • Parks in lot B • Parking attendant calls volunteer Z's cell to inform of arrival • Singer met by volunteer Z in lot and escorted to "green" room • Met and briefed in "green" room by: _____ Anthem singer technical check: • Time: _____ • Site: _____ • Singer escorted to staging area for technical check by: _____ • Wireless microphone provided by: ___ • technician on hand (with back-up mic) Anthem singer introduction: • Introduction confirmed/any changes to Public Address announcer by volunteer Z

Figure 4.2 Examples of level 1, 2, and 3 operational planning detail – Preparations for anthem singer

performance. Meanwhile, contingency issues are activities that could arise and impact an event; they cause deviations from the planned operational activities. An event manager ensures preparation, or the development of contingency plans, for a plethora of issues – just in case they occur.

Examples of event contingency issues include:

Personnel issues: such as a key person not showing up, whether a key staff member or volunteer, the anthem singer, a presenter, or the public address announcer, etc.;
Facility issues: such as the electricity shutting off, a pipe bursting and flooding the volunteer room, or issues that require janitorial staff;
Equipment issues: such as the microphone or the walkie-talkies not working;
Community issues: such as a protest that has nothing to do with the event but interrupts the transportation and entrance to the venue;
Security issues: such as when a streaker gets through security to interrupt performers – and, perhaps, promotes a sponsor written on their back.

Meanwhile, emergency issues are defined as requiring the use of emergency personnel, such as ambulance, fire, medical, police, security services, or structural engineers. Emergency plans are generally the responsibility of the facility manager for the venue and are not discussed in detail in this text. Examples of event emergencies include the 2013 Boston Marathon bombing, and the 2015 Stade de France bombing in Paris.

It is critical, however, that an event manager meet with the facility manager to discuss emergency plans and ensure access for emergency services. For instance, every event manager should be able to access the venue command centre, know how many minutes it will take to clear a section of the venue, as well as the full venue, in the event of an emergency. Additionally, they should understand how to make this evacuation happen and know pre-established routes and sites where the participants are to go once evacuated. It is important that a communication system for informing event participants and patrons of an emergency and the instructions for an evacuation are pre-established. This includes understanding what facility pre-set visuals and signage is available to aid in emergencies.

An event manager should work directly with the facility manager to adopt the specific emergency procedures that have been established and practised by the facility staff. The facility's emergency policies and procedures should be integrated within the event operational plan, and importantly, all event staff and volunteers should be trained in these procedures. It is important that the event and facility staff work in tandem during emergencies.

This integration process may not be applicable for a niche event that does not use a traditional venue. This niche situation means the event manager may be positioned to be uniquely responsible for the facility manager's role in developing the emergency policies and procedures. Knowledge in this vital role is crucial. It is recommended that event managers in this position advance their common and advancement knowledge in facility emergency management by reading pre-established policies and procedures, by talking with facility managers, and by developing relationships with emergency services staff. Always use professionals in emergency management to review your operational plans for emergencies and strongly consider their advice.

Interestingly, Rosselló, Becken, and Santana-Gallego (2020) stated a need for managers to also specifically plan for unexpected demands for change due to the natural environment or nature. Their research focused on tourism events, but is applicable to all events that can be impacted by extreme weather issues, such as high winds, major rain or snow/sleet events, sandstorms, forest fires/smoke, flooding, droughts, approaching tornadoes, or hurricanes/cyclones, etc.

Contingency and emergency planning involves two distinct strategies. First, the plans mitigate the potential issue prior to the event – to ensure that it does not happen. Mitigation strategies need to be developed for as many issues as possible. Second, for those issues that cannot be mitigated, strategies for managing the issue, should they occur, need to be generated. These plans are only instituted should the issue arise.

It is important to note that issues that have happened at previous events – or can be foreseen – and cause deviations within event operational plans are *programmed issues*. Those that cannot be foreseen are *non-programmed issues*. This implies that an event manager must be ready for both types of issues. Excellence in the event communication system is critical for managing issues.

Assignment B: Contingency issues

Using your work from Assignment A above, create a list of contingency issues or deviations that could happen when managing your event sponsor. Then develop action steps for mitigating and/or managing each issue. Determine if you will integrate these contingency plans within the operational plan, add them as a supplementary plan, or outline them in the appendix of the operational plan.

Mechanism 4: Update and test the communication system

The communication system was started in the first phase of the planning model – the Development Phase. In this second phase – the Logistical Phase – the communication system is advanced and contingency issue or emergency scenarios can be used to determine the effectiveness of the system.

What does an excellent communication system involve? It involves thinking through elements required such as:

- *Communication equipment:* obtaining cellular phones, landlines (hardwired phones), walkie-talkies, headsets, and batteries, along with back-up equipment;
- *Equipment maintenance:* ensuring equipment is charged (i.e., batteries for the walkie-talkies, and noting where back-up communication equipment will be placed);
- *Record maintenance:* including names and contact numbers, and where these numbers will be placed for easy staff/volunteer access (for example, on the back of the staff/volunteer accreditation passes);
- *Distribution of communication equipment and contact numbers:* the process for assigning equipment to staff/volunteers; the sign-out and sign back in process; determination of where back-up system equipment will be placed;
- *Testing the communication system:* ensuring those that need to be connected can converse within the communication system. This ensures access on the part of key individuals to those making decisions concerning plan adaptations, and to medical, security, and emergency personnel – this is a critical component;
- *Training to using the communication system:* ensuring all parties know which groups are to use which channel on the walkie-talkie; understanding the communication protocols (i.e., what if someone is conducting personal chatter and no one else can contact the individual when needed?).

Recognizing each communication system as unique means the equipment, system, and protocols must be designed for the individual event.

This mechanism is a critical aspect of an event, so, it is important to complete the assignment below to practice ensuring links for excellent event communication.

Assignment C: Develop a diagram of the communication structure

Draw a diagram indicating the communication connections for an event of your choice to be held at a recreational centre. This diagram should illustrate the communication options (who can talk to whom) for the event. Within the diagram, be sure to have a command centre that has access to emergency services (i.e., ambulance, fire services). Next, ensure that the heads of each event component can converse, such as the managers of transportation, accommodation, food and beverages, media, and participant management. Additionally, other connections are to be considered for your diagram, such as to the Service Department. When completed, test your communication system with the contingency issue of a fire down the street from the event venue, the smoke from which is severely impacting the air quality at your event. Do you have an effective communication system that can manage such an issue and allow for easy communication with staff/volunteers, performers, patrons, media in attendance, etc.? Did you, for instance, include the venue management in your communication options – or will they learn of the issue, and how you are managing it, via the media? Compare and contrast your communication diagram with another person's (or more than one) to review different communication organizational strategies.

Mechanism 5: Establish meeting agendas

Operational planning activities generally include meetings with the multiple groups involved in the event. These meetings may involve, for example, meeting with personnel from the venue, the media outlet, and/or the accommodation site. Thinking through the requirements for each meeting helps in devising an agenda to guide the meeting.

An event meeting agenda with the venue manager can include items that are diverse and encompass areas such as:

1. Date, time, and site of meeting
2. Those to be in attendance at the meeting
3. Welcome and introductions

Cheryl Mallen

4. Confirmation of date booked and venue rooms/areas to be used
5. Confirmation of parking requirements for event attendees and the associated costs
6. Venue access, including the specific gate/doors and the times they will be open
7. Security available during move-in activities, the event, and the move-out timeframe
8. Venue services, such as the availability and cost of having an electrician onsite, the need for electrical extension cords, ushers, food services, event marketing assistance, and the use of tables, chairs, and red carpets
9. Financial requirements, including event deposits and the final payment timeframe.

Now, think through five items that should be added to the venue meeting agenda list above.

Another example includes the development of a meeting agenda for the event manager and the contracted media outlet (i.e., television station producer) that can also span across a number of items such as:

1. Event overview (including the details to be provided to the media outlet prior to the event, such as the event activities and their timeframe, who will be involved in the opening ceremonies, and background information on key event participants)
2. Media truck arrival/departure times, along with the parking space required
3. Food and beverage requirements for media staff (including site, times, menu items, and who is responsible for paying for this service)
4. Media electrical requirements and who is responsible for paying for these services (the event or the media outlet)
5. Venue seats that need to be removed from being for sale due to camera positions/platforms
6. Specifics about what will be televised (i.e., the anthem singer, awards ceremonies, or intermission activities)
7. Sponsors and their contracted media requirements
8. Access or accreditation requirements.

A further example involves an agenda for a meeting between the event manager, the event accommodation manager and the accommodation personnel that includes items such as:

1. The number of rooms booked and the date/time that a final count must be provided
2. The number of people per room
3. Who will be paying for the rooms and the payment timeframe
4. Who is responsible for paying for services such as the mini-bar, movies, and room service
5. Signage
6. Parking availability and cost
7. Hospitality rooms.

Assignment D: Meeting agenda development

You are a manager of the opening ceremonies for an event. Establish the agenda for your first meeting with a presenting sponsor. What items need to be discussed? What would your agenda look like? Share your agenda (once completed) with others to observe agenda options.

Mechanism 6: Integrating the operational plans between event components

The development of operational plans generally begin as separate entities focusing on each event component. A key to successful event management; however, is the integration of the multiple detailed plans. Integrating, interlacing, or intertwining event elements creates multiple coherent, cohesive, and smoothly flowing plans for the overall event.

An example of integration for an accommodation plan is the interlacing of elements from the transportation plan within the accommodation plan. This integration can help to coordinate elements such as the transportation drop-off and pick-up sites at the accommodation venue. The integration can also ensure that transportation coincides with the accommodation check-in time arrangements. Integrating elements from the accreditation plan can also assist in the distribution of accreditation and room assignments all in one coordinated effort.

A successful integration process relies upon a key operational factor. This factor is the *establishment of integration exchange opportunities* for the operational network members. The integration process must be designed to provide an adequate number of exchange opportunities on a regular basis and must be adaptable to allow intermittent integration exchanges to meet the integration workflow requirements. Generally, there is a large amount of planning detail, and the integration process is complex (Matusik, 2002). An event manager facilitates an integration process and ensures that multiple exchange opportunities are arranged, if required. Common strategies for integration can include messages, bulletins, announcements, charts, drawings, diagrams, sketches, maps, and reports.

A particularly crucial strategy for integration is to set up *production meetings* between the members from different components. These meetings provide opportunities for each member to discuss and coordinate items from their component with the other components.

It is important to note that *network theory* indicates that operational network members can exchange planning data without the use of a hierarchy. The success of an event is, however, contingent upon the extent to which the event manager can facilitate the transfer of operational data across the planning nodes. The flow of the operational planning knowledge is contingent on the structure and strategies established to disseminate the transfer.

Assignment E: Integration of operational plans

You are the manager of an event component (of your choice, i.e., event transportation). Develop a list of areas that need to be integrated or coordinated with the other components – i.e., transportation needs to be coordinated with the food and beverage component to ensure performers make it to the meal venue during the correct time period, and must be coordinated with the performance schedule, as the drivers will field questions from the passengers and they should be able to provide answers (or be able to access answers) to ensure the event is seamless.

Mechanism 7: Prepare for event issues and political 'games' with a guiding ethical statement

Beyond contingency issues, event managers must be prepared to manage the political 'games' that can impact an event. Events can be rife with politics among organizers, sponsors, participants, and others. This can be referred to as the "game-within-the-game" (GwG). This is where those involved use their role in the conducting of the event for their own purposes, to promote themselves or their special interest. Who plays these games? Those playing the political game can be found anywhere in an event and can be a distraction from the business of planning and running the event. They also have the potential to detract from or even sabotage the success of the event. Every event is different and the GwGs can be unique to the event activities and individuals associated with the event. Consequently, the event management team must expect the GwG to occur and be prepared to identify situations where it can or has occurred and develop mitigating strategies for managing it should it arise.

Sometimes the GwG can benefit the organizers. For instance, an individual may be thrilled to be part of the organization committee of an event to advance their personal skills and résumé. This could provide additional motivation for this person to work hard and be very committed to their assignments which would be beneficial to the event. Or, conversely, this individual may only sign up to work at the event with the intention of putting it on their résumé without much interest in completing their tasks – they show up, but end up being detrimental to the overall effort. This usually results in someone else having to take on their tasks as well as their own which stretches the available resources in a negative manner. Something as trivial as a volunteer being assigned a walkie-talkie may prompt that individual to refuse to complete their tasks because others have been assigned this communication equipment. This may make them feel that they are not as valued by the event staff.

Therefore, the role of an event manager must include seriously considering potential GwG scenarios for their particular event and alerting the management team to also consider the potential of such activities for their component. Further, the event manager must ensure that there are operational plans to mitigate and manage such activity. This is necessary as GwGs can be a distraction, can interrupt planned event activities, and can monopolize the media attention that focuses on the event.

The issues of event issues and political games is discussed further in another chapter – but in this chapter, we suggest the follows strategy to be implemented. This includes ensuring that staff/volunteers understand that arising issues – including political issues – should be reported immediately to the component and/or event manager. The sooner an issue is reported, the quicker it can be managed. An event manager must create an environment that is open to revealing and managing issues as they arise.

Mechanism 8: Preparing for the activation of the operational plans

Once logical, sequential, detailed, integrated event operational plans have been developed, along with the contingency plans, emergency plans, and plans to mitigate and manage any arising political "games," the operational plans must be distributed to the staff and volunteers. One method to manage the dissemination of those plans involves hosting a training meeting with key representatives from each component. The operational plans are distributed, and the key points are reviewed verbally. Further, the component representatives in this meeting are responsible for reviewing and presenting ideas to refine the planning statements for a coordinated and efficient effort.

The refining process is intended to add detail to the plan and eliminate any questions that may arise when the plan is implemented. An example of a refining process was first formally illustrated by the 2002 Salt Lake Olympics Organizing Committee (SLOC). This committee instituted a peer review process as a refining technique along with what they called an "Executive Roadmap" (Bowen, 2006). The peer review process included an exchange of operational plans for consideration by others within the event operational network. Reviewers searched for gaps in the detail provided in the operational plan, ensured clarity in the planning statements, and determined any questions arising when reading the operational plans. The roadmap consisted of an executive summary of the key timelines that needed to be met and was used for quick reference. Skilled event planners completed the refining process to meet the goal of planning excellence.

Mechanism 9: Practice to develop your operational planning skills

To aid in your skill development, at the end of this text, in the Appendices section, there are examples of operational plans for you to review. Review these documents to learn more about the details necessary in an event operational plan and consider any questions that would arise if you were responsible for implementing the planning actions.

The event operational planning phase

Assignment F: Developing an operational plan

Develop an operational plan for the following scenario: You are responsible for managing an in-person and virtual media conference for a major tourism event (event of your choice). This media conference is to be held midmorning, one day prior to the launch of the event, and is to be held at a major hotel in the downtown area of your city or town. Create a written operational plan for managing the key elements to complete the media conference. Be sure to include the invitations for four key media outlets to attend, including one media outlet from each of the following outlets: newspaper, radio, television, and web-based media. Further, the operational details must include setting up the media conference room or area in the hotel, managing the media personnel as they arrive, checking credentials, providing accreditation, the provision of media conference activities, and a media question period. Remember the operational plan must include all communication requirements (for example, communicating to the venue staff the requirements for tables, chairs, microphones, platforms, rod and drape, and the hanging of signage and security). Build into the plan the speakers representing the event along with the media opportunities such as personal interviews and photo opportunities. Assume you have the funding to support your activities.

When your operational plan has been completed, share it with another person or group. The sharing process is designed to allow for comparison with respect to the detail in the operational plans, along with giving rise to questions that arise if someone else must implement your plan. This sharing process is to be a learning exercise and those involved are to practice event diplomacy when sharing perspectives.

Assignment G: Continue to practice developing operational plans

Develop an operational plan for the following scenario. Your event owns drones that were designed to perform athletic feats – including flying, searching/finding, and diving down to pick up an item and be able to return to the base site. You have 12 drones, and their operators, that are in training for their future use at the new on-campus sports arena. These drones will soon be used to deliver food and beverages to patrons in the parking lot of the venue during a tailgate party. You have been hired to complete the following: food and beverage orders – along with the payment – that will be made online; your job is to ensure their order is brought to their car during the tailgate party via a drone. Develop the communication system for the drone operators. With whom do they need to converse? Outline the communication system developed for the drone operators, etc. to ensure an efficient and easy system. Indicate where you are using cellular phones, walkie-talkies, landlines, and computers (or any combination). Also, consider a back-up communication system. Outline your communication system strategy in a diagram format – it can be hand drawn. The associated communication system must link the following: 12 drone operators, 4 staff drone technicians/trouble shooters, the food and beverage coordinator; the food and beverage staff/order managers, and you – the drone coordinator.

Consider any other linkages that you would like to integrate into your communication system, such as the medical team, security, and the Media Coordinator.

Be sure to include an operational plan for your communication system hardware (what do you need? That is, how many cellular phones or walkie-talkies? What else do you need with the walkie-talkies (i.e. a battery changing system)? Where will you get it? Store it? What is the distribution process, etc.).

Conclusions

In the second phase of the planning model, the Operational Planning Phase, network members complete intensive operational plans that include timed activities for each event component. The strength of an event operational plan is determined by the logical and sequential process, the amount of planning detail provided, the integration forged between the planned components, the extra preparedness based on the contingency plans and the process of refining and communicating the plans prior to their use. Facilitating quality operational plans can be developed with practice. The concept of quality in event operational planning is discussed further in Chapter 12, "Facilitating quality in event management." Overall, the operational plans are created in preparation for the next phase in the planning model, the implementation, monitoring, and management phase.

Chapter questions

1. Develop an overview of what an event manager does during the Operational Phase of an event and the skills required to complete the tasks.

2. What are the characteristics of contingency theory, complexity theory, agency theory, and the theory of marginal gains? How can the characteristics of these theories guide an event manager in the event operational planning phase?
3. Describe the difference between level 1, level 2, and level 3 planning, and the concept of weaving.
4. How does contingency theory relate to events and differ from contingency plans?
5. What do contingency plans provide, and why are they important in event management?
6. Describe three key issues that can arise in the event operational planning phase and then outline how an event manager can act to overcome these issues.
7. How much operational detail is required? Review the operational plans in the Appendix below. What information was missing if questions arise concerning your understandings for completing the tasks – and what would you add – to the operational plans to ensure excellence in communicating operational plans?

References

Bowen, H. (2006). *The Salt Lake organizing committee: 2002 Olympics*. Harvard Business School Publishing.

Doherty, N., & Delener, N. (2001). Chaos theory: Marketing and management implications. *Journal of Marketing Theory and Practice, 9*(4), 66–75.

Eisenhardt, M. K. (1989). Agency theory: An assessment and review. *The Academy of Management Review, 14*(1), 57–74.

Harrell, E. (2015, October 30). How 1% performance improvements led to Olympic gold. *Harvard Business Review*. https://hbr.org/2015/10/how-1-performance-improvements-led-to-olympic-gold

Keirsey, D. (n.d.). The dilemma of science. In D. Keirsey, *Existence itself: Towards the phenomenology of massive dissipative/replicative structures* (Chapter 2). http://edgeoforder.org/pofdisstruct.html

Matusik, S. F. (2002). An empirical investigation of firm public and private knowledge. *Strategic Management Journal, 23*(5), 457.

Owen, R. G. (2001). *Organizational behavior in education*. Allyn and Bacon.

Roselló, J., Becken, S., & Santana-Gallego, M. (2020). The effects of natural disasters on international tourism: A global analysis. *Tourism Management, 79*, 104080. https://doi.org/10.1016/j.tourman.2020.104080

Safari, A., & Sales, S. (2020). Key determinants of SMEs' export performance: A resource-based view and contingency theory approach using potential mediators. *Journal of Business & Industrial Marketing, 35*(4), 635–654.

Stacey, R. D. (1996). *Complexity and creativity in organizations*. Berrett-Koehler.

Victer, R. (2020). Connectivity knowledge and the degree of structural formalization: A contribution to a contingency theory of organizational capability. *Journal of Organization Design, 9*(7). http://doi.org/10.1186/s41469-020-0068-3

Wijngaard, J., deVries, J., & Nauta, A. (2006). Performers and performance: How to investigate the contribution of the operational network to operational performance. *International Journal of Operations & Production Management, 26*(4), 394–411.

Appendix A: Case study – An event volunteer management operational plan

Case assignment

Examine the following event volunteer management operational plan for (a) potential arising issues if you had to implement the plan, (b) additional detail you would add to the plan, (c) headings needed to find items easily, and (d) how the wording could be made more succinct.

(by Iain Sime)

Timeframe	Activity	Person responsible
Six months prior to event	**Volunteers** ***Develop and post volunteer recruitment information on event website; send to local team websites for posting*** Include: • event title/name • event dates • how to apply to volunteer • request volunteer name, address, email, telephone number, cell phone number, previous volunteering or work experience, checklist of volunteer opportunities and overview of tasks, minimum age requirements, deadline date for applications, mandatory volunteer orientation session date/time information, shirt size (men's/women's – small, medium, large, or extra-large), volunteer shirts distributed at volunteer session; volunteers to wear black pants and comfortable shoes, complimentary ticket policy for volunteers, and contact site for further information on the event and volunteer roles ***Word-of-mouth volunteer recruitment activities*** Develop a business-card-style information sheet indicating volunteers needed for event, including event name, dates, and website for further information • *Distribute business cards at league basketball games to potential volunteers* ***Online distribution to recruit volunteers***	Volunteer Coordinator and Volunteer Committee members

(Continued)

Timeframe	Activity	Person responsible
	Twitter and Facebook – call for volunteers (and other sites that groups use) • Direct all potential volunteers to the website **Develop newspaper volunteer recruitment posting** • Develop local newspaper ad(s) to attract volunteers (include event name, dates, and how to apply via the website)	

Five months prior to event	***Volunteer selection and confirmation***
	• Review volunteer applications and select pool of volunteers
	• Select six "rover" volunteers who will learn all roles and be able to fill in whenever necessary
	• Subdivide list between Event Committee members and ensure all volunteers are called
	• Establish an overall checklist to confirm each volunteer'sparticipation/confirmation and their attendance at the mandatory volunteer orientation session
	• Send all volunteers an email confirming their role, agreement to participate and the details concerning the mandatory volunteer orientation session (date; time; site; specific room; parking arrangements; whether coffee, tea, etc. will be provided; and event contact name/contact information)
	• Prepare for selection issues, such as:
	  i If more than enough interested volunteers are available, how you will respond to those not getting a role at the event
	  ii Keeping a reserve group of volunteers in case they are needed as replacements
		Volunteer Coordinator and two Volunteer Committee members

Four and a half months prior to event	***Order developed for Volunteer Room*** • Room to be set up by 8 am on date: _____ • Coat racks (3: to hold 20 coats per rack) • Eight tables (10' round; white tablecloths) positioned in two rows of four in room for volunteers • 10 chairs at each table for a total of 80 chairs • Arrange for two security staff to be stationed just outside the Volunteer Room doorway for the orientation session and the event date(s) • Arrange for food and beverages for volunteer orientation session (to be available 45 minutes prior to start of orientation session for 60 people; to include coffee/tea/orange juice/apple juice; four kinds of muffins and bread sticks; fruit tray, and vegetable tray) • Arrange for tables for food and beverages: three 3 × 8' tables, white tablecloths, basketball centrepiece (× 3), tables placed on north wall • Generate a diagram showing where tables, coat racks, food, etc. are to be positioned within the Volunteer Room	Volunteer Coordinator and Venue Manager

(Continued)

The event operational planning phase

Timeframe	Activity	Person responsible
Three weeks prior to event	**Confirm Volunteer orientation session** Date:____ Time:____ Venue:____ Room:____ Attendance required from ____ to ____pm Attendees:____ Set-up: 2–3 hours prior to orientation (see requirements in preparations above) • Place at each seat an information card welcoming all volunteers to the upcoming volunteer appreciation night; card to include the date, time, and site; agenda for the orientation session • Place emergency protocols sheet at each seat • Ensure that the Accreditation Committee is set up to begin taking headshots and adding required information for the printed and laminated accreditation passes one hour prior to the orientation session; lanyards to be available; distribution process pre-established • Ensure security staff in place 45 minutes prior to orientation session • Meet and greet all volunteers as they arrive *Orientation agenda* • Welcome and introductions (ask all volunteers to sign in next to their name on the volunteer sheet) • Review of volunteer roles (see list below) • Volunteer communication system explained • Emergency protocols discussed (provided in writing) • Review process for volunteer breaks during event • Facility tour • Dress code and distribution of volunteer golf shirts • Accreditation distribution • Parking pass distribution • Discuss volunteer complimentary tickets; how to order and pick up their tickets • Discuss the volunteer appreciation night	Volunteer Coordinator, Venue Manager, Event Accreditation Coordinator, and volunteers

(Continued)

Timeframe	Activity	Person responsible

	Examples of volunteer roles to be reviewed:
	Anthem singer – informed of timing, confirm introduction for public address (PA), where they are to walk/stand, direction to face, bilingual version anthem required, where they go after anthem, and pre-event technical check time and site on event day
	Team hosts – one per team; to ensure teams know their assigned warm-up and game schedules, etc.
	Statistics Managers – to gather pre-event team statistics, to distribute statistics to media and PA announcer at pre-assigned intervals throughout the event
	Game Sheet Manager – to manage the completion of the official game sheet for each team within a predetermined timeframe; information distributed to Media Manager
	Media Manager and volunteers – to meet and greet media in attendance, to develop and distribute a media package, to answer media questions
	Volunteer security – to ensure only those with the correct accreditation have access to the Volunteer Room, the team rooms, the Media Room, etc.
	Entertainment volunteers – to secure prizes and to design and conduct fan entertainment during team timeouts/between quarters and during halftime; to work directly with the public address (PA) announcer to ensure promotions are announced
	Communication Managers – if two-way radios are available, then the volunteers should be shown how to use them. If there are not enough radios for each volunteer, then assign the radios to the volunteers whom you determine need them the most
	  i Make sure volunteers stay in constant contact with one another as well as yourself
	  ii If any problems occur, make sure they are communicated to one another right away	

	Process for volunteer orientation for those missing the preparation session • Place a copy of the volunteer orientation information on the website • Confirm non-attendance of volunteers who did not attend the volunteer orientation session and then direct them to the website orientation information site • Answer any questions the volunteers have accordingly	Volunteer Coordinator
Two weeks prior to event	Volunteer management contingency plan development Generate "What if scenarios" and the response for each situation: • What if a volunteer doesn't show up? • Train three "floater volunteers" who are prepared to do any of a list of multiple volunteer jobs	Volunteer Coordinator

(Continued)

The event operational planning phase

Timeframe	Activity	Person responsible

	• What if a volunteer unexpectedly brings their young child with them?
	  • If you can do the event without their help, then you could inform them that their child cannot attend
	  • If you have a spot where the child could stay supervised, then they can leave their child supervised while the event is going on
	• What if they lose their accreditation or volunteer golf shirt?
	  • Make sure to keep extra shirts and accreditations on hand in case they are forgotten
	  • If there is more than one type of accreditation, then make sure you have some extra of each type	

Eight days prior to event	***Volunteer reminder notices*** • Send out an email reminding all volunteers about the event, including the date, time, and their role; and the fact that the orientation information has been posted on the website for their review/reminders • Update them on any new information regarding the event	Volunteer Coordinator
Five days prior to event	***Volunteer Room final preparations*** • Prepare to post on Volunteer Room bulletin board an overview of each volunteer position (reference material) – state name of volunteer assigned to complete each task • Double-check on the order for tables, chairs, food and beverages, and communication equipment	Volunteer Coordinator
Four to six hours prior to event	***Volunteer Room set-up*** • Post all job assignment overviews with name of volunteer to complete each job on the bulletin board • Set up food and drink in the locker room for volunteers • Volunteer Room security staff to be stationed at the entrance of the room	Volunteer Coordinator
Two hours prior to event	***Final volunteer meeting*** (Subdivided into their volunteer groups) • Have checklist used to know if all volunteers have arrived • If a volunteer has not arrived, replace with a "floater volunteer" • Distribution of volunteer communication system (sign-out list used) • Coordinator available in Volunteer Room for any questions and to manage issues • Answer arising questions	Volunteer Coordinator

(Continued)

Timeframe	Activity	Person responsible

Event time	**During the event**
	• Distribution of volunteer communication system of cell phones:
	• List of all contacts and their cell phone numbers provided with phones
	• Use checklist of volunteers to ensure that all are in attendance and in position; manage volunteer absentees
	• Monitor volunteer activities; manage arising issues
	• Volunteer breaks: ensure volunteers get at least one break during the event
	  – Stagger breaks so not all volunteers are on break at once
	  – Limit breaks to 15 minutes
	  – Make sure volunteers keep their radios with them during break in case of an emergency
		Volunteer Coordinator

At the end of the event	**After the event** Volunteer communication system collection say thanks and encourage attendance at Volunteer Appreciation Night	Volunteer Coordinator
One week post-event	**Confirm attendance for Volunteer Appreciation Night** • Confirm attendance • Establish agenda • Order awards • Establish a Master of Ceremonies for the night • Complete preparations for food and beverages	Volunteer Coordinator
Four weeks post-event	**Volunteer Appreciation Night** R Room set-up: • Set up tables and chairs. • Put out drinks and food on a "snack table" • Coat racks available • Music predetermined; have music and speakers ready to go – Master of Ceremonies briefing: • Written overview of event details (order of speakers) and their timing, along with specific announcements to be made to be provided to Master of Ceremonies; reviewed/discussed verbally – Awards: • Hand out awards to each of the volunteers by: _____	Volunteer Coordinator

Appendix B: Case study – Segments of operational plan for event transportation

Examine the following event volunteer management operational plan for (a) potential arising issues if you had to implement the plan, (b) additional detail you would add to the plan, (c) headings needed to find items easily, and (d) how the wording could be made more succinct.

(by Landon Fletcher)

Date/Time	Operational activity	Responsibility
11 months prior to event	**Transportation policies development meeting** Date: ____ Time: 11 am Location: _____ Lounge, _____ Attendees: _____ *Meeting agenda:* • Routes and schedules • Specific detours (road closures) • Types of transportation • Disabled transportation • VIP transportation • Athlete transportation • How will drivers know who can be transported (proper accreditation) • Transportation communication system • Event parking	Transportation Manager and staff

(*Continued*)

Date/Time	Operational activity	Responsibility
Seven months prior to event	**Staff meeting – re: general questions regarding transportation and parking** Date: ____ Time: 12 pm Location: ____ Lounge, ____ Attendees: transportation staff Confirmed attendance: by email *Meeting agenda:* Discuss team goals, organization goals, policies, procedures, and processes leading up to the event Questions that will be asked include: • Due to the fact that the event is three days in duration, who from the transportation staff will be available for which day? What hours can they work during those requested days? • What type of transportation method is best? (School bus, coach bus, public transit bus, limo, taxi) • How many vehicles will be needed each and every day? • Who will be in charge of directing traffic on the day of the event? • Where will the vehicles be stored overnight? And where does everyone suggest the best place to store the vehicles will be? • Security on vehicles? • Routes, schedules, and parking for fans, participants, special guests, and alumni as well as media • Communication distribution of transportation information	Event transportation staff led by Transportation Manager

(Continued)

The event operational planning phase

Date/ Time	Operational activity	Responsibility
Five months prior to event	**Security Manager meeting** Date: ____ Time: 12 pm Location: ____ Lounge, ____ Invitees: Confirmed: via email *Meeting agenda:* Discuss the role of security needed for transportation and parking • Hiring security guards (12) • Negotiate pre-made contract • Security will be assigned in groups of two in case one of them needs to use the washroom • Two security guards at the participants' hotel for transportation boarding area security • Two security guards will be located at venue Lot B • Two will be located at the rented parking lot across from the venue • Two will be located at the bus terminal located at the loop in the middle of the venue route • Two security guards available to ensure participants have safe access to their transportation areas at all times • Two security guards will be placed overnight to watch the vehicles • Contract to cover fees and payment process	

(Continued)

99

Date/Time	Operational activity	Responsibility
Three months prior to event	**Meeting with bus and limo companies** Date: ____ Time: 4 pm Location: online (Teams) Invitees: limo service, bus service, transportation manager Confirmed: via email *Meeting agenda:* Inquire and commit to the days of the event this meeting will ensure that: • **Finalize contract** *Bus:* • Discuss bus routes and times • Discuss bus fares/passes • Discuss detour routes • Discuss accreditation • Discuss bus maximum capacity • Negotiate contract (payments, people with disabilities, liabilities, length of contract) *Limo:* • Discuss routes and times • Discuss fares • Discuss accreditation • Negotiate a contract (payment, length, VIP transportation, dress code, special event shirts)	Transportation Manager to assign task

(Continued)

The event operational planning phase

Date/Time	Operational activity	Responsibility

Six weeks prior to event	**Meeting to re-connect with security staff**
	Date: ____
	Time: 2 pm
	Location: conference call
	Invitees: Manager of Security Services and any of their staff
	Confirm attendees
	Agenda
	• 12 security guards needed for November 6, 7, and 8 (with bright security shirts on)
	• Guards work in pairs; $___.00 per hour; from 7 am–10 pm
	• Responsibilities to include: ____:
	  • Two security guards located at the performers hotel lobby
	  • Two security guards located at Lot B, directing traffic
	  • Two security guards located at the rented parking lot across from ____ Complex ensuring that everyone who enters has a proper parking pass.
	  • Two security guards placed between the dressing rooms
		Transportation Manager to assign task

(Continued)

Date/Time	Operational activity	Responsibility
Six weeks prior to event	**Meeting re: opening and closing ceremonies** ***Opening ceremonies meeting*** Date: ___ Time: 12 pm Location: ___ Lounge, ___ Invitees: Ceremonies Manager and staff Meeting confirmed: by email ***Agenda:*** Discuss potential transportation opportunities Where the ceremonies are going to be held; date; participant transportation needed; activities Security requirements C ***Closing ceremonies meeting*** Date: ___ Time: 2 pm Location: ___ Lounge, ___ Invitees: closing ceremonies staff Meeting confirmed: via email ***Agenda:*** Where the ceremonies to be held; date and time Transportation requirements Security requirements VIP participation Awards required Technical requirements Public address announcer	Transportation Manager to assign task

(Continued)

The event operational planning phase

Date/Time	Operational activity	Responsibility
Five weeks prior to event	**Meeting with transportation staff** Date: _____ Time: 12 pm Location: _____ Lounge, _____ Invitees: entire transportation staff Meeting confirmed: by email **Agenda:** Discuss operations and contingency plans Communication system Roles (and driving license requirements) Insurance and contracts Where staff pick up their accreditation and uniform (day before event, at ___ between 12 pm and 8 pm)	Transportation Manager to assign tasks
Five to six weeks prior to event	**Transportation signage** Signs designed and printed/blue background; #; rectangular; to state: ___x___; to be erected on the wall with: mascin tape to direct folks to the venue sites	Transportation Manager to assign task

(Continued)

103

Date/Time	Operational activity	Responsibility
Four weeks prior to event	**Meeting: Tow truck company** Date: ____ Time: 12 pm Location: ____ Invitees: ____ Meeting confirmation: via email **Agenda** Discuss potential towing needs should event buses, limos, or cars break down, they can safely be towed back • Flat-rate contract $700; taken to: ____ • Explain emergency routes in case of an accident, meaning they need to get there in a hurry • 2 trucks on site at all times (for contingency purposes)	Transportation Manager to assign task
One day prior to event	Delivery of transportation signs to ____ Lounge, ____ and team ready to put them up	Transportation Manager to assign task

# Appendix C: Case study - Sections of operational plan on the hospitality component

Examine the following event volunteer management operational plan for (a) potential arising issues if you had to implement the plan, (b) additional detail you would add to the plan, (c) headings needed to find items easily, and (d) how the wording could be made more succinct.

(by Lauren Thompson)

Timeframe	Task	Responsibility
Three months prior to event	**Budget development** Obtain budget for the hospitality committee from host university • Develop budget overview chart to personally keep track of your hospitality spending • Continuously develop budget details to have a realistic picture of the budget at all times	Facilitated by the Event Hospitality Coordinator
	Hospitality preparation Create overview of hospitality areas to be set up in the competition venue, the potential capacity, constituents to cater to, food/beverage requirements for patrons and volunteers and equipment requirements • Include: staff/media buffet, locker rooms, officials' rooms, official evaluators' room, basketball committee room, black room/press conference area, media refreshment area, and breakfast/evening hospitality room at the host hotel • Include: constituents to cater to – athletes, coaches, officials, official evaluators, media, host university staff, volunteers, and basketball committee	Event Hospitality Coordinator

(Continued)

105

Timeframe	Task	Responsibility
	Competition venue Facility Manager meeting Meet the host venue's Facility Manager and event coordinators with host university staff • Go on a site visit and become familiar with the venue • Determine: the hospitality food and beverage areas, all set-up details, storage areas available, including size and access process • Obtain diagrams of the facility and create a specific sitemap of all event hospitality areas • Develop a written timeline and list of hospitality preparation or set-up details	Event Hospitality Coordinator and competition venue Facility Manager
	Confirmations Confirm set-up areas with the host university staff by: • communicating with the Facility Manager the sitemap timeline and details	Event Hospitality Coordinator
	Competition venue food services meeting Arrange meeting with the facility's Food Services Manager • Prepare for meeting by creating an outline for discussion of the different areas for hospitality services, the number of people to cater to, and the type of food/beverages to be served • Obtain the already existent sponsorship contacts and the list of products that will be provided that apply to the hospitality component of the event • Attend meeting; discuss the catering options based on the event budget and the type and number of people for catering service • Discuss event beverage sponsors who will provide certain products to be served • Determine the appropriate area and time for product drop-off • Develop potential catering contracts (determine approval process for approving and signing contracts) • Confirm catering contracts at venue with the host university staff • Communicate with the facility's Food Services Manager the final food/beverage requirements for the venue catering contracts. Notify them that the delivery times will be communicated at a later date, once game and practice times are established	Event Hospitality Coordinator and competition venue Food Services Manager

(Continued)

The event operational planning phase

Timeframe	Task	Responsibility
	Host hotel meeting Arrange meeting with host hotel to discuss hotel hospitality area and menu options/contracts for the daily media breakfast and evening drinks and snacks • Attend meeting with the host hotel and determine the area for media hospitality and the hours of operation, and establish the food and beverage contracts. Food and drinks should be served in a buffet-style format. During the evening hospitality time, a server will be required to serve alcoholic beverages. All of the details should be agreed upon based on the hospitality committee's budget • Confirm hotel catering contracts with the host university staff • Communicate with the host hotel the final food/beverage requirements for the catering contracts	Event Hospitality Coordinator and host hotel Food Services Representative
	• Work with the Sponsor Committee to communicate to event sponsors the details for hospitality product time and drop-off at the venue and host hotel	Event Hospitality Coordinator and the Sponsor Committee
Two months prior to event	**Hospitality volunteer development** Obtain the tentative schedule for event game and practice times from the host university • Determine the hospitality areas where volunteer staff will be needed • Determine the number of volunteer staff required to fulfil the duties of the hospitality areas • Determine the potential shift times for the volunteer positions based on the tentative schedule for game and practice times. • Communicate the staffing requirements to the Staffing Coordinator. Make sure to include extra bodies to help cover positions in case of dropouts or no shows. The Staffing Coordinator is responsible for volunteer recruitment and assignment	Hospitality Coordinator and Staffing Coordinator

(Continued)

Timeframe	Task	Responsibility
	Hospitality signage Determine all signage needs for the hospitality areas • Provide diagram of all signage placement in the venue and host hotel • Communicate to the host university the signage required and its placement (including date and time requirements)	Hospitality Coordinator and Signage Committee
One month prior to event	**Volunteer assignment** Obtain list of contacts who will be volunteering for the hospitality component from the Staffing Coordinator • Determine appropriate hospitality volunteer shifts for each of the four days of the tournament • Assign volunteers in the contact list to daily hospitality shifts • Prepare daily schedule of events, individual schedules, and list of responsibilities and duties to be included in the volunteer training packages for the Hospitality Committee to distribute at volunteer training. Also include the venue sitemap of the hospitality areas • Submit the Hospitality Committee documents for the volunteer training packages to the Staffing Coordinator and determine the volunteer training dates. The Staffing Coordinator will make all of the training packages and call each volunteer to inform them of their training times • Create volunteer training agenda for the volunteer training night. Following the main presentation, volunteers will be broken up into committees for 30 minutes for specialized training and a venue walk-through	Hospitality Coordinator and Staffing Coordinator
Two weeks prior to event	**Volunteer hospitality training** • Attend volunteer training sessions • Conduct specific training session to communicate all of the Hospitality Committee details to the assigned volunteers	Hospitality Coordinator and Staffing Coordinator

(Continued)

The event operational planning phase

Timeframe	Task	Responsibility
	Conduct walk-through of the venue and point out where all of the hospitality areas are as well as the beverage storage area to be used if beverages are running low before new delivery times • Show volunteers where the proper entrances and exits are and where radios (if necessary) and credentials can be picked up • Ensure time is allocated for a question-and-answer period • For those hospitality volunteers unable to attend the training, ensure arrangements are made for them to pick up their training package and uniform, and communicate any essential information from the training session *Credentials or accreditation:* • Arrange for the creation of credentials or accreditation for the Hospitality Coordinator and all of the hospitality volunteers for the competition venue and host hotel. The credentials indicate the name and access areas the person is allowed to enter • Arrange for the distribution of credentials for the Hospitality Coordinator and hospitality volunteers • Distribute information to all volunteers concerning their access, entrance areas for the competition venue and host hotel, and their credential access allowance • Understand the system for replacing credentials should anyone lose or forget their credentials	Hospitality Coordinator and Credentialling Coordinator
	Confirmations • Confirm game and practice times with the host university • Confirm and adjust the catering and staffing details, if needed • Contact Sponsor Committee and ensure food/beverage event sponsors' product and delivery times are confirmed, and exact delivery site and contact names are provided. Ensure all deliveries will take place the day before the event begins. Keep an overview of contact names and numbers to call should deliveries be delayed • Confirm with Facility Manager the set-up areas and where signage is to be hung (and how it is to be fastened)	Hospitality Coordinator

(Continued)

Timeframe	Task	Responsibility
	• Confirm signage has arrived at facility from the Signage Committee to the venue and has been delivered to the Facility Manager • Confirm with the Food Services Manager at host hotel: the catering contracts, all menu items, including breakfast and evening catering requirements, delivery times, clean-up times, sponsor product use and placement, the signage to be placed at the hotel directing patrons to the hospitality area, and the signage in the hospitality area to be hung by the event volunteers • Receive a copy of all finalized contracts from the venue and host hotel and review details again	
	Event daily review meetings • Arrange meeting time and location with the host university venue and host hotel facility managers for each morning of the event to ensure all hospitality details are reviewed and are correct	Hospitality Coordinator, competition venue Facility Manager, and host hotel Facility Manager
Day prior to event	***Final preparations*** • Arrive at venue and conduct a venue walk-through to oversee that all hospitality areas are in the proper spots, are set up correctly and that all of the necessary signage is present • Ensure all sponsor product has been delivered and is stored at the proper location • Check into the hotel • Conduct a walk-through of the host hotel hospitality areas and ensure all are correctly set and signage is up	Hospitality Coordinator

(Continued)

The event operational planning phase

Timeframe	Task	Responsibility
Day 1: practice day	***Event day activities***	
6:30 am	• Arrive at host hotel hospitality area, be sure to have credentials on hand • Ensure all breakfast set-ups are complete and that the proper food is out for the buffet, signage is out properly • Speak with the hotel representative in charge and retrieve an extension number to call if any food/beverage is running low	Hospitality Coordinator and Volunteer A
7:00 am–10:00 am	• Welcome media guests into the breakfast room • Check for proper credentials upon each person's entry	Volunteer A
8:00 am	• Go to the competition venue, be sure to have credentials on hand • Conduct walk-through of the competition venue hospitality areas to ensure all areas are set up correctly • Conduct a final volunteer briefing session	Hospitality Coordinator
8:30 am	• Meet with the competition venue Food Services Manager to confirm all daily catering details	Hospitality Coordinator and competition venue Food Services Manager
8:45 am	• Report to media refreshment area and go through your checklist to ensure that all food, beverages, and supplies (cups, napkins, bowls, tablecloths, cloths to wipe up spills, and so on) have been delivered to the media refreshment area • Ensure tables are set: one table for beverage distribution and the other for snacks to be distributed	Volunteers B, C, D, and Hospitality Coordinator

(*Continued*)

111

Timeframe	Task	Responsibility
8:30 am–5:00 pm	• Main duty is to be a floater and conduct regular checks on every hospitality area to ensure its smooth functioning as well as to fulfil any special requests and manage volunteers	Hospitality Coordinator
9:00 am	• Work areas and courtside areas open to the media	Competition venue Facility Manager
9:00 am–5:00 pm	• Work in the media refreshment area; drinks should be poured for the media by the volunteers to save product • Ensure that the area is kept tidy at all times • The food services staff will be doing regular deliveries; however, if product is running low, communicate to either the Coordinator or one of the food service staff. If necessary, use stock from the storage area • The janitorial staff will complete regular clean-ups as scheduled; however, if their services are required at other times, communicate to either the Coordinator or one of the janitorial staff directly • Volunteers at the media refreshment area will take turns eating lunch and take breaks as scheduled, ensuring the area is never unattended	Volunteers B, C, D
10:00 am	• Arrive at venue, be sure credentials are on hand • Gather beverages from storage areas and fill two coolers in each locker room with drinks and ice (one with water, and one with a sponsored replenishment drink). Ensure different flavours of the replenishment drink are present. The coolers and buckets of ice will already be placed in the locker rooms by the food services staff	Volunteer E
10:00 am–4:30 pm	• Conduct regularly scheduled check of the locker rooms to ensure coolers remain stocked with fresh ice throughout the duration of the day. Note: do not enter the locker rooms if they are occupied by the teams	Volunteer E
10:30 am	• Team entrance opens	Competition venue Facility Manager

(Continued)

The event operational planning phase

Timeframe	Task	Responsibility
10:30 am	• Ensure that the Basketball Committee room is set up and that their meals, beverages, and snacks are all in place	Volunteer F
11:00 am–2:00 pm	• Ensure that the Basketball Committee room stays tidy and meal food stays hot and fresh • The food services staff will be doing regular deliveries; however, if product is running low, communicate to either the Coordinator or one of the food service staff	Volunteer F
11:00 am–4:30 pm	• Ensure that the Basketball Committee room stays tidy and snacks and beverages stay stocked • The food services staff will be doing regular deliveries; however, if product is running low, communicate to either the Coordinator or one of the food service staff. If necessary, use stock from the storage area	Volunteer F
11:00 am	• Facility opens to the public	
11:00 am	• Arrive at venue and obtain credentials • Ensure that the media/staff buffet area is set up and that the correct food, beverages, and supplies are in place according to the catering contracts • Put up the "Staff Only" buffet sign in the staff/media buffet area	Volunteer G
11:30 am–12:30 pm	• Check the buffet area to ensure it is ready and then communicate over the radio that the staff buffet is ready and for all coordinators to send their volunteers when they are able to get away for their meal • Staff buffet takes place • Ensure the area remains tidy and stocked and that no bottles leave the area. All drinks must be poured into cups • The food services staff will be doing regular deliveries; however, if product is running low, communicate to either the Coordinator or one of the food service staff • The janitorial staff will be doing regular clean-ups; however, if their services are required, communicate to either the Coordinator or one of the janitorial staff	Hospitality Coordinator and Volunteer G

(Continued)

Timeframe	Task	Responsibility
12:00 pm–12:50 pm	Team #1 practises.	
12:30 pm–2:00 pm	• Ensure the "Media Buffet" sign is up in the staff/media buffet area • Welcome the media personnel into the buffet area • Check for proper credentials at the door • Watch for and keep any person without proper media credentials out of the area • Ensure the area remains tidy and stocked and that no bottles leave the area. All drinks must be poured into cups	Volunteer G
12:30 pm	• Ensure the delivery and proper set-up of Team #1's box lunches into their locker room is made on time	Volunteer E
12:30 pm	• Ensure that the area for the press conferences is set up and the beverages and supplies are stocked	Volunteer F

Issues and management strategies in event operational planning

Nicole Greco and Cheryl Mallen

Events in sport, recreation, and tourism are rife with emerging issues. Each event manager must develop strategies for managing such issues. The purpose of this chapter is to define issues management, to offer mitigation and management strategies from event managers in the industry – including best practices – and to encourage managers to think through management strategies so as to learn to manage arising event issues for their events by completing the case studies offered within this chapter.

Defining issues management

For decades, issues management was defined as the process by which a corporation can identify, evaluate, and respond to arising problems or concerns that significantly impact events (Johnson, 1983). By 2020, this area was being called "strategic issue management" (Bowen & Health, 2020). Another way to define these issues has been unofficially called "a game-within-a-game." This implies gamesmanship occurs to obtain an advantage within sport, recreation, and tourism event planning and hosting activities.

Knowledge in issues management

No matter how you define event issues, it is imperative that managers develop knowledge for issues management. This knowledge encompasses early detection whereby "the earlier a company can identify a potential threat or opportunity, and commit itself to appropriate action, the more likely it will be able to influence an issue" (Johnson, 1983, p. 22). For over two decades, it has been noted in the literature that managers need knowledge and skills "for the proficient execution of three interrelated activities" (Wartick & Heugens, 2003, p. 9), including an ability to scan for arising issues, an ability to interpret the issues, and an ability to develop strategies for managing such issues (Wartick & Heugens, 2003). Overall, these skills encompass "decision-making intelligences" (Bowen & Health, 2020, p. 1002) that can be difficult to master. As the topic of event issue management continues to mature and grow in significance (Lawal et al., 2012), these skills are becoming ever more significant in managing and resolving event conflicts.

Best practices

Over the decades continuous development of best practices has been supported as a valuable endeavour for improving performance (Cua et al., 2001; Fullerton et al., 2003) that leads to increased competitiveness (Voss, 2005). Dembowski (2013) described these best practices as "the process of developing and following a standard way of doing things that multiple organizations can use" (p. 12) and it "is the optimization of the effectiveness of an organization" (p. 13). Meanwhile, Blake et al. (2021) stated that knowledge sharing in best practices can act like blueprints that guide action.

Best practices can be framed with *coordination theory*. This theory originated in the late 1980s from the field of computer sciences and draws upon a variety of different disciplines including organization theory, management science, economics, and psychology (Malone, 1988). Crowston (1997) implied that organizations can perform the same task; however the processes can differ in how they are coordinated, and with coordination common patterns are generated. Meanwhile, *relational coordination theory* also applies as multiple stakeholders, such as those in sport, recreation, and tourism events, that need to harmonize their shared goals and knowledge with excellence in communication. This sharing within relationships can "support frequent, timely, accurate, problem-solving communication … enabling stakeholders to effectively coordinate their work" (Bolton et al., 2021). Working to coordinate event components, along with understanding successful patterns of action that aid in generating best practices, can result in legacies of excellence.

Events as legacies

Preuss (2007) defined an event legacy as follows: "irrespective of the time of production and space, legacy is all planned and unplanned, positive, and negative, tangible and intangible structures created for and by ... [an] event that remain longer than the event itself" (p. 211). Preuss built his definition on the work of Cashman (2005), who categorized legacies into fields such as economics, infrastructure, information and education, public life, politics, and culture. Meanwhile, Horne (2010) suggested two types of analysis for legacies; the first focused on the impacts/outcomes of the event for material development (economic, technological, urban infrastructure), and the second addressed the ideologies in media representations of the locations and the many groups involved and the relationship of these to national identities. This second type offered representational types of legacies that included intangible effects based on an awareness and imagery of host cities and countries.

Similar to Horne's two types of analysis, Rocha (2020) identified a dichotomy in sport event legacy literature with their longitudinal study of the 2016 Olympic Games held in Rio de Janeiro, Brazil. Rocha (2020) decided to divide "legacies into two groups: tangible (economic, tourism, and structural legacies) and intangible (sporting, cultural, and psychological legacies)" (p. 134). This researcher also pointed out that although support of major sport events "may be connected to expected positive legacies, negative legacies should not be ignored" (p. 134) and that "legacies are in the eye of the beholder" (p. 134). It is evident that the term legacies has been used in a variety of ways throughout the literature to highlight the lasting impacts of events. To perform with excellence, and to leave event legacies, event managers must first plan and execute the event, including managing the arising issues.

Event issues and management strategies

There are a plethora of typical event issues that arise and event managers need to understand and manage them all. Yet, the available event management literature revealed a general lack of research focusing on such issues. So, this chapter was framed on a research project conducted by Greco (2016). Her research specifically sought to determine the key issues and management strategies within an event. Additional research in this area is encouraged, and to support such endeavours, an overview of her research process is outlined in the Appendix of this chapter.

Greco's examination of event managers and their issues, as well as strategies for issues management, revealed several prominent event management issues. These emerging issues were placed into the following categories: timing, accountability/authority, knowledge management, funding, relationships, and turnover of staff/volunteers. It is important that event managers understand the types of emerging issues in event management, as well as how to devise mitigation or management strategies that advance the success of an event. Examples of these, along with further potential event arising issues, are now presented.

Timing issues

Timing issues were the most prominent issue encountered by event managers in the industry (Greco, 2016). Timing issues are described as "unmovable deadlines, decision making pace speeding up" (Parent et al., 2011, p. 350). There were several types of timing issues. One timing issue type involves the *timing of formal agreements*. It was noted that if formal agreements are *not done early enough in the process, then the event has no leverage with the host committee and/or local stakeholders such as hotels*. It was revealed by an event manager in the industry that "if you wait to negotiate them after you've won the [event], hotels are going to jack up the prices on you because they know you have no choice now" (Research Participant-A). A strategy identified to help solve this issue included developing and providing templates of details well in advance of agreements and ensuring the process is completed as early as possible. Additionally, it was noted that one organization "provides a template for such agreements and the agreements must be signed at the bid phase. This way granted the rights to host, agreements are already in place" (Research Participant-B).

The second timing issue involved *not communicating in a timely manner*. This could mean that staff/volunteers may get so consumed by their event activities that they do not consider others involved and may not respond to their inquiries in an appropriate timeframe. Event managers in the industry indicated that discussions needed to be held with event staff/volunteers concerning established communication protocols. These protocols can ascertain elements such as the appropriate timeframe expected for a response, as well as the process to be used for responses established to mitigate this issue.

The third timing issue involved *the time it takes for a decision to get made*. An event manager in the field noted that: "if I need approval to book flights and right now the flights are on sale – so I'm trying to save the organization money, but then their flight isn't approved until a month later when the seat sale is gone" (Research Participant-C). Thus, the ability to facilitate timely decisions is important. This implies that decision protocols must be established to clearly articulate areas such as who can decide and the process for requesting a decision and the impact of the timeframe. This issue is also linked to the accountability/authority issue discussed below.

The fourth timing issue was *not accomplishing tasks outlined in the strategic plan in the timeframe that has been established for them to be completed*. This issue means that an event manager must facilitate a strategy to provide feedback based on the monitoring and management of event activities. This feedback must ensure staff/volunteers understand the timeframe as well as the impact of missing the established timeframe, and that they act as a positive motivator that encourages tasks/activities to meet the scheduled time requirements. Further, two-way feedback is also important. This means that an event manager must establish a process and be open to hearing from those completing the tasks. These individuals can outline the reasons for the delays, the impact of the current resources, and can potentially provide suggested strategies to overcome the hurdles that are impacting the completion of tasks/activities in the established timeframe.

The fifth timing event management issue was the *timing of staff hiring*. It was noted by event managers in the industry that delayed hiring impacts work and, as well, hiring too early impacts the event finances. Event managers must facilitate the timing of hiring to be optimal for the budget and work requirements. Overall, an event manager must be continuously cognizant of time and facilitate the pace of planning activities, including agreements, communication, and decisions to be completed within the set time frame.

Accountability/authority issues

According to Greco (2016), the second most prominent event management issue category involved *accountability/authority*, a category that was described by Parent et al. (2011) as "assigned roles and responsibilities, who has the final say, [and] who has the power to make decisions" (p. 351). One issue within this category involves *role clarity – if roles are not clear, issues arise*. All of the individuals that play a role in the operations of events are stakeholders and it is important that their roles are clear in order to assist in the successful execution of events. Industry event managers suggest the need to "revise manuals and organizational charts with clearly defined roles and responsibilities for each area" (Research Participant-D). This issue implies that human resource management strategies are needed for mitigation purposes.

A second accountability/authority issue involved *different stakeholders not responding to communications [being accountable]*. Industry event managers have found that sometimes staff/volunteer participants "don't avail themselves of the information that is available and that is sent to them" (Research Participant-E). A mitigation strategy involves putting instructions in writing; and additionally, hosting production meetings to review instructions verbally. Alternatively, if the instructions were provided in a verbal format initially, then follow-up written material is necessary. Both a verbal overview and written reference material is necessary. This issue has direct links to the issue above regarding the timing of responses. This implies that communications are both an important timing and accountability/authority issue.

A third accountability/authority issue involves *making decisions based on wants and not on needs* and *decisions being made without consultation*. Overall, the prominence of these accountability/authority issues should be noted by event managers to prepare for the significant impact these issues could have on an event.

Knowledge management issues

Parent et al.'s (2011) description of knowledge management involves: "learning, information sharing/keeping people informed, information bottleneck, monitoring, knowledge transfer, communication inefficiencies, freedom of information, reporting, centralization of information, corporate memory" (p. 351). Communication and information were key words used in the description of these issues. In this category, Greco (2016) found that the key issues involved not enough communication taking place and that there is the assumption that everyone knows the necessary information. Additionally, she found that information does not flow from one function/department/area/position to another as well as it should or what Parent et al. (2011) described as "information bottleneck." Further, the misinterpretation of information was also an issue. This means that communication was implicated in issues based on timing, accountability/authority, and knowledge management – this makes communication a key issue for event managers, and advancement knowledge for managing communication a key skill. Event managers, thus, must facilitate the establishment of regular communication strategies to ensure operational participants feel abreast of the latest information, protocols, and decisions, and to ensure clarity in the interpretation of instructions. Regularly established meetings are best practices and suggestions from industry event managers include: "monthly meetings with set agendas;" "file sharing capabilities;" and easy access "conference calls" (Research Participant-E). This sharing of information can aid in engaging staff/volunteers in their roles.

Funding issues

Events would not be possible without the financial support necessary for the implementation of planned activities. The description of funding as an issue category provided by Parent et al. (2011) was "budget, economic situation" (p. 350). Issues in this category included the ideas that *there is never enough funding*, that events struggle *trying to balance the financial requirements of hosting*, and the *loss of revenue streams*. Industry event managers suggested that event managers must: "*Have a clear understanding of your budget;*" "*Be smart and creative to stretch your budget*" and *"Spend money in the right places. You can't cut corners on certain elements."* This means that event managers need advancement knowledge in managing event finances.

Becker et al. (2022) provided an example of funding issues in their study of four different major sport events in Norway. Their article tied some of the other issues from this chapter together including timing and accountability/authority issues. Becker et al. (2022) claimed "that the absence of a separate decision-control function comes along with undesired phenomena that are observed at sports events like insufficient knowledge transfer, soft budgeting, conflicts between stakeholders, and ultimately financial trouble" (p. 2). Similar to Greco (2016), the study by Becker et al. (2022) attempted to provide tangible solutions to event managers. One such solution is as follows: "allowing for both undercutting and exceedance of costs accompanied with appropriate strategies for profit and loss sharing might alleviate the problem of soft budgeting and discipline the initiators of events to submit more accurate and serious budgets" (p. 15). More research should be completed to fully understand the financial implications of and strategies for events.

Relationship issues

The issue of relationships was described by Parent et al. (2011) as "trust, fairness, openness about issues, embeddedness, right people around the table, individual/personal, intra/inter-departmental, intra/inter-governmental, involvement of community and/or other stakeholders, integration, temporary vs. enduring" (p. 352).

In event management, these relationships stem from the need to coordinate operational plans within as well as between event components.

A key relationship issue in event management involves *conflicting personalities among staff and/or volunteers*. An event manager in the field indicated that the issue arises as: "You're dealing with many personalities; different skill sets, different experiences and then you're building a team with them ... not everyone ... works well together" (Research Participant-F). This issue means that fostering an environment of cooperation for coordinating operational plans can be the greatest challenge an event manager faces. Cooperation problems stem from the variety of personalities, as well as the different skills, abilities, and knowledge, of the operational network members that are required to develop component plans. The multiple component operational plans, by virtue of their size and number also can create cooperation problems.

Industry event managers provided their best practices to help solve the issue of *conflicting personalities among staff and/or volunteers* in the relationship(s) issue category (Greco, 2016). Numerous strategies were suggested including, having good policies and principles around a respectful workplace; having a strong leadership and human resources department; and bringing the issues forward and having staff/volunteers provide their ideas for a resolution. It appears that different event managers have solved the issue of conflicting personalities in a variety of ways. This suggests that there is no one specific best practice to help solve conflict as complexity stems from the differing personalities and how they must be handled.

In addition, relationship issues emerge due to advancing virtual or dispersed work opportunities. Due to the wide footprint of major events, it is now possible to use that communication technology to coordinate activities out of many different venues. Coordinating activities off-site requires additional communication and demands clarity within the communication plans. Managing event staff/volunteer personalities and multiple additional event relationships adds complexity to the process of event operational planning.

Another relationship issue involves the government as a partner (Greco, 2016). Event managers in the industry indicated that there are two key political situations arising from this relationship that should not be ignored. The first relationship issue is that *government leaders change positions throughout the course of planning and executing an event*. Second, there is the issue that the *government may not view the event as a high priority*. Suggested mitigation strategies from event managers in the industry revolved around building and, importantly, maintaining relationships, such as with key elected officials and explaining the event economic impacts to government personnel.

Gao et al. (2020) provided a unique perspective concerning relationship issues in their study on interorganizational relationships and social leveraging at the 2019 Federation of International Basketball Associations World Cup held in China. This study repeats from above looked at comparisons and differences in event relationships. An example involved the study of government commitment for a major sport event. The study indicated that event managers must be cognisant of government leaders waivering concerning the priority of an event. Government officials can change positions concerning supporting an event over the course of the event planning and execution stages. In this case, Gao et al. (2020) identified that the Chinese government had a solid and consistent involvement in the management of the tournament throughout the planning and implementation stages, and that this may have impacted decisions concerning resource distribution. Importantly, Gao et al. (2020) identified that depending on what the government views as important or less important has an effect on other stakeholders – and this is a critical issue for an event manager.

A relationship not identified in the Greco (2016) study but discussed in Gao et al. (2020) involved the media. Gao et al. (2020) stated "the perceived threat of the interests of the media in the mega event itself and its tendency to amplify the misconceptions of the stakeholder, particularly in terms of the expectations that people have for the event and what it can do for society, may pressure the stakeholders" (p. 155). The role of the media in large scale sport events was also highlighted in Kim et al. (2015), who through their findings were able to ultimately "provide guidance for event managers and public relations executives of mega sport events in terms of how to communicate with the public" (p. 82). Kim et al. (2015) posited that "media relations are critical so that an understanding of the topics covered in the media is available to event organizers, who can plan for public reactions and create media communication talking points to avert certain reactions and promote certain legacy outcomes" (p. 82).

Turnover of staff/volunteer's issues

The study by Greco (2016) found that the turnover of staff/volunteers is a key issue that involves the *loss of quality staff – and managing how to replace them*. The best way to solve this issue could be impacted by different organizational factors such as whether completion bonuses are offered, ability to hire from within, and/or the expertise required of the position needing to be filled, all factors indicated by event managers. However, no single best practice to help solve the issue is available. Further, it is important to note that a strategy for the introduction and training of new staff/volunteers is key to making them productive sooner and keeping them longer. This means that an event manager must not just hire, but must facilitate a "turnover" training program. This would include areas such as ensuring that new personnel understand the event goals and objectives, their roles, the decision-making process, timing, and communication expectations and protocols. How often these training programs must be activated depends on the turnover rate.

Case assignments

The list of potential event issues can be expansive. There is the potential for the game-within-the-game issue to occur based on the wants and needs of an individual or group involved in an event. This includes government entities, the participants/entertainment, paying patrons, staff/volunteers, celebrities or very important people (VIP's), members of the media, the event sponsors, and so forth. Arising issues can be based on who gets an event staff/volunteer t-shirt and/or walkie-talkie and who does not; "games" that can be enacted to gain advantages over an opposing team (i.e., getting the better dressing room), coaches making statements to game officials for future calls that go their way, staff meeting high profile performers and then forgetting to do their event role, the list goes on.

Here are three case studies to consider. Assignments have been outlined for you to mitigate and/or manage these three cases for any event that you choose. The cases encompass the issue of free event tickets, releasing event attendance figures, and events as a forum for protest.

Assignment A: Event free tickets

A typical event game-within-the-game involves the determination to – or not to – distribute free tickets for an event. You are charged with developing an event policy concerning free event tickets for an event of your choice. The policy statement is critical for mitigating and managing potential arising issues concerning free ticket distribution. As you begin to develop this ticket policy statement, consider the following:

(i) If you stated 'no' (that free tickets could not be distributed to event staff or volunteers), what did you base your decision upon? If there is no clear policy that ensures no free tickets can be distributed – then others, such as the event ticket manager or others, could distribute free tickets. This could result in an issue whereby some staff/volunteers were turned down for free tickets, and yet others received tickets – depending on whom they asked. An event manager would then have to manage disgruntled staff or volunteers due to unequitable decisions with respect to ticket distribution.

Now, consider that you agreed to distribute free tickets for the event. Generate the event policy statement considering the following:

(ii) State the percentage of overall free event tickets or the number of free tickets your event will distribute.
(iii) Outline which staff and/or volunteers can access free event tickets.
(iv) Ensure the following items are detailed within your policy statement: the number of free tickets any one staff member or volunteer can access; the process for requesting free tickets and the deadline; the free ticket distribution process; and the policy dissemination strategy to ensure that all staff and volunteers know the details prior to the event.

Review your policy statement to ensure staff and volunteers will be treated consistently and fairly with respect to understanding the tickets they are eligible to access, how to request the tickets, and then how to obtain the tickets. Does your pre-established policy mitigate any potential arising issues?
   Next, consider free ticket requests from staff or volunteers for disadvantaged youth within the community.

(v) Add a statement in your policy concerning the support of community youth with free tickets.

In this scenario free tickets are available to support disadvantaged youth from the community to attend the event. It is important to determine if the tickets are going to a youth organization or to an individual that will bring the youth to the event. The answer dictates who will be responsible for the transportation of the youth to and from the event venue and the type of transportation that will be used. Further considerations include who will oversee the youth(s) while at the event, where they will be dropped off post-event, and whether any youth will be alone (such as in a vehicle alone) with the staff or volunteer member. Ensuring the safety of disadvantaged youths that are not accompanied by a parent is vital to ensure that one game-within-the-game does not include an adult gaining access to youth for the purpose of abuse. How will you ensure that the child is never in a vulnerable situation? This is not a typical situation, but one that must be kept in mind. If it only protects one child over the years, it is worth it.

Review your policy. Have you mitigated potential issues concerning safeguards for disadvantaged children from the community that would enjoy attending the event? For instance, can staff/volunteers access tickets for unaccompanied minors without you knowing? Can they give their free tickets to others to bring disadvantaged youth to the event? Are these items of concern? Go back and ensure your policy statements offer the necessary protection.

Now, review your policy again and consider that a request for tickets for disadvantaged youth is coming from a key volunteer that you have known personally for years. Are there exceptions for ticket distribution to individuals that you believe you can trust?

One more area of concern involves a request for free tickets for the media outlet that is responsible for the online and television viewing of the event. Do you accept the number of tickets requested by your media contact and hand over the tickets? Do you ask for names of the crew members that will be needing the tickets to ensure they will be used by working crew members? How are you mitigating the potential issue that members of this media group are not asking for more tickets than necessary as they have friends that want to get into the event for free. Also, once in the venue, what access does their media pass get them? For instance, can they gain access to dressing rooms to meet high valued performers – even if they are not working the event and simply gained access from a free ticket or media pass?

Overall, your developed policy should mitigate issues concerning free event tickets. There may continue to be arising issues despite your best efforts!

Issues and management strategies

Assignment B: Releasing event attendance figures

As the event manager, you know the true event attendance figures ... and the figures about to be released during the event are an exaggeration. How will you manage this situation? Consider that the numbers may impact areas such as the media's presentation of the event online, on television, and in print, along with sponsorships sought in the future. There is an ongoing political game concerning the release of these figures. Do you insist on the real attendance figure being released or are you okay with the exaggerated figures? Is it the role of the event manager to get involved in this aspect of the event?

Assignment C: Events as a forum for protest

Do event staff/volunteers, participants/performers, or others involved in events have the right to use an event for the purpose of protest? The ability to communicate a message to a wide audience makes events an appealing vehicle for protest! But consider the following: if "athletes were not allowed to politicize at the field of competition, or they could expect harsh sanctions. Now where did the principle of human rights go?" (Meeuwsen & Kreft, 2022, p. 5). So, should a performer be able to use an event for political purposes?

A key historical example of sport and protests involved apartheid in South Africa, where black and white individuals were segregated (Sikes et al., 2019). With respect to sport, this meant that black athletes did not play on white teams and the seating policies created a divided spectatorship. In protest to such policy, multiple countries around the world refused to play the South African Bok rugby teams until apartheid policies were removed (Sikes et al., 2019). For instance "Australia ceased all contact after hosting the Boks in 1971 as did Scotland in 1969 until the lifting of apartheid" (Thornley, 2020, n.p.). The pressure worked! Another key example involves the 1968 Mexico Olympic Summer Games held in Mexico City. In this case, two American athletes, Tommie Smith and John Carlos, stood on the podium and during the playing of the anthem they raised a black-gloved hand high in a "clenched fist salute" (Hartmann, 2019). Their actions were in support of the "Olympic Project for Human Rights" (Schweinbenz & Harrison, 2022). They were immediately sent home for their actions.

More recently, a professional American football quarterback for the San Francisco 49ers, Colin Kaepernick, kneeled on the sidelines during the USA national anthem played prior to 2016 Games. He did this to highlight and protest against inequalities between races and injustices in the USA social system (Doehler, 2021; Sikes et al., 2019). He played in the initial games – this meant that the event manager did not respond to the action. Shortly afterwards, however, he was out of the league (Doehler, 2021; Sikes et al., 2019) despite kneeling for a just cause.

Keep in mind that protests and conflicts can have negative impacts, particularly for tourism industry events (Monterrubio, 2017). Such protests/conflicts can be destructive to the required economic and social stability needed to draw patrons to tourism events. It is the position of Monterrubio (2017) that event managers "should adapt a proactive approach that involves understanding not only the *what* but also the *why* of the wider context of hazards, risks, and vulnerability in the tourism industry" (p. 40).

Your assignment is to select an event of your choice and then generate a statement that indicates how you, as the event manager, will mitigate any key event performer from using the event for the purpose of protest. Next, if a key performer does use the event for protest, record how you, as the event manager, will handle the situation – keeping in mind the human rights of the performer. Share your action statements with others to discuss and work toward a consensus as event managers.

What can event managers do about arising event issues?

Every event manager must remember that events are "rife with unpredictable shifts and fragmented initiatives" (Fullan, 1999, p. 88). There are no phases of an event that are immune to arising issues. This requires an event manager to pursue continuous learning to recognize, understand, mitigate, and manage each arising issue.

To begin, an event manager needs to hone what Robinson (2020) described as "the ability to effectively understand others at work, and then to use that information to influence others to behave in ways that enhances one's personal and/or organizational objectives" (p. 15). This understanding includes building strong ethical standards that can be articulated and used to guide decisions. These ethical standards are particularly helpful when an issue is so complex that no resolution can be found. In all cases, a strategy for managing involves "maintaining ethical standards and then those relationships can exist in whatever form is most intelligent for handling of issues" (p. 1002).

Experience in diplomacy and advanced political skills are also needed, skills that support an ability to manage what Fullan (1999) called "sub-plots" that can occur at every level. Event managers need to read about potential issues. Discussions on each of the arising issues outlined above can be advantageous to aid one's understanding as different perspectives on how to mitigate and manage are expressed. Event policy and rules must be pre-determined and circulated widely to ensure fair and equitable treatment of all members. Avoid creating and imposing rules on the spot as this may not prove to be fair to all. And remember, 'games-within-the-game' or political games at events cannot all be negated – be ready to be challenged to enforce policy and to manage unpredictable situations. Event managers need experience in the field to observe and evaluate how issues have been managed to advance their knowledge on management options.

Due to the time-consuming efforts to manage arising issues, *it is imperative that events are well planned prior to an event so that an event manager can devote time to the management of arising issues as the event unfolds based on the detailed instructions within an operational plan.*

Conclusions

This chapter defined issues management and examples of event operational planning issues, including the categories of timing, accountability/authority, knowledge management, funding, relationships, and turnover of staff/volunteers. Industry event managers offered suggestions for managing some of the issues and/or their best practices. Readers were encouraged to think through management strategies to mitigate issues by completing the case studies offered within the chapter. Overall, arising issues are positioned as a distraction for an event manager, but it is imperative that managers become adept in mitigating and managing whatever issues arise.

Chapter questions

1. Define four key concepts, including: a "game within a game," "best practices," "coordination theory" and "relational coordination theory" as they apply to event management.

2. Outline five (5) key event management operational planning issues outlined in this chapter. State your established strategy for mitigating/managing each issue. Consider the categories of timing, accountability/authority, knowledge management, funding, relationships, and turnover of staff/volunteers.
3. Define coordination theory and outline how it applies to event management.
4. Define the concept of an event legacy and state how these legacies relate to event management issues.
5. Think through the operational planning process and determine three (3) additional issues that must be managed in the process of any management.
6. Identify three (3) relationships inherent to an event and the types of potential arising issues within these relationships.
7. Determine three (3) areas of research that could expand our knowledge base of event operational planning issues.
8. Based on your experience, list any issues you have encountered whether through a paid or volunteer position at an event and strategies used to mitigate or manage the issues.

References

Becker, M., Arne Solberg, H., & Slåen Heyerdahl, G. (2022). The financial challenges of hosting sports events: A problem of insufficient separation between decision-making and decision-control. *European Sport Management Quarterly*. https://doi.org/10.1080/16184742.2022.2044366

Blake, O., Glaser, M., Bertolini, L., & te Brömmelstroet, M. (2021). How policies become best practices: A case study of best practice making in an EU knowledge sharing project. *European Planning Studies*, 29(7), 1251–1271. https://doi.org/10.1080/09654313.2020.1840523

Bolton, R., Logan, C., & Gittell, J. (2021). Revisitng relational coordination: A systematic review. *The Journal of Applied Behavioral Science*, 57(3). https://doi.org/10.1177/0021886321991597

Bowen, S., & Health, R. (2020). Intelligences in strategic issues management: Challenging the mutually beneficial relationship paradigm. *Partecipazione & Conflitto (PaCo)*, 13(2), 1002. http://dx.doi.org/10.1285/i20356609v13i2p1002

Costa, C. A. (2005). The status and future of sport management: A Delphi study. *Journal of Sport Management*, 19(2), 117–142.

Crowston, K. (1997). A coordination theory approach to organizational process design. *Organization Science*, 8(2), 157–175. http://dx.doi.org/10.1287/orsc.8.2.157

Cua, K., McKone, K., & Schroeder, R. (2001). Relationships between implementation of TQM, JIT, and TPM and manufacturing performance. *Journal of Operations Management, 19*(6), 675–694. http://dx.doi.org/10.1016/S0272-6963(01)00066-3

Dalkey, N., Brown, B., & Cochran, S. (1970). Use of self-ratings to improve group estimates: Experimental evaluation of Delphi procedures. *Technological Forecasting, 1,* 283–291. http://dx.doi.org/10.1016/0099-3964(70)90029-3

Day, J., & Bobeva, M. (2005). A generic toolkit for the successful management of Delphi studies. *The Electronic Journal of Business Research Methodology, 3,* 103–116.

Dembowski, F. L. (2013). The roles of benchmarking, best practices & innovation in organizational effectiveness. *International Journal of Organizational Innovation, 5*(3), 6–20.

Dietz, T. (1987). Methods for analyzing data from Delphi panels: Some evidence from a forecasting study. *Technological Forecasting and Social Change, 31,* 79–85. http://dx.doi.org/10.1016/0040-1625(87)90024-2

Doehler, S. (2021). Taking the star-spangled knee: The media framing of Colin Kaepernick. *Sport in Society, 26*(1), 45–66. https://doi.org/10.1080/17430437.2021.1970138

Fullan, M. (1999). *Change forces: The sequel.* Falmer Press.

Fullerton, R., McWatters, C., & Fawson, C. (2003). An examination of the relationships between JIT and financial performance. *Journal of Operations Management, 21*(4), 383–404. https://doi.org/10.1016/S0272-6963(03)00002-0

Gao, F., Heere, B., Todd, S. Y., & Mihalik, B. (2020). The initial intentions for social leveraging of a mega sport event among stakeholders of a newly formed interorganizational relationship. *Journal of Sport Management, 34*(2), 147–160. https://doi.org/10.1123/jsm.2018-0026

Greco, N. (2016). *Major sport event operational planning issues and strategies: A multi-case Delphi study.* Unpublished MA thesis. Faculty of Applied Health Sciences, Department of Sport Management, Brock University.

Hartmann, D. (2019). The Olympic "Revolt" of 1968 and its lessons for contemporary African American athletic activism. *European Journal of American Studies, 14*(1), 1–25. https://doi.org/10.4000/ejas.14335

Heugens, P. (2003). Strategic issues management and organizational outcomes. *Utrecht School of Economics Tjalling C. Koopmans Research Institute Discussion Paper Series.* https://www.researchgate.net/publication/23696027_Strategic_Issues_Management_and_Organizational_Outcomes

Horne, J. (2010). Material and representational legacies of sports mega-events: The case of the UEFA EURO™ football championships from 1996 to 2008. *Soccer & Society, 11*(6), 854–866. https://doi.org/10.1080/14660970.2010.510748

Johnson, J. J. (1983). Issues management – What are the issues? An introduction to issues management. *Business Quarterly, 48,* 22–31. https://doi.org/10.1016/S0272-6963(99)00013-3

Kim, A., Moonhoon, C., & Kaplanidou, K. (2015). The role of media in enhancing people's perception of hosting a mega sport event: The case of Pyeongchang's

Winter Olympics bids. *International Journal of Sport Communication, 8*, 68–86. https://doi.org/10.1123/IJSC.2014-0046

Lawal, F. M., Elizabeth, O. O., & Oludayo, O. (2012). Effect of strategic issue management on organisational performance. *Transnational Journal of Science and Technology, 2*(10), 17–29.

Mallen, C., Adams, L., Stevens, J., & Thompson, L. (2010, June). Environmental sustainability in sport facility management: A Delphi study. *European Sport Management Quarterly, 10*, 367–389. https://doi.org/10.1080/16184741003774521

Malone, T. W. (1988). What is coordination theory? *Massachusetts Institute of Technology; Sloan School of Management. Center for Information Systems Research.* http://dspace.mit.edu/bitstream/handle/1721.1/2208/SWP-2051-27084940-CISR-182.pdf?sequence=1

Martino, J. P. (1983). *Technological forecasting for decision making* (2nd ed.). North Holland.

Meeuwsen, S., & Kreft, L. (2022). Sport and politics in the twenty-first century. *Sport, Ethics and Philosophy.* https://doi.org/10.1080/17511321.2022.2152480

Monterrubio, C. (2017). Protests and tourism crises: A social movement approach to causality. *Tourism Management Perspectives, 22.* http://dx.doi.org/10.1016/j.tmp.2017.03.001

Nigh, D. D., & Cochran, P. L. (1987). Issues management and the multinational enterprise. *Management International Review, 27*(1), 4–12.

Parent, M. M., Rouillard, C., & Leopkey, B. (2011). Issues and strategies pertaining to the Canadian Governments' coordination efforts in relation to the 2010 Olympic Games. *European Sport Management Quarterly, 11*(4), 337–369. https://doi.org/10.1080/16184742.2011.599202

Powell, C. (2003). The Delphi technique: Myths and realities. *Journal of Advanced Nursing, 41*, 376–382. https://doi.org/10.1046/j.1365-2648.2003.02537.x

Preuss, H. (2007). The conceptualisation and measurement of mega sport event legacies. *Journal of Sport & Tourism, 12*(3/4), 207–228. https://doi.org/10.1080/14775080701736957

Rocha, C. M. (2020). Temporal variations in the relationship between legacies and support: A longitudinal case study in Rio 2016 Olympic games. *Journal of Sport Management, 34*(2), 130–146. https://doi.org/10.1123/jsm.2019-0039

Schweinbenz, A. N., & Harrison, C. K. (2022). They didn't do anything wrong but they did everthing white: Examination of the 1968 Harvard Crew's support of the Olympic Protest for Human Rights. *Sport History Review, 54*(1), 90–108. https://doi.org/10.1123/shr.2022-0002

Sikes, M., Rider, T., & Llewellyn, M. (2019). New perspectives on sport and apartheid: Local and global. *The International Journal of the History of Sport, 36*(1), 1–6. https://doi.org/10.1080/09523367.2019.1653559

Thornley, G. (2020, May 13). Sporting controversies: Rugby's relationship with apartheid all there in black and white. *The Irish Times.* https://www.irishtimes.com/sport/rugby/international/sporting-controversies-rugby-s-relationship-with-apartheid-all-there-in-black-and-white-1.4251990

Tracy, S. J. (2013). *Qualitative research methods: Collecting evidence, crafting analysis, communicating impact*. Wiley-Blackwell.

Voss, C. A. (2005). Alternative paradigms for manufacturing strategy. *International Journal of Operations & Production Management*, 25(12), 1211–1222. https://doi.org/10.1108/01443570510633611

Wartick, S. L., & Heugens, P. R. (2003). Future directions for issues management. *Corporate Reputation Review*, 6(1), 7–18. https://doi.org/10.1057/palgrave.crr.1540186

Appendix: A research strategy for determining event issues and strategies

There was such limited research on event issues and strategies that this chapter would not have been possible without the completion of a specifically focused research project. This research utilized a modified Delphi Technique. This technique is outlined and additional research in this area is encouraged.

A modified Delphi research technique

According to Day and Bobeva (2005), the Delphi technique is "a structured group communication method for soliciting expert opinion about complex problems or novel ideas, through the use of a series of questionnaires and controlled feedback" (p. 103). Dietz (1987) outlined the basic process for the Delphi technique as follows:

> First, a panel of experts on the topic(s) under study is created. A series of questionnaires is sent to each member of the panel, soliciting both a forecast for each event being studied and a brief statement as to why the panellist has made that particular forecast. The second round questionnaire…[provides] summaries of the overall panel response on the previous round and a brief summary of the reasons offered for each forecast. The third round questionnaire provides panellists with information from the second round, and so on.
>
> (p. 80)

In this study, a modified Delphi research technique was utilized. First in-depth interviews were completed, then the interviewees were provided with the results via a questionnaire that solicited further data; and this was repeated with another questionnaire. Three feedback rounds with respondents is common practice in a Delphi, and the participants also remain anonymous (Costa, 2005; Day & Bobeva, 2005; Mallen et al., 2010; Powell, 2003). Overall, Martino (1983) outlined that the value of the technique was that the total information available to a group can be many times that possessed by any single member and that the number of factors that can be considered by a group can be at least as great as the number which can be considered by a single member.

The interview and questionnaire framework

The interviews and questionnaires were designed with a focus on operational planning and execution issues arising in the management of a major sport event and the strategies used to address these issues. The framework followed an adaptation of Parent et al.'s (2011) eight strategy types including: (1) communication processes; (2) decision-making frames; (3) engagement; (4) flexibility; (5) formalized agreements; (6) human resource management procedures/principles; (7) strategic planning; and (8) structural framework (Parent et al., 2011).

The Delphi participants

The typical instance sampling (Tracy, 2013) included male and female managers, responsible for the operational planning and execution of previously held major sport events. Martino (1983) stated that experts are considered to be experts in the sense that they know more about the topic to be forecast than do most people. Martino (1983) suggested selecting a slightly higher number of panellists than the researcher deems necessary due to the possibility of panellists dropping out. Previous Delphi studies have utilized anywhere from 17 panellists (Costa, 2005) to 31 panellists (Mallen et al., 2010). Dalkey et al. (1970) determined that starting with 15-20 panellists was a suitable number. This study had 15 participants. The average industry experience of the participants was 15 years, with participant experience ranging from five to 33 years and encompassing titles such as Director, Tournament Director, Assistant Director, Senior Manager, General Manager, and Chief Executive Officer, among others.

Panellists were contacted via email to request their participation with email addresses obtained via event websites and official event documents where available. Participation in the three rounds had a high retention rate of 66.6%.

Data analysis

Upon completion of interview data collection, this study followed a five-step analysis process. These steps involved: human coding and identifying themes, including identifying the operational planning and execution issues within the themes. The initial themes included context-based issues outlined by Parent et al. (2011) and comprised time, geography, funding, other resources, and political situations; the other issue types included accountability/authority, activation/leveraging, knowledge management, legal, operational, planning, power, relationships, social issues, structure, and turnover (Parent et al., 2011); this research is also open to additional issue types. The next step was determining the strategies used to manage the issues, following Parent et al.'s (2011) strategy types previously outlined; this research is also open to additional strategies. There was then a comparison between issues and strategy management; and an examination of what went well in terms of issues management or best practices.

Stage A analysis occurred between rounds one (interviews) and two (1st questionnaire) of the modified Delphi technique and involved the following three steps including: human coding; identifying themes, including identifying the operational planning and execution issues; and determining the strategies used to manage the issues. Stage B analysis took place following completion of the Round Two (1st questionnaire) and three (2nd questionnaire) During this stage the data was analysed based on the participants' rankings of the issues identified during stage one. Stage C analysis took place following the completion of the Round Three (2nd questionnaire) and the analysis was based on the participants' ratings of the frequency of utilizing strategies, to determine best practices in operational planning. Steps four and five of analysis also occurred including a comparison between issues and strategy management and finally, step five involved examining what went well in terms of issues management or best practices.

6

The event implementation, monitoring, and management phase of the event planning model

Lorne J. Adams

This chapter emphasizes the role of the event manager in making the operational plan work when it counts most – at the event itself. While many may be aware of the detail within the operational plan, no one knows it as well as you, the event manager. That is why you will be called upon to facilitate the work of the people who implement the plan, monitor the various elements of the event, and manage and provide guidance for the unforeseen problems that may arise. How you manage all of this will determine not only the success of the event but your success as a quality event manager (Figure 6.1).

A lot will be asked of you as the event unfolds. Understanding yourself and your role is critical to the success of the event. You will not be a dispassionate observer; you will be totally immersed in the event and all it entails. You will also bring your unique set of skills and abilities, predispositions, and biases with you. They are as much a part of the event as the people and systems that you are attempting to manage.

Implementation: executing the plan

Implementation involves the execution of the plan by moving the planned operational concepts and processes from the members that completed the planning to a myriad of event staff and volunteers that are tasked with executing the plan (Bowen, 2006). Facilitating the implementation of the operational plans does not take place in a passive world; it is purpose driven, goal

DOI: 10.4324/9781003391098-6

Implementation, monitoring, and management

oriented, and dynamic, as we live in a unique change-based time (Mallen, 2006), and the forces of change demand that we react and manage the repercussions of that change. In this environment, implementation is not easy. The first step entails coordinating and getting all of the people implementing the plan on the same page.

Event Development Phase
The event manager facilitates the development of event structures for governance, event networks, policies, volunteer practices, and participation

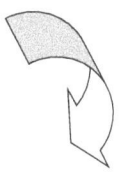

Event Evaluation and Renewal Phase
The event manager facilitates the selection of event components to be evaluated, the completion of the evaluation tasks, and the implementation of the evaluation recommendations

Event Operational Planning Phase
The event manager creates and facilitates the development of written operational plans that are logical, sequential, detailed and integrated, along with contingency plans and the activation of a plan refining process

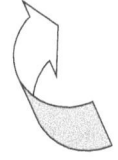

Event Implementation, Monitoring and Management Phase
The event manager facilitates the implementation of the written operational plans, monitors activities looking for deviations, and manages all deviations from the plans

Figure 6.1 An event planning model

Disseminating implementation requirements and hosting production meetings

A much broader group or team will be responsible for implementing the plan than that which created the plan. They need an opportunity to hear, understand, and assimilate the plan in their unique area of responsibility and in the larger context of the plan. *Production meetings* are held to provide this opportunity. There are several key elements required in the art of hosting production meetings. These meetings include a variety of event invitees that are involved in the integral act of implementing the event operational plans. These meetings need to have a pre-established detailed agenda, offer supplementary materials that ensure understandings of the goals and objectives of the organization as well as the event, delineate the specific roles and responsibilities, and offer facility tours to ensure all of those implementing the event plans know the facility.

Who is involved in these meetings? In some cases when the event is small, it is possible to involve everyone in the production meeting. However, as the size and complexity of the event increase, the less practical and possible it is to involve everyone. Your plan should have identified managers for each event component. It is essential that these people are in attendance. They in turn will be responsible for holding implementation meetings with the staff and volunteers that make up the network members associated with their unique area of responsibility.

What does hosting an implementation meeting entail? To begin, a detailed agenda needs to be developed. This will help you prescribe an adequate amount of time for the meeting and an agenda. You want to maximize the use of people's time and keep them focused. A detailed agenda with some general guidelines allotting time for each item helps to maintain attendees' focus and will allow for a logical progression to the meeting.

Be considerate of people's time; be sure to provide the agenda in enough time for participants to review and analyse the material. This is a subjective guideline. If you send it too early, you risk having it set aside and forgotten; if you send it too late, people may be reviewing materials as the meeting unfolds. This will lead to needless discussion and can derail a meeting quite quickly. As a rule of thumb, 7 to 10 days of advance notice is a reasonable time frame for many people.

Supplementary materials should also be provided with the agenda. This includes providing the written operational plans. Once again, as these are the people who are going to train others and keep them on track, a high level of detail is required. Throughout the plan, each member's personal responsibilities should be highlighted in some way. This can be as simple as a bolded text or a coloured highlighter. This personalized plan takes time, but for each member it is a focusing agent. Also, the inclusion of an executive summary can minimize questions. In addition, providing an organizational flow chart will help delineate responsibilities and establish a context for each node involved in the plan. Finally, a diagram of the facility with detailed and accurate instructions will further the understanding of locations and placement of equipment. The pictorial representation will save a lot of verbal explanations that could be misinterpreted.

When members attend production meetings, never assume that everyone has read the material provided in advance. People don't intend to derail a

Implementation, monitoring, and management

meeting, nor do they deliberately attempt to hold up the process by shirking their responsibility to review the material. However, they may have busy, complex lives, and sometimes even the well-intentioned have to deal with issues not associated with your event, no matter how important it may seem to you. As the facilitator, it is your responsibility to provide a verbal review to ensure they understand the written operational plans and the specific tasks for which they are responsible.

Production meetings provide opportunities to ensure that each member implementing the plan understands the goals and objectives of the event. They must also know their responsibilities, including required actions. Creating specific responsibilities limits the possibility of someone thinking that someone else was responsible for a particular task and thereby increases accountability.

It is also important that team members understand the interrelatedness of their role with the other elements of the plan. They need to see what they are doing that contributes to the larger plan and that what they are doing is valued. When it becomes clear that what they are doing is not an end in itself, but an important part of a much larger whole, commitment and motivation are enhanced.

In addition to written materials and their discussion at the production meeting table, a tour of the facility or facilities to discuss elements at the site in the context of the operational plan is essential. During a tour, managers of each event component may be able to assess specific needs or problems, such as access to electrical outlets, sound system, running water, internet access, and so on.

At the end of production meeting(s) and facility tour(s), component managers and the constituent managers within each component should be aware of the specific goals of the event, their unique responsibilities, and how they fit into the plan. They should also be familiar with the venue(s) and be prepared to motivate and train those who will report to them. Their questions should have been answered and, if you have done the job well, they will be excited about getting started.

Monitoring the dynamic and fluid operational environment

During implementation, you as the facilitator need to focus on the details of the plan using a "zoom lens." Two key areas of focus are monitoring the issues of timing and progress. For example, you need to monitor whether enough time has been allotted for getting essential materials to the venue in a timely manner so that people are not sitting around waiting to do their work. Also, have you allocated enough time for set-up and to test the equipment? If people need to be at two or more venues at specific times, is there enough time for travel between each venue? Monitoring involves questioning to determine if people are attending to the task that will lead to successful implementation of the plan in the time scheduled.

As a facilitator, it is important that you see - and are seen - by the event staff and volunteers. You should employ an operating principle that involves "the five P's of implementation." Use your *presence* and *profile* to support *positive* and *productive performance*. Presence is the concept of management by walking around. When you are present it is easier for dialogue to occur. Implementers can ask you questions, and you in turn can question them. This will reduce ambiguity in the first instance, and in addition, provide the sense that what they are doing is important and a worthwhile contribution. Your presence also reinforces your perception of attention to detail. Ultimately you will have a working knowledge of all phases of the plan.

Your presence also raises the profile of the specific components. If it is deemed important enough for you to visit them, it raises the value of that unit to the people completing the task. Like it or not, as an event manager you have a profile, and you can use that profile in positive, productive ways. When you have taken the time to visit, ask, and respond to questions, a subtle process of accountability has been introduced. If you have addressed the concerns of the front-line workers, have listened to their suggestions and provided your vision of the project or event, people will be more committed to doing the work and doing it well. They are people, and you are seen as a person, not an object. If workers have the sense that we are all important to the eventual success of the project, they will be more committed to ensuring that success with their productive performance.

Managing operational plan implementation

As the event manager, it is your responsibility to facilitate the management of deviations from the operational plan that may happen for any reason. This will be a tough task. According to Wijngaard and deVries (2006), tacit knowledge is required to make judgments on the precision of performance. Tacit

Implementation, monitoring, and management

knowledge, you will recall, is related to advancement knowledge. As the text has pointed out, tacit knowledge has been acquired through personal experience. It is the know-how you have acquired over the years as a student, as a volunteer, as an emerging professional. It is that "job sense" that comes from having been there. Schön (1983), in his book *The Reflective Practitioner*, refers to professionals being able to work "in the indeterminant zones" that their training has not explicitly prepared them for. This requires an application of knowledge. Several tips can assist you to keep implementation on track:

- Determine deviations from the operational plans through a variety of mechanisms, such as periodic progress reviews; anecdotal reports; direct observation.
- Create a climate in which people are not afraid to report implementations in a timely way, including arising problems and issues.
- Do not wait for progress reports; be out on the front lines of implementation, observing and asking questions.
- Every implementation plan contains risks – some unforeseeable. Create a contingency plan for all foreseeable issues and be prepared with a strategy to assess and manage unforeseeable issues (adapted from 'How to stay the course: Sensing and responding to deviations from plan,' (HBS Press, 2006).

Once you have noted that there is a deviation from the plan, you will require the knowledge and ability to develop a strategy for bringing things back on track. A skilled and knowledgeable event manager is needed to handle issues, to create a decision-making process, and complete the adaptations to ensure that the planned activities conform to timelines and acceptable levels of completeness. The decisions on how to manage issues must be aligned with the overall objectives and priorities of the event. You will need to determine (ahead of time) the process to be used, who will be involved, a strategy to resolve conflict, and an implementation stage; you will also have to be mindful of time constraints, and the need to act quickly.

Overcome foreseeable failure when managing deviations from the plan

You need to be conscious of the fact that managing deviations from the operational plan can invoke a predictable response that can result in a negative impact for the event. You need to overcome this predictability to improve your decision-making abilities during event implementation. This predictability was revealed by Dörner (1996) as he outlined in detail how well-intentioned, intelligent people can experience difficulty in complex, dynamic systems. He developed a game with a hypothetical population and simulated the real-world environment and found participants responded in a consistent and patterned manner.

His research indicated that participants tended to *act without prior analysis of the situation*, that is, they accepted things at face value without much consideration of prior events or history that were germane to sound decision-making. The lack of an immediately obvious negative effect of an action deluded them into thinking that their decision had solved the problem. Participants *failed to anticipate side effects and the long-term consequences of a particular course of action*. In addition, participants *failed to take into account the lag time between action and consequences* and were forced to react quickly at a future point as a consequence of their prior decision. This "domino effect" was repeated in the simulations and in most cases compounded the problem or created new ones that needed to be handled with increasing urgency. In his terms, problems increased exponentially, not in a linear fashion, and created a catastrophic conclusion. In his words, participants demonstrated "an inadequate understanding of exponential development and an inability to see that a process that develops exponentially will, once it has begun, race to its conclusion with incredible speed" (p. 33). Dörner (1996) concluded: "People court failure in predictable ways" (p. 10).

When you consider that events are run under strict time constraints, Dörner's (1996) work is worth remembering. Certainly, no one intends to fail, nor would you actively court that outcome. However, if you do not understand yourself or the system (event) you are dealing with, the possibility exists that your desired outcome will not be achieved. In addition, when called upon to make decisions, it's worth noting that decision-making is not a single activity, something that takes place at a particular time. Decision-making is best described as a process, one that takes place over time and is "replete with personal nuance and institutional history" (Garvin & Roberto, 2001, p. 1).

It would behove you to go back and look at the material on complexity theory, contingency theory, and systems theory presented earlier in this text. Knowledge of theories will help you make the decisions that will need to be made during the implementation of an event. In addition, consider how you will analyse situations (including taking into consideration the history, side effects, and consequences of actions).

Predetermine the decision-making team and process

When managing deviations from the written operational plan, the decision-making team must be pre-determined. Basically, you are answering the questions, who's in and why? There is no magic formula for this or guidelines for answering these two questions. There will be key players that your advancement knowledge will make obvious. Certainly, anyone who will be directly impacted should be considered.

The process that the decision-making team works within must be pre-determined.

- Who gets brought into the issue?
- How are they informed?
- How much time is needed to assemble or obtain a decision?
- How quickly must the decision be disseminated?
- Is there a need for a dispersed decision process (teleconference)?
- How will the decision-making process unfold (consensus, simple majority, majority, advisory to an ultimate decision maker)?
- How will conflicts in the decision-making process be handled?

As we have already indicated, any response to a plan deviation needs to relate to the vision and goals of the event. Mintzberg et al. (1976) described a process model as a situation in which the goals are clear, but the methods needed to attain them require decision-making. These researchers indicate that decision-making in a process model includes an environment in which "the entire process is highly dynamic, with many factors changing the tempo and direction of the decision process" (p. 263). In a process model, the decision-making process has historically been divided into three areas, including *identification*, *development*, and *selection* (Mintzberg et al., 1976). Identification provides the recognition of the situation and the communication through the system that a decision is required. Development involves the search for options as solutions. Selection includes the evaluation of options and the finalization of the chosen decision for implementation.

Once a decision is rendered, a decision-making implementation process must be followed. This process determines how decisions will be implemented.

- Who will implement the decision?
- What processes will be put in place to ensure that the decision is being acted upon?

What monitoring will be put in place to ensure that the decision is achieving its desired outcome?

The process of implementing decisions must be facilitated for efficient and effective application of decisions. To help to achieve this state, programmed decisions are created.

Programmed and non-programmed decisions

As you have spent many hours developing the plan for your event, you will have asked yourself the question "What if?" on many occasions. In event management, a significant aspect for decision-making in the operational network is prescribed and automatically implemented at a designated time. The prescribed decisions are stated in the contingency operational plans. When the situation(s) arises, the decisions are enacted. These decisions are programmed or pre-established.

In contrast, there will be situations when the decision-making is not programmed. During these situations, the communication system that was pre-established becomes vitally important to achieve operational network membership negotiation, coordination, decision-making, cooperation, and for the integration of actions within the overall operational plan. It has been noted for years by Wijngaard and deVries (2006) that when completing operating plans outside of the programmed decisions, a pattern of decision-making and work functionality is established that requires support from the system. Facilitating the communication system is a priority to manage non-programmed decisions.

Inherent implementation, monitoring, and management issues in operational network practice

In operations management, be sure to allow staff and volunteers to "contribute significantly to the performance of the system" (Wijngaard & deVries, 2006, p. 408). These event members are positioned within the planning and control framework to implement tasks and manage emerging issues and problems. These members, thus, need some level of autonomy. Yet, "this autonomy adds also to the unpredictability and ambiguity of the system of control" (Wijngaard & deVries, 2006, p. 395). This is because, although the planning and control elements eliminate as many potential situations as possible, they "can never be complete; there are too many tacit elements in the situation to control" (Wijngaard & deVries, p. 405).

Clearly, operational implementation performance cannot be fully controlled, and the concept of control may even be a misnomer in a dynamic and fluid environment. However, as an event manager you will be looking for *scope control*. Scope control asks that people stay within the confines of the project and not add or introduce elements that are not part of the plan. While we attempt to control as much as we can and operate within the parameters of the plan, "basically the system is not 'closed'. That is, the system is open to all kinds of unexpected influencers" (Wijngaard & deVries, 2006, p. 395).

If planning and control frameworks can never provide full control, then the system is open to providing inadequate planning and control (Konijnendijk, 1994). This inadequacy includes ambiguity, which in turn provides opportunities for individual interpretations of planned tasks (Wijngaard and deVries). Without the possibility of full control, the planning and control frameworks can offer what Wijngaard and deVries call "perceived control" (p. 405) and a base line from which deviations can be determined. This implies that full control is not possible, and the event environment will involve handling arising issues.

Maintaining control is a complex issue in events, but regardless, it is your job to ensure the required level of quality in the control aspect of the event. In addition, it is your task as a facilitator to anticipate and manage their stress levels when attempting to obtain some semblance of control over the event implementation aspects. Knowledge of strategies for this can be studied by watching those in the field and how they handle these situations.

Issue: operational plan detail and implementation performance

If the operational plans are not detailed in nature, or if circumstances arise that require deviations from the operational plans, then there is a need to allow for a degree of operational freedom, and the importance of decision-making increases. For members of the operational network to be effective in their decision-making, the operational network members implementing the plan need "a good understanding of the system to control, the specifics of the actual situation, as well as of the underlying rationale of the planning and control framework" (Wijngaard & deVries, 2006, p. 398). In addition, the operational network members adapting the plan need a solid understanding of the event goals and expected outcomes.

If the operational plans are detailed in nature, the operational network need only initiate the steps as prescribed. A detailed plan limits the degree of decision-making and operational change or freedom to make changes.

Issue: implementation knowledge and performance

One of the issues that may impact implementation performance is the knowledge level of the operational team members. You will need to ascertain whether the implementation network members understand and have a working knowledge of the event requirements and objectives. Obviously, you can't give a test to ensure that this has happened, but they should be given opportunities with forums to demonstrate their depth of knowledge and understanding of the event requirements.

An initial way to help ascertain if the level of knowledge has been transferred to the implementation network members is simply to check the attendance records in the minutes of production meetings. For instance:

- Have the members attended the meetings regularly so they can learn the requirements and the objectives?
- If they have missed meetings, what steps have they taken to obtain the information provided at the meeting? What steps have you taken to assist those who have missed access to the information?

Another issue that arises is the implementation team's knowledge regarding their role(s). As an event manager, this might be a good time to look in the mirror and ask yourself questions. The questions may include:

- How well did I facilitate the process to ensure every member understands their role?
- Did I make assumptions because of my own deep familiarity with what is required?
- Did I use language that is clear and understandable?
- Was a time frame allotted to every task, and was it realistic?
- Was the integration process completed?

The answers to these questions illustrate the complexities within the role of event facilitation.

Issue: Deviations from the plan

There are any numbers of reasons that an activity may not be completed as planned. Some of the issues that may contribute to that outcome are now highlighted. One of the most obvious problems is that an operational team member(s) adapts the role or the event due to an individual's level of understanding, or lack thereof. Further, sometimes people take it upon themselves to alter the activity for reasons known only to them. Perhaps prior experience; it's the way it's "always" been done; it's not the way we used to do it; they can make it better, and so on.

One of the main contributors to activities not being completed as planned is the communication system and the communication skills of the members. In addition, communication is a key factor in the capacity of the intraorganizational network members to function as a team. Communication assists in the level of cooperation present to complete tasks. Your role is to facilitate the communication process to ensure general communication problems are overcome. These problems can advance if information is withheld, if information is available to only a select few, or if decisions that affect a particular role or task are not communicated.

Issue: Implementation conflict

Conflict may not be inevitable, but any time you bring a group of people together to work toward a common goal the potential exists for conflict to occur. "Ironically, one of the important characteristics of a well-structured team – diversity of thinking, backgrounds and skills – is itself a potential source of conflict" (Keeping on Track, HBR, 2006, p. 8). One of the purposes of bringing people together is to examine options, to engage in critical thinking and collaborative thinking, and ultimately to embark on the best course of action. Obviously, this kind of focus can engender great debate and people can have widely divergent thinking. As meetings unfold, there may come a time when, in trying to decide between two alternative positions, people become entrenched in one camp or another. The longer this goes on, the greater the likelihood conflict will result. Garvin and Roberto (2001) point out that conflict comes in two forms – cognitive conflict and affective conflict.

> *Cognitive conflict* is the kind of healthy debate that is focused on the task at hand. It is substantive in nature, open to other alternatives and ultimately is designed to solve problems. The exchanges can be quite intense, but they are not personal; they are about the exchange of ideas with the goal of coming up with the best possible plan.
>
> *Affective conflict*, on the other hand, is personal. It may arise from a clash of personalities, a visceral dislike for someone or a defensive reaction to criticism. When you have interpersonal conflict, people are less likely to cooperate, to listen to new ideas, to move the project forward. They may become entrenched in a particular position, as noted above, and are less accepting if a decision is made that is at odds with their firmly held stance.
>
> To promote cognitive conflict and to reduce affective conflict, Garvin and Roberto (2001) provide a framework comprised of the "three C's" of effective decision-making, including *conflict*, *consideration*, and *closure*, and, as they point out, each of them need to be handled carefully. The conflict portion has been outlined above but bears repeating. As an event manager you want to facilitate as much cognitive conflict as possible while at the same time minimizing affective conflict.

The second "C," consideration, is a simple concept, but one that in practice is often ignored. As we have pointed out, when there are two sides to an issue, one side will be chosen and the other set aside. Obviously, then, some people are going to have to support and implement a course of action that they did not, at one point in time, prefer. The concept of consideration is sometimes referred to as due diligence or procedural justice. At its heart, it refers to a sense of fairness. It is a far different thing to not be heard, than it is to be considered. Considered indicates that your ideas have been listened to carefully, been weighed in the context of what must be, and that your ideas are clearly understood.

Consideration requires the facilitation of members that listen actively, ask questions, take notes, ask for explanation, are patient during explanations of positions, and keep personal opinions or preferences to themselves. At all costs, avoid looking as if you already have made up your mind.

Implementation, monitoring, and management

Facilitating communication

The facilitation of an effective communication processes is crucial for an event to run properly. Experience indicates that most communication issues arise in the first hours of the opening of an event. This can often cause mass confusion over the communication lines (such as radios, walkie-talkies, or clear comms) established for an event. From my experience at a National Collegiate Athletic Association (NCAA) Men's Basketball Championship and the San Francisco International Children's Games, where over 400 volunteers and 100 staff were involved in each event, at least a third of the operational network members needed to be connected to the communication system radios. Therefore, an event manager must facilitate the proper use of the communication system as a key element in helping to resolve situations in a fast and timely manner. In addition, the proper use of the communication system aids to keep the airways clear in case of an emergency.

Facilitating motivation and direction

Sport, recreation, and tourism events that are staged for longer than one day in length require an event manager to facilitate a high level of morale and energy throughout the members of the operational network, and this can be a challenge. You may be aware of the phrase "it's all about the first impression." However, in event management it is also the reverse; the last impression of the event is also vitally important to participants, spectators, sponsors, and all partners. It is important for the event manager to consistently facilitate the interactions with network members staging the event to maintain the professionalism from the first to the last day of the event.

One way to facilitate a high level of motivation is to constantly show a presence. The event manager must be available and responsive to network members' issues. This involves facilitating the care and concern of each member for a fair and effective process for providing breaks or rotating positions. It is also the event manager's role to provide a sense of appreciation throughout the event. A simple comment such as "good job" can mean a lot to a member.

Facilitating appropriate direction to operational network members during the staging of an event is also an important role for an event manager. The following are a few strategies for facilitating direction with a process for continuous dialogue to aid production.

After an initial briefing meeting prior to the start of an event, a daily production meeting can be held. This meeting can be offered at the end of the event day or held in the early morning hours each morning of the event. It is important that this meeting be facilitated to stay on the agenda topics and to be conducted in a short timeperiod (such as in one hour's time).

Another process can be a debriefing page posted for members to review. This provides members with an overview of changes and can confirm activities as well as can be presented in an inspirational and upbeat message to aid morale.

Figure 6.2 Suggestions for facilitating the implementation, monitoring, and management phase of the planning model by Scott McRoberts

Whatever process is used, it is important that an event manager facilitates event changes with the operational network members and eliminates the occurrence of repeated problems. An event is conducted in an environment of change and interpretations that can lead to issues or problems. A process for continuous dialogue needs to be established and facilitated to allow key personnel the opportunity to collectively provide input on the current state of the implementation, monitoring, and management of an event and to provide positive suggestions for moving the event forward.

Facilitating through credentialing issues
A key challenge in event management involves the credentialing or accreditation process at an event. This involves the pass that provides access to specific areas within the event venue. Credentialing can be a large issue if an event anticipates a significant media presence. The following are suggestions for alleviating many issues:

Facilitate a process for developing an understanding of the number of individuals that may attend but have not registered for a credential or accreditation pass and a system for managing these individuals upon arrival. It is important to have a plan in place as well as personnel to deal with this issue. It is also important to monitor the process and to adapt to be able to provide additional personnel should they be needed or to reassign members should there be only a few unregistered individuals arriving.

There will be credentials that have misspelled names or provide the wrong access within the event venue. Having a credential machine on site with a dedicated and qualified person to operate the machine will help resolve these issues in a timely manner.

For distribution of the credential passes, subdivide all credentials alphabetically and spread out the distribution sites of each group of alphabetical credentials to make the process efficient without a lot of congestion.

Facilitating personality issues
It is important for an event manager to facilitate the management of common situations that arise due to the personalities of the members within the operational network. There are three common issues that every event manager should be cognizant of and be prepared to manage the fan versus the worker scenario, personality conflicts, and the need to rotate members to other positions for the purpose of advancing their experience.

The *fan versus worker scenario* is common in the majority of events. Volunteers apply for a role in an event because they have an interest in the product. This situation can produce one of two potential outcomes. The first outcome is a terrific operational volunteer who, because of their interest in the event, maintains professionalism and attention to their position or duties. The second outcome is a member that becomes a spectator and is looking for access to participants, autographs, and perks that mean they do not pay attention to their position or duties. It is important for an event manager to establish, communicate, and facilitate the rules for participation at the outset and create a zero-tolerance policy for infractions. These infractions are witnessed in all types of events and can have an adverse effect on the motivation, direction, and professionalism of others involved in the event.

Figure 6.2 (Continued)

Personality conflicts abound in event management. It is important for an event manager to position members within their strengths and to manage personality conflicts as they arise. Long hours at an event can lead to short fuses or those that are impatient with others they are working with. Other conflicts arise from individuals who think tasks should be completed in a particular manner that differs from what is in the operational plan. Facility managers must be cognizant of these types of situations and facilitate the efficient and effective management of the conflicts in a timely manner. One way to establish a process that aids to alleviate such conflicts is to rotate members within a series of positions.

Facilitating a rotation of members between a series of event positions is a good way to meet the needs of members that ask to expand their experiences and develop their skills, to help keep members alert during events that are staged over many days, as well as to alleviate personality conflicts. A process that does not impede the outcome of a successful event must be developed to offer the opportunity to "shuffle" event operational members to a new post or a series of new posts. While doing this it is important that event managers be cautious, as they must first provide the training to cover the new duties and must involve the members in the production meetings that update the members. In addition, the member must be flexible and competent to manage a changing environment of tasks.

Learning the strengths of the members is difficult, especially when there are potentially hundreds of members involved in staging an event. In some situations, there may be members that are better suited to positions that require continued interaction with people, whether it involves celebrities, event members, or consumers. Having an upbeat and positive member that can think on their feet will only reflect positively on the event as a whole. Furthermore, you may be able to determine if an individual is better suited to one specific task, one which may not involve decision-making. Therefore, rotating members is a difficult activity to facilitate and, once begun, it requires constant monitoring and management. If facilitated effectively, a rotating process can leave event members happier and more experienced in the end.

Overall, the role of the event manager is very complex. The environment is forever changing. It is important that the event manager facilitates the event implementation, monitoring, and management activities to ensure the vision of the event is accomplished. Therefore, the vision must be conveyed to all event operational members, and they must be reminded of the vision throughout the staging of the event, especially as common implementation issues are being managed.

Remember, an important person in the entire process is the event manager. This means you must facilitate your own process to maintain control of your emotions, remain calm, be positive, and present a positive perspective while managing all implementation issues. This includes presenting an attitude that situations can be solved positively, in a timely manner, and with demonstrated professionalism and confidence. The manner in which an event manager conducts themselves highly influences the operational network members and ultimately the outcome of the event.

An important element for an event manager is to enjoy the facilitation process and seeing the fruition of well-prepared tasks or activities happen over many tireless nights. Relaxation techniques aid an event manager to worry about only the elements they can control and to have an overall perspective of the event to be able to determine which elements these involve.

Figure 6.2 (Continued)

Consideration also means that once you have decided, you communicate what the final choice is and why it is the best course of action. Referencing the input you have received – and how it impacted your choice – will go a long way to achieving acceptance by the group.

Providing closure is also a balancing act. Debate can't go on incessantly, nor should it be halted prematurely. In many cases, the event itself will dictate the time frame by which a decision is to be rendered, but even if that is the case, there is a need for closure. It is a skilful facilitator who knows when to "call the question." The skilled and experienced event manager knows when enough information has been gathered, when repetitiveness is apparent, and when to avoid the trap of paralysis by analysis.

Issue: Implementation communication

Throughout this text you will find both explicit and implicit exhortations to communicate frequently and effectively. Effective communication is essential at every stage for an event manager. So much has been written about communication that it is beyond the scope of this text. However, we encourage you to constantly work on the development of your communication skills. Be an active listener and all that it entails, including eye contact, bridging, paraphrasing, body language, asking the right questions, being non-judgmental, not personalizing issues and so on.

Finally, be generous with your praise. Publicly acknowledge the accomplishments and successes of those who are carrying out the plan. Additional suggestions in Figure 6.2 for facilitating the implementation, monitoring, and management phase of the planning model are offered by Scott McRoberts at the end of this chapter.

Conclusions

Clearly, a lot is expected of an event manager facilitating the event implementation phase, and your skills will be tested. Event managers need to understand themselves and the complex systems that are part of any event. It is also quite clear that careful preplanning and well-articulated goals and processes are essential to a successful event.

You need to be aware that decisions you make will have both short-term and long-term effects on the eventual success of the event. Event managers have the ultimate responsibility of monitoring and managing the implementation effort. You will be called upon to use direct observation and tacit knowledge. As you will be responsible for keeping the operational plan on track, you are also responsible for putting in place the processes for implementing, monitoring, and ensuring that deviations are managed. Be cognizant of the two different types of conflict that were discussed (cognitive and affective). during your facilitation activities. Also, remember the importance of improving communication skills.

Chapter questions

1. Develop an overview of what an event manager does during the Implementation, Monitoring, and Management Phase of an event and the skills required to complete the tasks.
2. Describe a production meeting (including why the meeting is held, who participates in the meeting, and what is accomplished at the meeting).
3. What are two key areas of focus when monitoring an event?
4. Describe the 5 Ps of implementation and the 3 C's of decision-making. a.
5. What can you do to overcome foreseeable failure when managing the implementation of events?
6. There are inherent issues when implementing an event; what are the issues and how do they influence an event?

References

Bowen, L. (2006). A brief history of decision making. *Harvard Business Review*, 1–7. https://hbr.org/2006/01/a-brief-history-of-decision-making

Dörner, D. (1996). *The logic of failure: Recognizing and avoiding error in complex situations* (R. Kimber & R. Kimber, Trans.). Perseus Books.

Garvin, D., & Roberto, M. (2001). What you don't know about making decisions. *Harvard Business Review*, 1–8. https://hbr.org/2001/09/what-you-dont-know-about-making-decisions

HBS Press (2006). How to stay the course: Sensing and responding to deviations from plan. *Harvard Business School Press*, 1–19.

HBS Press. (2006). Keeping on track: Monitoring control. *Harvard Business Review*, 1–24. https://hbsp.harvard.edu/product/6297BC-PDF-ENG

Konijnendijk, P. (1994). Coordinating marketing and manufacturing in ETO companies. *International Journal of Production Economics, 37*, 19–26.

Mallen, C. (2006). *Rethinking pedagogy for the times: A change infusion pedagogy.* Unpublished Ed.D. dissertation. University of Southern Queensland.

Mintzberg, H., Raisinhani, D., & Théorét, A. (1976). The structure of 'unstructured' decision processes. *Administrative Science Quarterly, 21*(2), 246–275. https://doi.org/10.2307/2392045

Schön, D. (1983). *The reflective practitioner: How professionals think in action.* Temple Smith.

Wijngaard, J., & deVries, J. (2006). Performers and performance: How to investigate the contribution of the operational network to operational performance. *International Journal of Operations & Production Management, 26,* 394–411. https://doi.org/10.1108/01443570610650558

7

The event evaluation and renewal phase of the event planning model

Scott Forrester and
Lorne J. Adams

This chapter focuses on the evaluation and renewal phase of the event planning model. The discussion begins with background knowledge on evaluation and renewal for the event manager and the decisions or evaluation considerations required before evaluating. It is important to note that preparation for the evaluation and renewal phase begins in the development phase of the planning model and continues through all four phases (Figure 7.1).

Background knowledge for the event manager

Event managers need to understand six key questions in the process of an event evaluation, including: 1 – What is an evaluation? 2 – Why is an evaluation necessary? 3 – What are the key evaluation questions to ask? 4 – What are the other areas of consideration when designing an evaluation? 5 – What does an event manager need to know about the general steps for conducting an evaluation, along with 6 - what decisions must the event manager make to successfully facilitate the evaluation process?

What is an evaluation?

To answer the first question posed, Henderson et al. (2017) defined evaluation as "the systematic collection and analysis of data to address criteria to make judgments about the worth or improvement of something" (p. 3). Based on this definition, there are key components within an evaluation, including the *purpose*, the *data*, and *decisions*.

Event Development Phase

The event manager facilitates the development of event structures for governance, event networks, policies, volunteer practices, and participation

Event Evaluation and Renewal Phase

The event manager facilitates the selection of event components to be evaluated, the completion of the evaluation tasks, and the implementation of the evaluation recommendations

Event Operational Planning Phase

The event manager creates and facilitates the development of written operational plans that are logical, sequential, detailed and integrated, along with contingency plans and the activation of a plan refining process

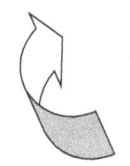

Event Implementation, Monitoring and Management Phase

The event manager facilitates the implementation of the written operational plans, monitors activities looking for deviations, and manages all deviations from the plans

Figure 7.1 An event planning model

Why is evaluation necessary?

An evaluation is a necessary step in the event planning model so that data-based decisions can be made regarding the merit, worth, value, or significance of the event, which informs decisions regarding the disposition of the event. An event manager can also use evaluations to justify the allocation of resources, scrutinize the competing interests, and analyse the finite budgets under which most events operate. Results from carefully and systematically executed evaluations are essential to sound decision-making. Further, event managers are increasingly being held accountable for numerous aspects relating to the production of an event such as human resources, including staff and volunteer management.

Henderson et al. (2017), in their summary of evaluation, identified five key purposes:

> *Determine accountability:* this involves establishing the extent to which the allocation of resources, revenue and expenses, marketing, promotion and sponsorship efforts, activities, and processes "effectively and efficiently accomplish the purposes for which an [event] was developed" (Henderson et al., p. 25).

Assess goals and objectives: events can be evaluated in terms of whether or not the goals and objectives were met for the event. This may also help determine the appropriateness of the stated goals and objectives and whether they need to be modified for future events.

Ascertain outcomes and impact: the extent to which festivals, conferences, conventions or local, regional, national, or international sporting events have encouraged tourism can be measured by the economic impact of the event through examining the direct and indirect financial benefits through tourist expenditures on a local economy. Or the event manager may wish to determine the impact that a local festival has on the quality of life in a community.

Identify keys to success and failure: evaluating the event may also serve the purpose of identifying what worked well and why, what didn't work well, why it didn't work well, and how that could be avoided or improved upon in the future.

Improve and set a future course of action: evaluations can also help identify ways that particular aspects of an event can be improved, as well as assist in the process of making decisions regarding the implementation, continuation, expansion, or termination of an event.

In addition to the purposes outlined above, evaluation can also identify and solve problems, find ways to improve management, determine the worth of the event or its programs, measure success or failure, identify costs and benefits, identify and measure impacts, satisfy sponsors and authorities, or help the event gain acceptance/credibility/support (Getz, 2005).

Further, it has been noted over time since Chelimsky (1997) stated that evaluations can aid in reflections that can strengthen an event and improve event performance and offer a measurement of efficiency, which provides information to decision makers. Also, knowledge from an evaluation, or the acquisition of a deeper understanding surrounding the factors and processes underpinning an event, can contribute either to its success or its failure. In general, regardless of what aspect of the event is being evaluated, the purpose of evaluating an event is to measure the effectiveness in terms of meeting its stated goals and objectives and to measure the quality of the performance of the event, such as whether or not the event was profitable. Regardless of the specific purpose, evaluation is a key component in the event planning model.

What are the key evaluation questions to ask?

In addition to ascertaining whether or not the event was successful in achieving its goals and objectives, there are a number of other questions that evaluations can answer. Evaluation questions typically fall into one of five recognizable types according to the issues that they address (Rossi et al., 2018):

Questions about the need for the event (needs assessment): needs assessments are often used as a first step in determining the initial ability to host an event or when designing a new event or restructuring an established event.

Questions about event conceptualization or design (evaluating program/event theory): evaluating the conceptualization or design of an event involves explicitly stating in written or graphic form the theory guiding the event and then measuring how appropriate it is. This is most essential when planning brand new events and when pilot testing events in their early stages.

Questions about event operations, implementation, and service delivery (evaluating event processes): process evaluations provide information for monitoring a specific procedure or strategy as it is being implemented so that what works can be preserved and what doesn't work can be eliminated.

Questions about the outcomes and impact of the event (impact evaluation): evaluating impacts involves examining both the intended and unintended impacts of the event.

Questions about event cost and cost effectiveness (evaluating efficiency): evaluating event efficiency involves examining the benefits of the event in relation to the costs incurred by the event. Cost benefit analysis can be used to evaluate the relationship between event costs and outcomes/impacts (benefits) by assigning monetary values to both costs and outcomes/impacts. Cost effectiveness analysis also uses event costs and outcomes but examines them in terms of the costs per unit of outcome achieved.

Henderson et al. (2017) have suggested that "it is essential to clearly identify what questions are to be addressed or what criteria to evaluate before data are collected for an evaluation or research project" (p. 18). The data refer

Event evaluation and renewal

to the information that will be systematically collected in order to address the purpose of event evaluation. Additionally, the decision-making component involves determining the "significance," "value," or "worth" of the event based on the analysis of the information (data) collected in relation to the purpose of the evaluation. These decisions come in the form of interpretations and conclusions stemming from the data analysis, as well as recommendations, or proposed courses of action regarding what needs to be done based on the conclusions. These findings often suggest how the data might be applied in practice and subsequently inform the renewal phase of event planning. Throughout the process of evaluation, there are key aspects to consider.

What are the other areas of consideration when designing an evaluation?

Beyond the points outlined above, there are multiple topics to consider within an evaluation process. Examples include the following:

1. What type of event is it, and where is the event in terms of the program life cycle?
2. Is it a traditional or niche event? If traditional, what type of sport (see overview on traditional events in Chapter 1), staged for what reasons (recreational, competitive, and/or tourism), and at what level (local, regional, provincial/state, national, or international)?
3. Or, what type of niche event is it (festival, banquet, conference, convention, stampede, or other type of show)?
4. Also, if niche, what is the history of the event, how did it evolve, and is the event growing, remaining stable, or declining? Regardless of whether or not the event is traditional or niche, the event manager should consider where the event is in relation to its life cycle. That is, has the event lost its impact or freshness; does it appear to have gone flat or to have lost its appeal?
5. Should an evaluation be conducted?

After reviewing the previous issues, the event manager must still decide whether or not to evaluate the event. While it is a step in the event planning model, "it is possible that after having looked at the mix of evaluation issues, resource constraints, organizational and political issues, research design, and measurement constraints, the [event] evaluator … recommends that no evaluation be done at this time" (McDavid et al., 2018, p. 32). There is no sense in wasting the significant amounts of money, time and resources needed to evaluate an event if the results of the evaluation are not going to be used. If a decision has been made to continue with an evaluation, additional considerations are listed below.

Have any evaluations been conducted in prior years?

Evaluation projects are different each time they are conducted. In order to reflect the uniqueness of the situation and the particularity of what is being evaluated, event managers can take advantage of evaluations of similar events in other settings or evaluations conducted in prior years. Rather than simply accept evaluations that have been previously conducted, the event manager should take into consideration the following questions:

1. What issues did the evaluation address?
2. What was evaluated, and how similar is it to what is currently being evaluated?
3. Who conducted the evaluation?
4. Who were the stakeholders?
5. How credible is the evaluation?
6. What measures were used, and what aspects are applicable to the current evaluation effort?

What is to be evaluated?

Before deciding whether to conduct a formative or summative evaluation, the event manager needs to determine what exactly is being evaluated.

Henderson et al. (2017) discussed the *"five P's of evaluation"* in relation to what aspects of an event could be evaluated. These include: *personnel, policies, places, programs,* and *participant outcomes*. They further suggest that programs can be evaluated based on inputs, through puts, or outputs of the event. The inputs are the resources used to implement the event, through puts are the organizational processes within the event, and outcomes include such items as the economic impact of an event.

McDavid et al. (2018) observe that evaluating program effectiveness is the most common reason for conducting evaluations. They also suggest several other aspects of events that can be evaluated, such as event efficiency (including a cost-benefit analysis of the event), the cost effectiveness of the event, or how well the event was implemented. Event managers should be aware that basically any aspect of an event can be evaluated, including: the development and implementation of the event plan, the outfitting of the venue, ticketing and accreditation, security, communications, information and signage, transportation, parking, and so on. Before making any decisions with respect to evaluation approaches or data collection strategies, the event manager must clearly determine what aspect of the event is being evaluated, why it is being evaluated, and the criteria to be used to evaluate it.

Should you use a qualitative or quantitative method – or both?

One area of consideration involves the method of the evaluation. A review of the evaluation literature indicates that there are two main types – quantitative methods and qualitative methods. Both types are useful for sport, recreation, and tourism event evaluations. While there are many texts devoted to delineating their differences, a rule of thumb is that *quantitative methods* are numerically based (such as the number of attendees, revenue raised, tickets sold, etc.), while *qualitative methods* are opinion based (such as how much you enjoyed the event, or what your experience was).

Should you use a formative or summative evaluation – or both?

Another consideration is that an event manager may wish to take advantage of two different types of evaluation, *formative* and *summative* evaluation. These evaluations are differentiated based on their timing. Formative evaluation takes place while the event is ongoing and tends to be process oriented. Summative evaluation typically takes place after an event has concluded and tends to examine whether or not the event achieved its goals and objectives. The advantage of formative evaluations is that they can take place at any time and allow for changes to take place as the event unfolds and perhaps before something becomes a problem. For example, in a formative evaluation we could ascertain whether or not volunteers are satisfied with their position, and whether or not they are getting the support they require (Gotlieb, 2011).

Summative evaluations involve a post-event process whereby an event manager makes judgment decisions about whether or not the event goals and objectives have been met. For some, this type of evaluation allows for accountability to be assessed and to make decisions about whether or not an event should be renewed. In short, it allows you to identify what worked, what did not work, and what needs to be improved.

Who are the key stakeholders of the evaluation?

Stakeholders refer to all individuals, groups or organizations having a significant interest in how well an event operates. For example, those with decision-making authority over various aspects of the event, sponsors, administrators, personnel, participants, clients, visitors, political decision makers, members of governing bodies, community leaders, or intended beneficiaries all have vested interest in the event. As evaluations are typically user driven, the event manager should identify early in the process the stakeholders and consider their information needs when designing the evaluation project.

What resources are available to evaluate the event?

While most resources are typically dedicated to the production of an event, there is generally a scarcity of resources available to evaluate the event. When planning the event evaluation, the event manager should consider what resources will be required in order to effectively evaluate the event. These resources could be related to money, time, personnel, necessary expertise required, organizational support, or any other resources that the event manager would need in order to effectively evaluate the event.

What kind of environment does the event operate within?

You will recall that complexity theory suggests that organizations adapt to their environment by creating event structures that are not overly complex and are also contingent upon the contextual factors of the environment. Questions relating to size of the event, competition with other events, available resources, or the degree of formalization, complexity, or centralization in the event structure all need to be taken into consideration when preparing to evaluate.

Which approach to event evaluation will be used?

There are multiple approaches to evaluation that can be utilized, including the following:

> *Goal-based approach:* Although two main types of evaluation, formative and summative, have previously been distinguished based on the timing and intended uses of the evaluation, numerous evaluation models have been developed over the years. Among the first was the goal-based model developed by Tyler (Isaac & Michael, 1995) in the 1930s. The purpose of this goal-based, goal-attainment (Henderson et al., 2017), or evaluation by objectives (Fitzpatrick et al., 2022) approach is to determine whether or not the event is achieving its goals and objectives. In this approach, goals and objectives are used as the criteria by which the event is evaluated. Goals are a broad statement about what is to be accomplished (Rossman & Schlatter, 2019), whereas objectives are specific statements that describe how the goal will be accomplished. Goal-based evaluation can be used with either outcome or organizational objectives. Outcome objectives examine the impacts or effects of the event on individual behaviours in one of four behavioural domains: cognitive (such as thinking, knowledge), affective (such as feeling, attitudes), psychomotor (such as movement, acting), or social (such as how people relate to each other). Organizational objectives refer to internal processes within the event and relate to both the operation of the event and the amount of effort to be expended in the delivery of the event. For this approach to be effective, the goals and objectives of the event need to be well written. As Rossman and Schlatter (2019) recommend, objectives should be: specific, clear, and concrete for understanding, measurable for objective assessment, pragmatic (attainable and realistic), and useful for making programming decisions. In addition to being one of the most common approaches used, the advantage to goal-based approaches for evaluating an event is the objectivity that this approach provides for establishing accountability. The drawback to using this approach is that the event needs to have well-written goals and objectives.
>
> *Goal-free approach:* In response to the criticism of goal-based approaches to evaluation, namely that they do not take unintended

outcomes into consideration, Scriven (1991) developed the goal-free approach. This approach seeks to discover and judge effects, outcomes, and impacts of the event without considering what they should be. When facilitating the use of this approach, the event manager should begin with no predetermined idea of what might be found. The overall purpose of this approach is to find out what is happening with the event. According to Henderson et al. (2017), in this approach the evaluator will "usually talk to people, identify program elements, overview the program, discover purposes and concerns, conceptualize issues and problems, identify qualitative and/or quantitative data that needs to be collected, select methods and techniques to use including the possibility of case studies, collect the data, match data and the issues of audiences, and prepare for the delivery of the report" (p. 72). The advantage to this approach is that it examines the actual effects of the event (regardless of whether or not they were intended) and allows for in-depth analysis, usually through the collection of qualitative data. The drawback to this approach is that it can be very time consuming, and some effects may be difficult to measure.

Responsive approach: In response to criticisms that evaluations were not being tailored to the needs of stakeholders, Stake (1975) developed the responsive model of evaluation. This approach stresses the importance of being "responsive to realities in the program and to the reactions, concerns, and issues of participants rather than being pre-ordinate with evaluation plans, relying on preconceptions and formal plans and objectives of the program" (Fitzpatrick et al., 2022, p. 159). Stake suggested that an evaluation is responsive if it "orients more directly to program activities than to program intents; responds to audience requirements for information; and if the different value-perspectives present are referred to in reporting the success and failure of the program" (p. 14). The purpose, framework, and focus of a responsive evaluation "emerge from interactions with constituents, and those interactions and observations result in progressive focusing on issues" (Fitzpatrick et al., p. 160). When taking a responsive approach, the event manager must continuously interact with individuals from various stakeholder groups. The manager needs to determine what information is needed and must present it in a way in that will result in understanding.

Empowerment evaluation: Fetterman et al. (2015) developed the empowerment evaluation model. This model uses evaluation concepts, techniques, and findings to foster improvement and self-determination. The focus of empowerment evaluation is on programs. It is designed to help program participants evaluate themselves and their programs in order to improve practice and foster self-determination. The evaluator-stakeholder relationship is more participatory and collaborative than Stake's responsive evaluation. As a result, evaluators taking this approach work toward building the capacity of the participating stakeholders to conduct evaluations of their own. This approach enables managers to use the results from evaluations for advocacy and change and to experience some sense of control over the event being evaluated. The process of empowerment evaluation: "is not only directed at producing informative and useful findings but also at enhancing the self-development and political influence of the participants" (Rossi et al., 2018, p. 58).

The Content, Input, Process, and Product (CIPP) Model, A Systems Approach to Evaluation: The CIPP model (Stufflebeam, 2003) is intended to provide a basis for making decisions within a systems analysis of planned change. The CIPP model defines evaluation as the process of delineating, obtaining, and providing useful information for judging decision alternatives. This definition, in effect, incorporates three basic points. First, that evaluation is a continuous, systematic process. Second, that this process includes three pivotal steps: beginning with stating questions requiring answers and specifying information to be obtained; then moving to acquiring relevant data, and finally, is providing the resulting information as it becomes available to potential decision makers. The manager can then consider and interpret information in relation to its impact upon decision alternatives that can modify or improve the event. Third, evaluation supports the process of decision-making by allowing the selection of an alternative and by following up on the consequences of a decision.

The CIPP model of evaluation is concerned with four types of decisions: planning decisions, which influence selection of goals and objectives; structuring decisions, which ascertain optimal strategies and procedural designs for achieving the objectives that have been derived from planning decisions; implementing decisions, which afford the means for carrying out and improving upon the execution of already selected designs, methods, or strategies; and recycling decisions, which determine whether to continue, change, or terminate an activity or even the event itself. In addition, there are four respective kinds of evaluation: context, input, process, and product; hence the acronym CIPP.

Context evaluations yield information regarding the extent to which discrepancies exist between what is and what is not desired relative to certain value expectations, areas of concern, difficulties, and opportunities in order that goals and objectives may be formulated. *Input* evaluations provide information about strong and weak points of alternative strategies and designs for the realization of specified objectives. *Process* evaluations provide information for monitoring a chosen procedure or strategy as it is being implemented so that its strong points can be preserved, and its weak points eliminated. *Product* evaluations furnish information to ascertain whether the strategies, procedures, or methods being implemented to attain these objectives should be terminated, modified, or continued in their present form.

Event managers can use the CIPP model of evaluation as a framework for ensuring a complete and comprehensive evaluation of any event or aspect of it. Utilizing the CIPP model as a guideline, event managers can evaluate not just the outcome of the event but the entire planning process, the event itself and the intended and unintended outcomes of the event. The CIPP model is designed to evaluate: the selection of goals and objectives, optimal strategies or program designs for achieving these objectives, methods to improve the execution of already selected program designs, methods or strategies, and whether or not to continue, modify or terminate the event or aspects of it.

Professional judgment approach: Should the event manager feel that s/he does not have the necessary expertise required to facilitate the event evaluation, one option, and another approach, would be to hire an outside professional consultant. If a high degree of objectivity is required or if the evaluation requires expertise beyond that of the event manager, then s/he may want to consider hiring an external expert. This may be the case if the event manager is interested in undertaking some sort of economic evaluation of the event. Hiring a professional consultant requires less time for the event manager to evaluate the event and is generally easier for the organization. In addition, the event manager obtains the results from a neutral, external expert. This adds a degree of objectivity to the evaluation process which may be important where there are political issues surrounding the event. On the other hand, hiring an expert can be expensive and the external consultant should have a degree of familiarity with the event, which may reduce the pool of experts that manager has in which to choose.

The decision regarding which evaluation approach to use should be based on the purpose of the evaluation as well as what is being evaluated. If experts and standards exist, *professional judgment* might be best. If goals and measurable objectives exist for a program, evaluating by using those goals and objectives (*goal attainment*) as the foundation will be preferable. If one is interested in finding out what is happening without comparing to established goals, the *goal-free approach* may be superior. If the event manager is interested in evaluating one component of the event in relation to the inputs, throughputs, and outputs, then a systems approach such as the *CIPP model* will enable them to choose the elements to examine in relation to the broad purpose of the event. Regardless of the approach taken, event managers should also ensure that the evaluation is responsive to stakeholders. Evaluation reports are used for making decisions to improve the event, to continue, modify, or terminate the event or aspects of it, and, in the process of doing so, help clients or participants evaluate themselves and their events.

What evaluation tool will be utilized?

Based on both the research design and the type of data desired, the event manager will need to decide which tools to use to evaluate the event. These include: questionnaires, interviews, focus groups, observations, expert panels, SWOT analysis, multi-criteria analysis, cost effectiveness analysis, and cultural and social analysis. See EuropeAid's description of evaluation tools for more information (https://europa.eu/capacity4dev/evaluation_guidelines/wiki/evaluation-tools-0).

The wise event manager includes thinking about evaluation right from the event pre-planning stage. A SWOT Analysis (Valentin, 2001), for example, is a useful tool that can help you identify and analyse the event: S = strengths, W = weaknesses, O = opportunities, and T = threats; these are categories that can be used pre-event, during the event, and updated post-event.

> *Strengths*: These are parts of your event and organizational structure that will aid you to achieve your goals and objectives. For example, an experienced organizing committee, adequate and well-trained volunteers, and community support.

Weaknesses: These are parts of your event and organizational structure that might get in the way of achieving your goals and objectives. For example, turnover in staffing, inexperienced volunteers, lack of sponsorship, and limited media availability.

Opportunities: These are external factors that contribute to achieving your goals and objectives. For example, the novelty of the event, no other events as competition, community engagement, and economic impact.

Threats: These are external factors (sometimes out of your control) that can detract from you achieving your goals and objectives. For example, bad weather, poor infrastructure, competition/time of year (such as a number of golf tournaments being held in the same time frame), and a lack of community support.

Conducting a SWOT analysis as part of pre-event planning allows you to document all the components of your analysis. This documentation will then be valuable later when it is time to evaluate at later stages of the event. To some degree, it will provide a baseline against which you can evaluate. Further, creating this type of analysis report may help you with other aspects of planning the event such as obtaining sponsorships or community buy-in.

In addition to conducting a SWOT analysis, the creation of event goals and objectives in the context of a mission statement is important. These goals and objectives become a critical piece in terms of evaluation. Setting goals and objectives for an event is easier said than done. Dudley (2020) has indicated that "goals and objectives provide a central anchor or reference point for conducting most evaluations" (p. 138). While Dudley's work was oriented to intervention in social work, he has pointed to some pertinent questions about goals that can be easily contextualized for use in event management evaluations. These questions include:

1. *What are the goals of the [event] program?*
2. *Are measurable objectives crafted for each of these goals?*
3. *Are the goals and objectives logically linked to clients' problems, unmet needs, and underlying causes?*
4. *Is there a logical link between the goals and objectives and how the program is implemented to reach these goals?*

(Dudley, 2020, p. 138)

It is not hard to extrapolate Dudley's questions to the event management milieu, and to appreciate their contribution to creating and evaluating an event. The more care invested in the beginning stages of planning, the easier it will be to create an evaluation strategy that will allow for decisions to be made. "Measurable goals are critical to any successful program… They are important because they provide… a direction to pursue and an outcome to reach" (Dudley, 2020, p. 140).

While examining considerations for an event evaluation, an event manager should also be seeking to understand the role of theory in event evaluation. Examples of such theory are outlined below.

What is the role of theory in evaluating events

When evaluating an event, it is important to view the event from a theoretical perspective. *Systems theory* suggests that event structures can be created and managed (as well as evaluated) by understanding the inputs, throughputs and outputs required to deliver the event. While it may not be feasible to evaluate all the resources (inputs), activities (throughputs), and outcomes (outputs) of the event, it is important to view the event from a systems perspective.

Theory of change (ToC) describes (most often graphically) how and why a desired change is expected to happen. ToC explains the process of change by identifying short, intermediate, and longer-term goals and then works backward to identify all the conditions that must be in place, and how these relate to one another causally, for the goals to occur. ToC can begin at any stage of the event, depending on the intended use. When developed at the beginning ToC is best at informing the planning of the event. A ToC also helps identify what data are necessary to test whether the change happened as hypothesized (Taplin et al., 2013). Event managers are encouraged to use program logic models (Knowlton & Phillips, 2012) if using systems theory or theory of change to evaluate the event.

Process theory involves using the overall event plan to describe the assumptions and expectations about how the event is supposed to operate. These assumptions and expectations should be examined before evaluating the event to determine whether or not the expectations for the event were met and if aspects of the event are operating as planned.

Contingency theory can also help event managers realize that the choice of organizational structures and control systems depends on, or is contingent on, characteristics of the external environment in which the event operates (Jones et al., 2022). That is why no two evaluation studies are identical. Even if the event has not changed dramatically from previous years, aspects of the external environment likely have. This in turn influences the operation of the event, which needs to be accounted for when evaluating the event from year to year.

Complexity theory suggests that organizations adapt to their environment by creating event structures that are contingent upon the contextual factors of the environment. Complexity theory emphasizes the interactions and accompanying feedback loops that continually change systems. Although complexity theory proposes that systems are unpredictable, they are also constrained by order-generating rules (Burnes, 2005).

Institutional theory (IT) considers the processes by which structures become established as authoritative guidelines for social behaviour. IT can be used to explain why some organizational practices become adopted despite their inability to improve organizational effectiveness, as the retention of many of these practices are often dependent on pressures for conformity rather than economic performance (Suddaby, 2013).

Resource dependency theory (RDT) assesses how external resources of organizations affect the behaviour of the organization. The procurement of external resources is an important aspect of managing any event. RDT can be used to examine the optimal structure of events, recruitment of employees and volunteers, production strategies, contract structure, external organizational links, and many other aspects of organizational strategy and managing events (Hillman et al., 2009).

So, while evaluation projects are not designed to develop or test theory, these theories can help event managers develop a deeper understanding of the event and help focus on what aspects of the event to evaluate.

What are the general steps for conducting evaluations and making decisions?

Five general steps are outlined for event evaluations. First, based on an adaptation from McDavid et al. (2018), before evaluating an event, these authors recommend that event managers should know the following background information: who wants the evaluation done and why, are there any hidden agendas or concealed reasons for wanting the event evaluated, and what are the main issues that the evaluation should address (need, event design, event operations and delivery, outcomes and impact, cost and efficiency)? Second, while different stakeholders will have varying views and agendas, it is important that the event manager be aware of these groups and their views when designing the event evaluation in order to avoid contaminating the data. Third, the focus moves to the selection of the evaluation method. While the details of different quantitative or qualitative research designs are beyond the scope of this chapter, "an important consideration for practitioners is to know the strengths and weaknesses of different designs so that combinations of designs can be chosen that complement each other" (McDavid et al., 2018, p. 30). The selection of a design is critical in the success of an evaluation. Fourth, the tool to be used, and the data to be collected in order to address the evaluation questions, must be finalized. Event managers should consider whether there is any existing data that can be used to serve their evaluation purposes, as well as whether quantitative or qualitative data will best meet the needs of the evaluation effort. And finally, fifth, the approach that seems appropriate must be selected.

The Three Horizons for event renewal and growth over time

An important aspect of an event is to keep it successful over time. With this in mind, McKinsey and Company (2009) devised an overview on the concept of business growth over time that entails what they called the *Three Horizons*. Each Horizon is applicable to event management. An application of the Three Horizons means to act simultaneously on hosting a sport, recreation, or tourism event, as well as positioning the event for growth over the next five years and beyond. Each of the Three Horizons are described as follows:

> *Horizon 1:* is concerned with the dominant focus or current business activities over the timeperiod of 1 to 3 years. In event management, this means focusing on hosting the event. This focus can include a number of areas to ensure event excellence such as communication, resource management (people, finances and technology management), and event marketing and sales.
> *Horizon 2:* is concerned with the activities that will ensure that business growth will continue in 3 to 5 years' time. In event management,

this means focusing on ensuring an event is not stagnant in terms of growth over the medium term. This focus includes areas such as obtaining patron evaluation feedback about the event and using it to re-design future marketing and sales strategies; testing new rules today to be incorporated within the event in the future; testing new technologies for future use; and/or re-designing elements of the event for future application.

Horizon 3: is concerned with business activities for the distant future of 5 to 10 years. Keeping an event relevant over the long term can be difficult. This Horizon involves activities that will position it for a viable long-term future. In event management, this can involve revamping the event for the needs of an upcoming generation and continuously incorporating elements that are on-trend.

If all Three Horizons are developed simultaneously, an event has a better chance of maintaining growth over the current-term, medium-term, and long-term.

Conclusions

This chapter focused on providing the event manager the background knowledge to successfully facilitate the evaluation phase of event planning. In so doing, evaluation was defined as the systematic collection and analysis of data in order to make judgments regarding the value or worth of a particular aspect of an event. The chapter also explained why evaluation is necessary and identified several key evaluation questions.

Overall, an evaluation should be conducted in the context of a theoretical framework.

Also, the chapter outlined areas for consideration that an event manager must make decisions concerning the direction, strategy, and scope of an evaluation. The decisions might include the following: informal versus formal evaluations, formative versus summative evaluation, a determination as to what to evaluate, the selection of the quantitative or qualitative method (or both), and dealing with political evaluation issues. To aid in organizing an event evaluation, five general steps when evaluating an event were detailed. Lastly, the chapter presented the Three Horizons for event renewal and growth over time.

Event evaluation and renewal

Chapter questions

1. Develop an overview of what an event manager does during the Evaluation and Renewal Phase of an event and the skills required to complete the tasks.
2. Why is evaluation necessary in event management?
3. What questions does the event manager have to consider before evaluating an event?
4. What are the five key evaluation questions according to Rossi, Freeman and Lipsey?
5. List and describe six approaches to evaluating an event.
6. Describe each of the Three Horizons and how each acts to guide an event manager to build event growth.
7. What theories did this chapter outline that can be used to guide event evaluations?
8. What additional sport, recreation, or tourism theories can be used to evaluate an event?
9. What are the five 'Ps' of evaluation?
10. What is a SWOT analysis?
11. Describe five key purposes of evaluation according to Henderson and Bialeschki.
12. What are the four components of the CIPP model of evaluation?

References

Burnes, B. (2005). Complexity theories and organizational change. *International Journal of Management Reviews, 7*(2), 73–90. https://doi.org/10.1111/j.1468-2370.2005.00107.x

Chelimsky, E. (1997). The coming transformations in evaluation. In E. Chelimsky & W. R. Shadish (Eds.), *Evaluation for the 21st century: A handbook* (pp. 1–26). Sage Publications. https://doi.org/10.4135/9781483348896

Dudley, J. R. (2020). Crafting goals and objectives. In J. R. Dudley, *Social work evaluation: Enhancing what we do* (3rd ed., pp. 138–156). Oxford University Press.

EuropeAid Co-operation Office. (2022, December). *Evaluation tools.* European Commission. https://europa.eu/capacity4dev/evaluation_guidelines/wiki/evaluation-tools-0

Fetterman, D. M., Kaftarian, S. J., & Wandersman, A. (Eds.). (2015). *Empowerment evaluation 2: Knowledge and tools for self-assessment, evaluation capacity building, and accountability.* Sage Publications. https://doi.org/10.4135/9781483387079

Fitzpatrick, J. L., Sanders, J. R., & Wingate, L. A. (2022). *Program evaluation: Alternative approaches and practical guidelines* (5th ed.). Pearson.

Getz, D. (2005). *Event management and event tourism* (2nd ed.). Cognizant Communication Corporation.

Gotlieb, L. (2011). *Evaluation: Your tool to volunteer program success*. https://charityvillage.com/evaluation_your_tool_to_volunteer_program_success/

Henderson, K. A., Bialeschki, M. D., & Browne, L. P. (2017). *Evaluating recreation services: Making enlightened decisions* (4th ed.). Sagamore Venture Publishing.

Hillman, A. J., Withers, M. C., & Collins, B. J. (2009). Resource dependence theory: A review. *Journal of Management, 35*(6), 1404–1427. https://doi.org/10.1177/0149206309343469

Isaac, S., & Michael, W. B. (1995). *Handbook in research and evaluation: A collection of principles, methods, and strategies useful in the planning, design, and evaluation of studies in education and the behavioral sciences* (3rd ed.). EdITS Publishers.

Jones, G. R., George, J. M., & Haddad, J. W. (2022). *Essentials of contemporary management* (7th ed.). McGraw Hill.

Knowlton, L. W., & Phillips, C. C. (2012). *The logic model guidebook: Better strategies for great results* (2nd ed.). Sage Publications.

McDavid, J. C., Huse, I., & Hawthorn, L. R. L. (2018). *Program evaluation and performance measurement: An introduction to practice* (3rd ed.). Sage Publications. https://doi.org/10.4135/9781071878897

McKinsey & Company. (2009, December). Enduring ideas: The three horizons of growth. *McKinsey Quarterly*. https://www.mckinsey.com/capabilities/strategy-and-corporate-finance/our-insights/enduring-ideas-the-three-horizons-of-growth

Rossi, P. H., Lipsey, M. W., & Henry, G. T. (2018). *Evaluation: A systematic approach* (8th ed.). Sage Publications.

Rossman, J. R., & Schlatter, B. E. (2019). *Recreation programming: Designing, staging, and managing the delivery of leisure experiences* (8th ed.). Sagamore Venture Publishing.

Scriven, M. (1991). Prose and cons about goal-free evaluation. *Evaluation Practice, 12*(1), 55–62. https://doi.org/10.1177/109821409101200108

Stake, R. E. (1975). *Evaluating the arts in education: A responsive approach*. Charles E. Merrill Publishing.

Stufflebeam, D. L. (2003). The CIPP model for evaluation. In T. Kellaghan & D. L. Stufflebeam (Eds.), *International handbook of educational evaluation* (pp. 31–62). SpringerLink. https://doi.org/10.1007/978-94-010-0309-4_4

Suddaby, R. (2013). Institutional theory. In E. H. Kessler (Ed.), *Encyclopedia of management theory* (pp. 379–383). Sage Publications. https://doi.org/10.4135/9781452276090

Taplin, D. H., Clark, H., Collins, E., & Colby, D. C. (2013, April). *Theory of change technical papers: A series of papers to support development of theories of change based on practice in the field*. https://www.actknowledge.org/resources/documents/ToC-Tech-Papers.pdf

Valentin, E. K. (2001). SWOT analysis from a resource-based view. *Journal of Marketing, Theory and Practice, 9*(2), 54–69. https://doi.org/10.1080/10696679.2001.11501891

Safeguarding the natural environment in event management

Greg Dingle, Chris Chard, and Matt Dolf

This chapter focuses on understanding environmental management strategies as well as the roles and responsibilities of event managers to produce a quality event while simultaneously considering the impacts of events on the environment. The call to manage events in a more environmentally sustainable manner has been amplified, as there is increasing pressure to (a) reduce direct harm caused to the environment, (b) satisfy the interests of stakeholders (both internal and external), (c) integrate risk management, (d) communicate in a credible manner, (e) ensure events can operate in a safe and healthy environment, and (f) meet all legal requirements.

In the following chapter, specifically, the focus is on environmental sustainability and why it is important in event management. Next, the focus moves to advancing knowledge on five key environmental management strategies that are important for an event manager, including the triple top line, the triple bottom line, life cycle assessment, the carbon footprint, and the ecological footprint. This is followed by a discussion on the various roles and responsibilities for event managers to design events in a more sustainable manner. Finally, we offer assignments to work through to apply your knowledge.

What is environmental sustainability?

In this chapter, environmental sustainability (ES) follows the established definition by the United Nations (UN) Brundtland Report (1987). This report sets out ES as the capacity of an organization to safeguard the natural environment by "meeting the needs of the present generation without compromising the ability of future generations to meet their own needs" (p. 1). This definition offers elements of choice, as both the present and the future can be considered in any organizational decision-making. Entwined in these "now" or "later" considerations, sustainability requires that organizations evolve and broaden the metrics to assess long-term success. However, we also note that estimates of the number of definitions of sustainability have varied between 100 and 300 (Johnston et al., 2007; Moscardo et al., 2013; Parkin, 2000), so this plurality of views offers the opportunity for a nuanced understanding of this concept. For example, Parkin (2000) argued that sustainability means that:

> something has the 'capacity for continuance.' Sustainability is therefore a quality. It is an objective not a process. Something either has or has not got the quality of sustainability—the intrinsic capacity to keep itself going more or less indefinitely. We want the environment to have it, so it can support life. It is the growing number of indications that it has not got it (most worryingly manifest in climate change) that have prompted current concern.
>
> (p. 3)

Importantly, contrasting definitions illustrate a consensus around the critical importance of ensuring that the natural environment is at the heart of sustainability efforts.

The terminology is evolving, too. Since Robinson (2004) argued that while "sustainable development" is more commonly used by private sector and government organizations, the term "sustainability" is gaining widespread use among Non-Governmental Organizations (NGOs) and academics. This is because the word "development" is tied to growth, whereas sustainability refers to the concept of preservation, or absolute limits. Robinson (2004) suggested that sustainability is positioned as a "value change" and sustainable development as a "technical fix." Although the terms sustainability and sustainable development are often used synonymously in practice, the philosophical distinctions are important. There is general agreement that achieving Gross Domestic Product (GDP) growth while at the same time shrinking resource use is a difficult task for humanity (UNEP, 2011; United Nations International Resource Panel, 2019). While Jackson (2017) proposed that prosperity can be achieved without GDP growth, this type of progress is likely a distant prospect. In the meantime, event managers need to be cognizant of the challenge to, on the one hand achieve growth, and on the other to improve quality of life through de-coupling resource use (Jackson & Victor, 2019) from the event management process.

Why is environmental sustainability important in event management?

Barrett and Scott (2001) noted that every organization, small to large, must consider environmental issues such as transportation, personal and organizational consumption, and waste management. Such issues materialize in a context of global economic growth and the associated multi-decadal growth in the consumption of natural resources, which has been supplemented by a corresponding multi-decadal global growth in the generation of waste. Since the 1970s, the global human population has doubled, and the global GDP has quadrupled (United Nations International Resource Panel, 2019). Such trends are underpinned by a rapid increase in consumption of natural resources, from a "material footprint" (United Nations International Resource Panel, 2019) of only 27 billion tonnes in 1970, to 92 billion tonnes by 2017 (United Nations International Resource Panel, 2019). Global waste generation is anticipated to reach 3.4 billion tonnes per year by 2050 if business-as-usual conditions persist (World Bank, 2018).

As a consequence of these trends, the most recent United Nations Environment Programme (UNEP) *Global Environmental Outlook* (UNEP, 2019) report noted clear evidence of long-term global environmental change (GEC). Defined as "planetary-scale changes in the Earth System" (Pyhälä et al., 2016, p. 1), GEC spans large-scale changes, from changes in the global geosphere and biosphere (e.g., carbon cycle, biodiversity loss) to changes at local or regional scales driven by human activities (e.g., waste production, land use change) (Zalasiewicz et al., 2011). GEC reflects changes occurring across all five major environmental domains: atmosphere, oceans, freshwater, land, and biodiversity, and is supported by a vast body of scientific evidence (e.g., Rockström et al., 2009; Steffen et al., 2015b; Tong et al., 2022; UNEP, 2005, 2007, 2012, 2019). The principal driver of such environmental degradation is human activities (UNEP, 2019). Consistent with these findings, other research has identified that humanity has exceeded nine critical planetary boundaries that are essential to a resilient Earth System (Steffen et al., 2015a; Stoknes & Rockström, 2018).

If we accept that the actions of all individuals collectively contribute to environmental change, then surely the responsibility to enhance sustainability is in the hands of everyone: governments, businesses, and citizens. Indeed, it can be argued that every event manager should be held accountable for their actions with respect to sustainability. Here, accountability is defined as "being called to account for one's actions" (Mulgan, 2000, p. 555).

Indeed, where no accountability is taken by any individual party for a mutual entity, the outcome may be the deterioration or destruction of said entity. In the case of ES, that entity is a vibrant planet. While this assertion may seem dramatic, it has been two decades since Perelman (2003) noted that, "in a complex world where the environment is now at the breaking point, the continued experiment with this dangerous system of organization represents a grave risk to everybody and everything" (p. 221). Yet, safeguarding the natural environment is not the norm when considering events.

Business as usual within the events industry can't continue. Our industry can't keep producing mountain ranges of rubbish or leave clouds of CO_2 in legacy. No matter the type of event, every coming together of people for a purpose can be done so with consideration for sustainability (Meegan Jones, 2011, Australian Delegation Head of ISO 20121).

Environmental change, vulnerability, and the need for resilience and adaptation for sport, recreation, and tourism events

Whilst the sustainability of the natural environment is of critical importance in broader sustainability discourse, it is also clear that the sustainability of humans, and our various institutions – including those in sport, recreation, and tourism – are of equal importance. Indeed, these industrial sectors are as fundamentally dependent on natural resources as others (e.g., finance, retail, manufacturing), and in some ways directly – or indirectly – dependent in ways that other industries are not. Specifically, much sport, recreation, and tourism depend on natural resources for the basic elements of their success. For example, sport and sport tourism depends indirectly on natural resources to design, build, and operate the facilities in which it is staged (Dingle et al., 2022; Kellison, 2015; Mallen & Chard, 2012; McCullough et al., 2019).

Many of the sport, recreation, and tourism sectors, however, also depend directly on eco-systems to provide the right environmental conditions that make them both possible and popular. In this way, sport, recreation, and tourism are similar to other nature-dependent industries such as agriculture (Hyytiäinen et al., 2022; Sayğı, 2020). For example, sports such as downhill skiing and snowboarding depend on the global climate system to provide the stable and sufficiently cold local climates for their success. Equally, sports such as tennis, golf, baseball, and cricket depend on stable warm climates that are essential for their success, while sailing depends on nature for the winds that enable competition.

Similarly, recreation and tourism activities (e.g., aquatic activities, visits to national parks) also depend on nature to provide either the natural attractions for such activities, and/or the stable environmental conditions that enable these. This fundamental nature-dependence – which includes *climate-dependence* (Dingle et al., 2022; Packard & Reinhardt, 2000) – underpins significant elements of the sport, recreation, and tourism sectors. Yet, it also highlights the potential for significant vulnerability of these sectors to changes in the natural environment, and the need for building resilience in their physical sites, and adaptive capacity in the organizations that manage them.

Consistent with the notion of Global Environmental Change (GEC), it is now recognized that the concepts of *vulnerability*, *resilience*, and *adaptation* are important to understanding the human dimensions of this change (Janssen & Ostrom, 2006). While *vulnerability* has been defined in a range of ways (Füssel, 2007b; Gallopín, 2006; Janssen et al., 2006; Smit & Wandel, 2006), Adger's (2006) definition is still perhaps the most appealing: "the state of susceptibility to harm from exposure to stresses associated with environmental and social change and from the absence of capacity to adapt" (p. 268). Such harms may be either direct and short-term, or long-term (Winn et al., 2011). In the context of GEC, vulnerability for sport, recreation, and tourism may also be direct and short-term harm (e.g., natural disasters: damage to sport facilities, national parks, or tourist precincts from hurricanes or forest fires), or longer-term and/or indirect (e.g., higher insurance premiums, operating costs, or adaptation costs from changed regulatory or market conditions).

Resilience (Füssel, 2007b; Gallopín, 2006; Janssen & Ostrom, 2006) has been defined as the: "the ability to absorb shocks and still maintain function" (Folke, 2006). When applied to organizations, resilience has been described as a "sufficiently wide coping range" (Linnenluecke & Griffiths, 2015). Within the context of present global environmental changes, resilience in sport, recreation, and tourism is a quality that has already been demonstrated (e.g., Louisiana tourist operators recovering from Hurricane Harvey in 2017, California National Parks recovering from forest fires in 2020, Japanese sport stadiums recovering from Typhoon Hagibis at the 2019 Rugby World Cup).

In contrast, *adaptation* (Füssel, 2007a; Gallopín, 2006; Janssen et al., 2006) has been described as: "an adjustment in social–ecological systems in response to actual, perceived, or expected environmental changes and their impacts" (Janssen & Ostrom, 2006, p. 237). In essence, such adjustments are aimed at enabling such a system (e.g., a household, group, organization, or country) to "better cope with" changed conditions, hazards, or risks (Smit & Wandel, 2006, p. 282). Adaptation research identifies different forms of adaptation. These include *incremental adaptation* (Termeer et al., 2017; Wise et al., 2014), small but familiar changes to existing practices to maintain an existing system; and *transformative adaptation* (Berrang-Ford et al., 2021; Field et al., 2012; Tàbara et al., 2019), fundamental qualitative change involving new paradigms, perceptions, and underlying norms and values. The justification for transformative adaptation has been expressed as the "continuous changes required to create resilience" (Glaas et al., 2022, p. 179), especially in the context of long-term climate change, and is focused on fundamental systems change.

For sport, recreation, and tourism, incremental adaptation may be demonstrated in different ways (e.g., outdoor sports introducing synthetic playing surfaces in response to drought conditions, recreation centres, or tourism operators reducing energy use in response to carbon pricing regulations). Similarly for sport, recreation, and tourism, transformative adaptation may also be demonstrated in different ways (e.g., integrating climate change risks into the long-term strategy of the organization; or relocating a sport or tourism event away from a site identified as having long-term flood risk, and thus considering time and spatial scales at the same time).

Roles and responsibilities for environmental sustainability in event management

The United Nations Environment Programme (UNEP) lists ways that events can impact the natural environment including:

- Development of fragile ecosystems or scarce land
- Noise and light pollution

Consumption of non-renewable resources
Consumption of natural resources
Emission of greenhouse gases
Ozone layer depletion
Soil and water pollution from pesticide use
Soil erosion during construction and from spectators
Waste generation from construction of facilities, and from spectators (UN, 2010, n.p.)

Recognizing this, it has been argued that event managers should be responsible for doing their part in protecting the natural environment (Mallen & Chard, 2011). Such responsibility has begun to be embraced by some sport organizations. For example, the environment has been recognized as the "third pillar" of the Olympic Movement alongside sport and culture (Cantelon & Letters, 2000). Indeed, the Olympic Movement's *Agenda 21* report highlights the commitment of the organization to environmental sustainability. Other examples of organizations embracing event management environmental sustainability initiatives in sport can be found including the Fédération Internationale de Football Association (FIFA) Women's World Cup Sustainability Strategy (FIFA, 2023), the English Football Association's Sustainable Events Policy (English Football Association, 2022), the 2022 Birmingham Commonwealth Games Sustainability Strategy (2022 Birmingham Organising Committee, 2022), and the Tokyo 2020 Olympics and Paralympics Sustainability Policy and Plan (International Olympic Committee, 2021).

At a micro-level, Hums (2010) notes that "students need to know the actions they can take with their events and their facilities to contain the impact of sport on the environment" (p. 5). Thus, it appears that environmental sustainability in event management is gaining support from the university classroom to the Olympic boardroom. At a practical level the question remains, who is ultimately responsible for environmental sustainability and how might this responsibility be proactively and effectively managed?

Part of the management process involves understanding the situation by measuring the impacts. A growing number of events have been examined with qualitative environmental management research techniques, and Scrucca, Severic, Galvan, and Brunori (2016) have proposed a design model for a quali-quantitative method; few, however, carry out quantitative assessment or modeling (Jones, 2008). According to Dingle (2016), the impacts of events on the natural environment, as well as the impacts of environmental change on events, has not been fully studied. Decisions are therefore often based on intuition, visibility, and ease of implementation rather than on an empirical understanding of major contributors to environmental harm.

There is a famous management axiom: "You can't manage what you can't measure." In monetary terms we rely on budgets and accounting procedures to make planning decisions and reflect the value of goods and services. As we have discussed earlier in this chapter, the environmental and social costs are not fully captured in current financial valuations. For example, the value of water loss from a water-stressed region is not reflected in the price of goods and services. As event managers, we therefore need additional indicators to make decisions about how we organize our events and answer questions such as: what is the biodiversity impact of fertilizers used on our pitches? By how much will installing solar panels on our stadium reduce the impact of electricity use? Should we build temporary or permanent venues? Further, what are the environmental impacts of tourism on a local economy?

It is common to see events target waste reduction and recycled paper as part of their "green" initiatives. But are these the most important things to focus on? Arguably not, since we know that Canada's greenhouse gas (GHG) emissions in 2022 showed that the impact of waste was 4% percent compared to 80% for energy (of which 24% was transport) and 8% for agriculture (Government of Canada, 2023). While not ignoring the symbolic importance of the visibility factor of trash and the expectation of fans to see recycling

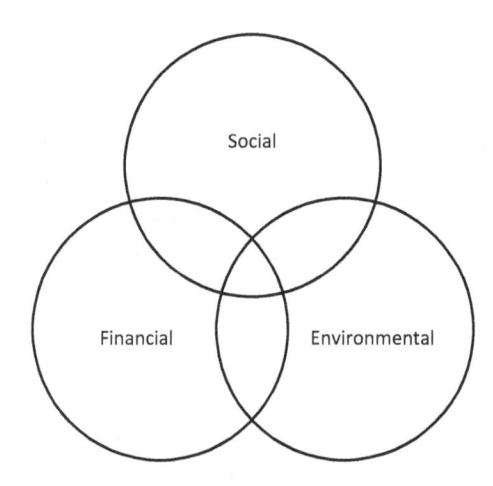

Figure 8.1 The three overlapping spheres of sustainability

bins, organizers need tools to help them focus on the areas where they can affect the greatest change.

Overall, sport, recreation, and tourism providers have varying levels of vulnerability to climate and need to develop resilience and learn to adapt to changed natural, regulatory, and market environments. In the process of understanding the role of the event manager in safeguarding the natural environment, six key environmental management strategies will now be outlined, including the triple top line and triple bottom line, life cycle assessment, carbon footprint, and the ecological footprint.

The triple top line and the triple bottom line

The "Triple Top Line" and "Triple Bottom Line" are examples of paradigms that embrace this wider scope to organizational management and assessment. In traditional business accounting, the top line relates to incoming revenue for an organization while the bottom line is what is left of this revenue after expenses have been accounted for. Similarly, the Triple Top Line moves "accountability to the beginning of the design process" (McDonough & Braungart, 2002, p. 252), by encompassing financial, social, and environmental concerns. Essentially, the Triple Top Line focuses the event manager's lens on every aspect of planning for an event. For example, knowing there will be $150,000 in revenue for a youth soccer tournament is not enough, we should know "how" the $150,000 is generated, socially and environmentally. Likewise, the Triple Bottom Line assesses the "bottom line" results of an event; how did the event perform? Again, consideration is given to the three sustainability measures. For example, considering our youth soccer event, if the event manager shows $28,000 in net profit, financially the tournament is deemed a success. However, if environmental degradation and social injustices occurred to achieve these fiscal gains, a Triple Bottom Line approach would account for these deficiencies.

McDonough and Braungart (2002) noted that frameworks such as these are great tools for integrating sustainability into the business agenda by balancing traditional economic goals with social and environmental concerns. The key word here is *balance*. Of vital importance when interpreting 8.1 is the need for *all* of the spheres to be strong. A common misconception of sustainable management is that it is *only* focused on environmental concerns. This is simply not true! Environmental sustainability at the expense of economic viability is in itself unsustainable. Randjelovic et al. (2003) addressed this point, noting the "need to develop competences ... which can create economic value *and* reduce environmental impacts/risks" (p. 251).

Hannah Jones, Nike's Sustainability Chief, addresses the concept of organizational sustainability by noting the desire at Nike to produce ROI[2] (Return on Investment) – or an exponentially strong return on both the financial investment with environmental safeguards. The thought process at Nike is that environmental sustainability does not, and should not, come at the expense of increasing shareholder value. "We can do well and do good at the same time" said Jones (Hollender & Breen, 2010, p. 121).

Life cycle assessment

Sport event organizers can take advantage of a multitude of environmental sustainability assessment methods, tools, and indicators (Ness et al., 2007), but no internationally accepted agreement exists on how governments, let alone events, should measure and report on impacts. We will focus on Life Cycle Assessment (LCA) as a promising method for measuring environmental impacts over the life of a product or service: from cradle to grave. LCA is being widely adopted by both the public and private sectors to assess impacts, report on performance, and as a basis for policies and regulations (Finnveden et al., 2009). Specifically, it can be a powerful tool for deciding between alternatives: *does product/solution A or product/solution B have the lower environmental impact?*

According to the International Organization for Standardization, which sets out the ISO 14044 (www.iso.org) guidelines and requirements for carrying out an LCA (2006), two of the key features of this method are (a) life cycle stages: raw material acquisition, production, use, end-of-life treatment, recycling, and final disposal; and (b) phases for carrying out an LCA study: goal and scope definition, inventory analysis, impact assessment, and interpretation. It is useful to understand each phase in a bit more detail (see Figure 8.2). *Goal and Scope:* defines the purpose of the study, the system boundaries, and the major assumptions. *Inventory Analysis:* defines the inventory of data, environmental inputs (resources) and outputs (emissions, wastes) of the system under study, and the methods for data collection and analysis. *Impact Assessment:* translates the inputs and outputs into indicators of potential environmental impact (e.g. human health, climate change, ecosystem quality). *Interpretation:* provides meaning to the results of the inventory and environmental impact assessment relative to the goals of the study.

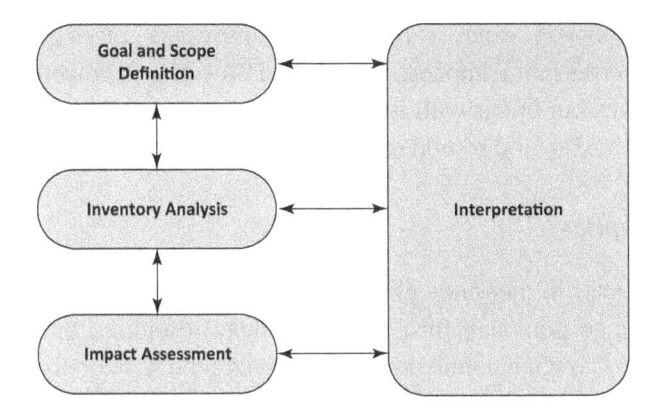

Figure 8.2 The four iterative phases of a Life Cycle Analysis (LCA) study according to the International Standards Organization (ISO) 14044.

Thinking with a life cycle perspective encourages both producers and consumers to consider the upstream and downstream impacts in the supply chain. For event management, this means not only understanding the environmental harm caused on-site by activities, such as air quality being affected by transportation emissions, but also the off-site impacts from purchased food, materials, and the generated waste. LCAs are used for a widening range of applications including business strategy, product and process design, environmental labeling, and product declarations. A key strength of LCA is its ability to characterize environmental impacts across multiple damage categories such as human health, ecosystem quality, climate change, and resource depletion (Jolliet et al., 2003). While LCA focuses on environmental impacts, it can be complemented by a broader set of Life Cycle Management (LCM) tools including Life Cycle Costing (LCC) and Social LCA.

There are, however, some considerations with using LCA for event management. Firstly, LCA results should not be used as a basis for comparison unless system boundaries, data sets, assumptions, and included processes are the same; we need to compare apples with apples. Secondly, the complexity of LCAs can be resource intensive if it requires extensive data collection and expertise. This can be a challenge for events with limited budgets or staff time. A third consideration is communication; while we all understand the value of a dollar, it can be challenging to interpret the importance of one tonne of carbon or one liter of polluted water. This leads us to a fourth issue, how one selects between opposing results, such as: which is more important, carbon or water? The answer of course depends on many issues such as geographic location, water scarcity, stakeholder values, placing importance on current versus future impacts, and so on. LCA can be a powerful planning tool for events but brings with it a need for increased expertise, education, stakeholder buy-in, and resources to implement effectively.

Carbon footprint

A carbon footprint measures global warming potential (synonymous with climate change potential) of a defined activity resulting from associated Greenhouse Gas (GHG) emissions over a given time horizon that is usually 100 years (Wright et al., 2011). The potential impacts for a number of GHGs (some common ones are carbon dioxide, methane, and nitrous oxide) have been characterized by the United National International Panel on Climate Change into carbon 'equivalents' (IPCC, 2007). The unit of measure is therefore the mass of carbon dioxide equivalents: kg CO_2-eq. The carbon footprint is the most widely used 'single' environmental impact category in the sports industry, with a host of mega events such as the London 2012 Olympic Games, and FIFA World Cup 2022 integrating it into their event management strategies. For instance, FIFA estimated that the carbon footprint of the FIFA 2022 World Cup in Qatar would be approximately 3.63 million tonnes of CO_2-equivalent emissions (CO_2-eq) with 51.7% due to, and 20.1% from accommodation, and 18% from permanent venue construction (Setterwall & FIFA, 2021).

Some benefits to applying a carbon footprint approach are that: it is a widely used and understood benchmark for environmental impacts; it has also become fairly well known and is therefore easily communicated to the public; it has the advantage of being applicable globally since global warming is not regionalized; and it benefits from a strong consensus in the scientific community on the existence of the problem and on the characterization of impacts (IPCC, 2007). A key drawback of events using a single indicator approach, however, is that it does not provide a full and contextual understanding of other impacts such as water use, land use, or resource use (Collins et al., 2009; Weidema et al., 2008).

Ecological footprint

The Ecological Footprint method developed by Wackernagel and Rees (1996) puts a focus on the carrying capacity of the earth. By estimating the total human consumption of resources and comparing it to the rate at which the planet can replace them, it can calculate whether our activities are meeting or exceeding its regenerative capacity. The unit of measure is the bioproductive area in hectares required to maintain human consumption. This can also be communicated in terms of the number of planet earths required to support our activities. According to the latest World Wildlife Federation (WWF) *Living Planet* (2022) report, the collective impact of global human population on the regenerative capacity of Planet Earth's ecosystems exceeds by 1.75. That is, to sustain humanity at current levels of natural resource consumption requires 1.75 Planet Earths.

The London 2012 Olympic Games, for example, embedded the ecological footprint as a measure for achieving their sustainability platform of a "One Planet Olympics." Collins et al. (2007) applied this assessment framework to measure the impact of the FA Cup international soccer match in Wales. They were able to show that spectators at the event increased their ecological footprint seven times over the daily average of a Welsh citizen.

Whatever environmental impact assessments managers choose to use, it is vital to become literate in the concept of examining impacts with a life cycle approach and across multiple indicators. As new tools develop for the event industry, managers can increase the sophistication level of their assessments and demonstrate increased accountability to their stakeholders.

It is important to be able to apply one's knowledge in practice. To aid in that process, assignments are now outlined to encourage this application.

Assignment A: Understanding event-related, environmentally focused organizations

There are a number of organizations that the event manager can partner with to advance their environmental actions. Select two of the organizations below and investigate their activities and record how they can aid an event manager. Your list can be advanced during your research.

- Global Sustainable Tourism Council
- Green Sports Alliance
- Sport Environment Alliance
- Sport for All and the Environment
- UNFCCC Sports for Climate Action

- The International Ecotourism Society
- The Sport Ecology Group
- Outdoor Alliance
- World Wide Fund for Nature (WWF)
- 350.org

Assignment B: Event decision-making for environmental sustainability

Suppose you are a manager of an annual golf event that is the cornerstone fundraising vehicle for your charitable organization. The tournament has been held at the same nearby golf course for the past 6 years. While no contracts exist, there is a "general understanding" that the tournament will be held at the same golf course for the coming year; your volunteers and staff have operated under this assumption in all planning. Two months before the event, however, you are approached by the General Manager (GM) of a new private course located 50 minutes north of your town. The GM offers financial incentives to move the event to their course; the proposal would increase net revenues from the event by 50%. As you contemplate the change of venue, other considerations spring to mind such as the increased travel for volunteers, staff, and participants to attend the event, the longer hours for volunteers, the impact that the loss of the event could have on the local golf course, and negative image issues arising from deserting the local golf course at the last minute. Lastly, the GM tells you the new club is experiencing a host of environmental challenges with pesticide use and water run-off to the local pond.

Clearly, the financial benefit of changing golf courses is evident, but how will you weigh these against the other social and environmental issues?

As can be seen from the scenario above, decision-making frameworks based entirely on the "bottom line" only account for the financial consequences of actions and are insufficient for contextualizing social and environmental considerations. Fundamentally, sustainability is about managing 3 P's: people, planet, and profit! Figure 8.1 provides a visual representation of sustainability in action; here, understanding the interactions between economic, social and environmental contexts forces managers to recalibrate their thinking, their managerial decisions, and their organizational assessment.

Assignment C: Ace Corporation Triathlon Group (ACTG) sustainability ownership and accountability

Imagine you are the marketing manager of the Ace Corporation Triathlon Group (ACTG). At a recent managers meeting, which included the head of finance, legal, human resources, operations, information, and yourself, the mandate from the President of ACTG was to move environmental sustainability to the forefront of the company's event delivery for the coming year. After the meeting, everybody is excited to integrate environmental sustainability into their division's practices.

At the following managers meeting the President asks for an update on the company's sustainability initiatives. Who steps forward to give the breakdown of ACTG's progress on this initiative? If challenges are put forth by the management team who "owns" these event management environmental sustainability initiatives; who will be charged with the task of finding solutions?

While environmental sustainability is certainly in its embryonic stage for event management, work has begun to move initiatives forward on the managerial agenda. For example, the Sport Event Environmental Performance Measurement (SE-EPM) model designed by Mallen et al., (2010) provides a comprehensive framework for evaluating a sport event's environmental performance. Key items of consideration within the framework include:

- The Environmental Organization System (environmental policies, environmental management committee, involvement in environmental programs).
- The Environmental Activities, Stakeholder Disclosure and Relationships (information transfer, disclosure and communications).
- The Environmental Operational Countermeasures (proactive initiatives such as renewable energy sources used, recycling, reduction, environmental training).
- Environmental Tracking (are items such as energy use and waste reduction being measured).
- Indicators and Measurement Items: Inputs and Outputs (paper, raw materials, CO_2)

The benefit of frameworks such as the SE-EPM is its ability to guide event managers on environmental sustainability initiatives. Moreover, a clearly defined

Greg Dingle, Chris Chard and Matt Dolf

rubric to guide assessment on event environmental performance can assist event managers in making individuals accountable for their assigned environmental sustainability projects. This type of guideline should serve event managers well in the coming years. Indeed, as the introduction of formal policies becomes commonplace, such as ISO 20121: Event Sustainability Management Systems (www.iso.org), the future of event management, and the requirements asked of the event manager will change. Here, the requirement to be compliant around sustainability will be mandated and policies to ensure observance of set standards will need to be integrated into event planning decisions.

Assignment D: Using a carbon footprint to minimize accommodation impact

You are organizing a baseball tournament for 8 teams of 15 people each. You are in the process of selecting a sponsor hotel to house the teams during the 7-day (and 7-night) event. One option, *Dandelion Inn*, is certified with a 'green hotel' program, partly because they have achieved significant reductions in energy use, water use, and waste generated compared to the industry average. However, they are located 10 kilometers away from the venue. A second sponsor choice, *Median Hotel*, is an industry average hotel and is located only 1 km away. In either case, you need to send a shuttle bus to the hotel twice per day to pick up and drop off the teams. A recent LCA study tells you that Dandelion Inn has an impact of 6 kg carbon dioxide equivalents (kg CO_2-eq) per person per night and Median Hotel has an impact of 12 kg CO_2-eq per person per night. You also know that the shuttle bus travel impact is 0.050 kg CO_2-eq per person per km (Figure 8.3).

1) Determine the hotel, travel and total Carbon Footprints of each option. Which has the lowest impact?
2) What other environmental sustainability considerations are there for an event manager when selecting between hotels? (Figure 8.4)

Hotels	Hotel carbon footprint	Travel carbon footprint	Total carbon footprint
Dandelion Inn	kg CO_2-eq	kg CO_2-eq	kg CO_2-eq
Median Hotel	kg CO_2-eq	kg CO_2-eq	kg CO_2-eq

Figure 8.3 Scenario data chart

Safeguarding the natural environment

> To determine the hotel carbon footprint:
> Dandelion: —— people × —— nights × <u>6</u> kg CO_2-eq/person/night = —— kg CO_2-eq
> Meridian: —— people × —— nights × <u>12</u> kg CO_2-eq/person/night = —— kg CO_2-eq
> To determine the travel carbon footprint from hotel to venue:
> Dandelion: —— people × —— km × <u>0.050</u> kg CO_2-eq/person/night = —— kg CO_2-eq
> Meridian: —— people × —— km × <u>0.050</u> kg CO_2-eq/person/night = —— kg CO_2-eq

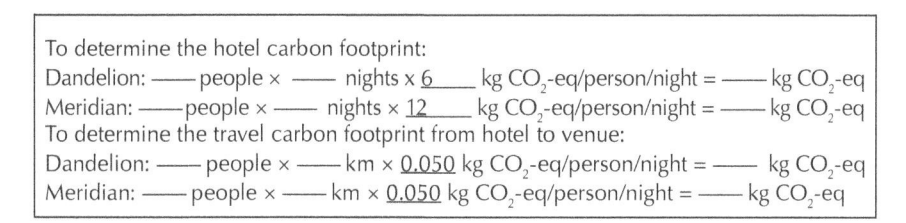

Figure 8.4 Guidelines for determining the carbon footprints in Assignment C

To determine the hotel carbon footprint:
Dandelion Hotel: 120 people × 7 nights × 6 kg CO_2-eq/person/night = 5,040 kg CO_2-eq
Meridian Hotel: 120 people × 7 nights × 12 kg CO_2-eq/person/night = 10,080 kg CO_2-eq

To determine the travel carbon footprint from hotel to venue:
Dandelion Hotel: 120 people × 280 km (10 × 7 × 4) × 0.050 kg CO_2-eq/person/night = 1,680 kg CO_2-eq
Meridian Hotel: 120 people × 28 km (1 × 7 × 4) × 0.050 kg CO_2-eq/person/night = 168 kg CO2-eq

Hotels	Hotel carbon footprint	Travel carbon footprint	Total carbon footprint
Dandelion Inn	5,040 kg CO_2-eq	1,680 kg CO_2-eq	6,720 kg CO_2-eq
Median Hotel	10,080 kg CO_2-eq	168 kg CO_2-eq	10,248 kg CO_2-eq

Figure 8.5 Answer to the scenario assignment concerning choice of hotels

3) How else could you lower the carbon footprint of accommodation?
4) What are the considerations of applying carbon as the only environmental impact category?

Conclusions

Alexander (2007) captured the inherent challenge for many managers considering changing business operations to implement environmental sustainability practices: how to convince those who currently enjoy economic success to enter into a process that could reduce their financial standing. From a similar perspective, Lothe et al. (1999) noted that "a conflict does not exist when the environmental strategies save on raw materials, reduce government penalties, make waste into positive gross margin products or increase sales because 'green' is marketable.... A conflict does exist, however, when the environmental strategies require extra investment" (p. 314–315).

The call to manage events in a more environmentally sustainable manner will surely increase in the future. Reducing the direct harm caused to the environment is the responsibility of everyone. Clearly, event managers have a part to play in environmental sustainability. Indeed, managing events with consideration for each of the three spheres of sustainability should be a priority for every event manager in the future.

Chapter questions

Drawing from your understandings of this chapter, please answer the following questions:

1. What is the difference between "sustainability" and "sustainable development"?
2. What are the three perspectives that are used to describe, manage, and assess sustainability?
3. Define "vulnerability" and "resilience" and apply the terms to the event manager working toward environmental sustainability.
4. "If you cannot measure it, you cannot manage it." Describe how this can be applied to environmental sustainability initiatives in event management.
5. Within an organization, who or what department should "own" environmental sustainability?
6. For the concept of "adaptation," think of an example of *incremental adaptation* of a sport event. And then for the same event, think of an example of *transformative adaptation*. Contrast the two examples, and reflect on which is likely to (a) be more challenging for a sport event manager to do? And (b) have a greater impact on the activities of a sport event organization?
7. Consider a road race and think of the multiple environmental sustainability initiatives that an event could adopt. Think of at least 3 other Event Management Environmental Sustainability initiatives.

References

2022 Birmingham Organising Committee. (2022). *Birmingham 2022 Commonwealth Games sustainability report*. C. G. Limited. https://resources.cwg-qbr.pulselive

.com/qbr-commonwealth-games/document/2022/11/08/05c0b10c-00c3-4ab7-88f4-e8396acc5834/Birmingham-2022-Sustainability-Report.pdf
Adger, W. N. (2006). Vulnerability. *Global Environmental Change, 16*(3), 268–281. http://www.sciencedirect.com/science/article/pii/S0959378006000422
Alexander, J. (2007, December). Environmental sustainability versus profit maximization: Overcoming systemic constraints on implementing normatively preferable alternatives. *Journal of Business Ethics, 76*(2), 155–162.
Barrett, J., & Scott, A. (2001, December). The ecological footprint: A metric for corporate sustainability. *Corporate Environmental Strategy, 8*(4), 316–325. https://doi.org/10.1016/S1066-7938(01)00132-4
Berrang-Ford, L., Siders, A., Lesnikowski, A., Fischer, A. P., Callaghan, M. W., Haddaway, N. R., Mach, K. J., Araos, M., Shah, M. A. R., & Wannewitz, M. (2021). A systematic global stocktake of evidence on human adaptation to climate change. *Nature Climate Change, 11*(11), 989–1000. https://doi.org/10.1038/s41558-021-01170-y
Cantelon, H., & Letters, M. (2000). The making of the IOC environmental policy as the third dimension of the Olympic movement. *International Review for the Sociology of Sport, 35*(3), 294–308.
Collins, A., Flynn, A., Munday, M., & Roberts, A. (2007). Assessing the environmental consequences of major sporting events: The 2003/04 FA Cup Final. *Urban Studies, 44*(3), 457–476. https://doi.org/10.1080/00420980601131878
Collins, A., Jones, C., & Munday, M. (2009). Assessing the environmental impacts of mega sporting events: Two options? *Tourism Management, 30*(6), 828–837. https://doi.org/10.1016/j.tourman.2008.12.006
Dingle, G. W., Dickson, G., & Stewart, B. (2022). Major sport stadia, water resources and climate change: Impacts and adaptation. *European Sport Management Quarterly*, 1–23. https://doi.org/10.1080/16184742.2022.2092169
Dingle, G. (2016). Sport, the natural environment, and sustainability. In R. Hoye & M. Parent (Eds.), *SAGE handbook of sport management* (pp. 531–557). Sage Publicaitons.
English Football Association. (2022). *The FA group event sustainability policy*. E. F. Association.
Field, C. B., Barros, V., Stocker, T. F., Qin, D., Dokken, D. J., Ebi, K. L., Mastrandrea, M. D., Mach, K. J., Plattner, G.-K., Allen, S. K., Tignor, M., & Midgley, B. P. (2012). *Managing the risks of extreme events and disasters to advance climate change adaptation. A special report of Working Groups I and II of the Intergovernmental Panel on Climate Change*. C. U. Press. https://www.ipcc.ch/site/assets/uploads/2018/03/SREX_Full_Report-1.pdf
FIFA. (2023). *Sustainability strategy*. FIFA Women's World Cup AU/NZ 2023. https://digitalhub.fifa.com/m/4c8c5e88c80b704b/original/FIFA-Women-s-World-Cup-2023-Sustainability-Strategy.pdf
Finnveden, G., Hauschild, M. Z., Ekvall, T., Guinée, J., Heijungs, R., Hellweg, S., Koehler, A., et al. (2009). Recent developments in life cycle assessment. *Journal of Environmental Management, 91*(1), 1–21. https://doi.org/10.1016/j.jenvman.2009.06.018

Folke, C. (2006). Resilience: The emergence of a perspective for social–ecological systems analyses. *Global Environmental Change, 16*(3), 253–267.

Füssel, H. M. (2007a). Adaptation planning üor climate change: Concepts, assessment approaches and key lessons. *Sustainability Science, 2*(2), 265–275.

Füssel, H.-M. (2007b). Vulnerability: A generally applicable conceptual framework for climate change research. *Global Environmental Change, 17*(2), 155–167.

Glaas, E., Hjerpe, M., Wihlborg, E., & Storbjörk, S. (2022). Disentangling municipal capacities for citizen participation in transformative climate adaptation. *Environmental Policy and Governance, 32*(3), 179–191. https://doi.org/10.1002/eet.1982

Government of Canada. (2023). *Canada's Eighth National Communication and Fifth Biennial Report on Climate Change (2022) – Executive summary*. Environment and Climate Change Canada. Retrieved March 22 from https://www.canada.ca/en/environment-climate-change/services/climate-change/greenhouse-gas-emissions/fifth-biennial-report-climate-change-summary.html

Hollender, J., & Breen, B. (2010). *The responsibility revolution: How the next generation of businesses will win*. Jossey-Bass.

Hums, M. A. (2010). The conscience and commerce of sport management: One teacher's perspective. *Journal of Sport Management, 24*, 1–9. http://dx.doi.org/10.1123/jsm.24.1.1

Hyytiäinen, K., Kolehmainen, L., Amelung, B., Kok, K., Lonkila, K.-M., Malve, O., Similä, J., Sokero, M., & Zandersen, M. (2022). Extending the shared socioeconomic pathways for adaptation planning of blue tourism. *Futures, 137*, 102917. https://doi.org/10.1016/j.futures.2022.102917

Intergovernmental Panel on Climate Change (IPCC). (2007). *IPCC fourth assessment synthesis report: Climate change 2007*. Cambridge University Press.

International Olympic Committee. (2021). *Sustainability post-games report: Tokyo 2020*. T. O. S. Centre. https://library.olympics.com/Default/doc/SYRACUSE/1327958/sustainability-post-games-report-tokyo-2020-the-tokyo-organising-committee-of-the-olympic-and-paraly

International Organization for Standardization (ISO). (2006). *ISO 14044:2006 environmental management – Life cycle assessment - Requirements and guidelines* (First.). ISO. http://www.iso.org/iso/catalogue_detail?csnumber=38498

Jackson, T. (2017). *Prosperity without growth: Foundations for the economy of tomorrow* (2nd ed.). Routledge. http://www.sd-commission.org.uk/data/files/publications/prosperity_without_growth_report.pdf

Jackson, T., & Victor, P. A. (2019). Unraveling the claims for (and against) green growth. *Science, 366*(6468), 950–951. https://doi.org/10.1126/science.aay0749

Janssen, M. A., & Ostrom, E. (2006). Resilience, vulnerability, and adaptation: A cross-cutting theme of the International Human Dimensions Programme on Global Environmental Change. *Global Environmental Change, 16*(3), 237–239. http://dx.doi.org/10.1016/j.gloenvcha.2006.04.003

Janssen, M. A., Schoon, M. L., Ke, W., & Börner, K. (2006). Scholarly networks on resilience, vulnerability and adaptation within the human dimensions of global environmental change. *Global Environmental Change, 16*(3), 240–252.

Johnston, P., Everard, M., Santillo, D., & Robèrt, K. H. (2007). Reclaiming the definition of sustainability. *Environmental Science and Pollution Research International, 14*(1), 60–66.

Jolliet, O., Margni, M., Charles, R., Humbert, S., Payet, J., Rebitzer, G., & Rosenbaum, R. (2003). IMPACT 2002+: A new life cycle impact assessment methodology. *The International Journal of Life Cycle Assessment, 8*(6), 324–330. https://doi.org/10.1007/BF02978505

Jones, C. (2008). Assessing the impact of a major sporting event: The role of environmental accounting. *Tourism Economics, 14*(2), 343–360. https://doi.org/10.5367/000000008784460382

Jones, M. (2011, Spring). Sustainable event management, ISO 20121. *The Business of International Events*. https://www.iso.org/files/live/sites/isoorg/files/store/en/PUB100302.pdf

Kellison, T. B. (2015). Building sport's green houses. In J. Casper & M. Pfahl (Eds.), *Sport management and the natural environment: Theory and practice* (pp. 218–237). Routledge.

Linnenluecke, M. K., & Griffiths, A. (2015). *The climate resilient organization: Adaptation and resilience to climate change and weather extremes*. Edward Elgar Publishing.

Lothe, S., Myrtveit, I., & Trapani, T. (1999, November/December). Compensation systems for improving environmental performance. *Business Strategy and the Environment, 8*(6), 313–321. https://doi.org/10.1002/(SICI)1099-0836(199911/12)8:6%3C313::AID-BSE219%3E3.0.CO;2-C

Mallen, C., & Chard, C. (2011). A framework for debating the future of environmental sustainability in the Sport Academy. *Sport Management Review, 14*, 424–433. http://dx.doi.org/10.1016/j.smr.2010.12.002

Mallen, C., & Chard, C. (2012). "What could be" in Canadian sport facility environmental sustainability. *Sport Management Review, 15*(2), 230–243. https://doi.org/10.1016/j.smr.2011.10.001

Mallen, C., Adams, L., Stevens, J., & Thompson, L. (2010, June). Environmental sustainability in sport facility management: A Delphi study. *European Sport Management Quarterly, 10*, 367–389. http://dx.doi.org/10.1080/16184741003774521

McCullough, B., Orr, M., & Watanabe, N. (2019). Measuring externalities: The imperative next step to sustainability assessment in sport. *Journal of Sport Management, 34*(5), 393–402. https://doi.org/10.1123/jsm.2019-0254

McDonough, W., & Braungart, M. (2002, August). Design for the triple bottom line: New tools for sustainable commerce. *Corporate Environmental Strategy, 9*(3), 251–258. http://dx.doi.org/10.1016/S1066-7938(02)00069-6

Moscardo, G., Lamberton, G., Wells, G., Fallon, W., Lawn, P., Rowe, A., Humphrey, J., Wiesner, R., Pettitt, B., Clifton, D., Renouf, M., & Kershaw, W. (Eds.). (2013). *Sustainability in Australian business: Principles and practice*. John Wiley & Sons Inc.

Mulgan, R. (2000). Accountability: An ever expanding concept? *Public Administration, 78*(3), 555–573. https://doi.org/10.1111/1467-9299.00218

Ness, B., Urbel-Piirsalu, E., Anderberg, S., & Olsson, L. (2007). Categorising tools for sustainability assessment. *Ecological Economics, 60*(3), 498–508. https://doi.org/10.1016/j.ecolecon.2006.07.023

Packard, K. O., & Reinhardt, F. (2000). What every executive needs to know about global warming. *Harvard Business Review, 78*(128). https://hbr.org/2000/07/what-every-executive-needs-to-know-about-global-warming

Parkin, S. (2000). Sustainable development: The concept and the practical challenge. *Civil Engineering, 138*(November), 3–8. https://doi.org/10.1680/cien.2000.138.6.3

Perelman, M. (2003). Myths of the market: Economics of the environment. *Organization & Environment, 16*(2), 168–226.

Pyhälä, A., Fernández-Llamazares, Á., Lehvävirta, H., Byg, A., Ruiz-Mallén, I., Salpeteur, M., & Thornton, T. F. (2016). Global environmental change: Local perceptions, understandings, and explanations. *Ecology and Society, 21*(3). https://doi.org/10.5751/ES-08482-210325

Randjelovic, J., O'Rourke, A., & Orsato, R. (2003, July/August). The emergence of green venture capital. *Business Strategy and the Environment, 12*(4), 240–253. https://doi.org/10.1002/bse.361

Robinson, J. (2004). Squaring the circle? Some thoughts on the idea of sustainable development. *Ecological Economics, 48*(4), 369–384. https://doi.org/10.1016/j.ecolecon.2003.10.017

Rockström, J., Steffen, W., Noone, K., Persson, Å., III Chapin, F. S., Lambin, E., Lenton, T. M., Scheffer, M., Folke, C., Schellnhuber, H., Nykvist, B., De Wit, C. A., Hughes, T., van der Leeuw, S., Rodhe, H., Sörlin, S., Snyder, P. K., Costanza, R., Svedin, U., Falkenmark, M., Karlberg, L., Corell, R. W., Fabry, V. J., Hansen, J., Walker, B., Liverman, D., Richardson, K., Crutzen, P., & Foley, J. (2009). Planetary boundaries: Exploring the safe operating space for humanity. *Ecology and Society, 14*(2), 1–33.

Saygı, H. (2020). Adverse effects of climate change on agriculture: An evaluation of fruit and honey bee farming. *Asian Journal of Agriculture and Rural Development, 10*(1), 504–514. https://doi.org/10.18488/journal.1005/2020.10.1/1005.1.504.514

Scrucca, F., Severi, C., Galvan, N., & Brunori, A. (2016). A new method to assess the sustainability performance of events: Application to the 2014 World Orienteering Championship. *Environmental Impact Assessment Review, 56*, 1–11. https://doi.org/10.1016/j.eiar.2015.08.002

Setterwall, S., & FIFA. (2021). *Greenhouse gas accounting report*. FIFA World Cup Qatar 2022. https://digitalhub.fifa.com/m/283d8622accb9efe/original/ocv9xna0lkvdshw30idr-pdf.pdf

Smit, B., & Wandel, J. (2006). Adaptation, adaptive capacity and vulnerability. *Global Environmental Change, 16*(3), 282–292. http://www.sciencedirect.com/science/article/pii/S0959378006000410

Steffen, W., Richardson, K., Rockström, J., Cornell, S. E., Fetzer, I., Bennett, E. M., Biggs, R., Carpenter, S. R., de Vries, W., de Wit, C. A., Folke, C., Gerten, D., Heinke, J., Mace, G. M., Persson, L. M., Ramanathan, V., Reyers, B., & Sörlin, S. (2015). Planetary boundaries: Guiding human development on a changing planet. *Science*. https://doi.org/10.1126/science.1259855

Stoknes, P. E., & Rockström, J. (2018). Redefining green growth within planetary boundaries. *Energy Research & Social Science, 44*, 41–49. https://doi.org/10.1016/j.erss.2018.04.030

Tàbara, J. D., Jäger, J., Mangalagiu, D., & Grasso, M. (2019). Defining transformative climate science to address high-end climate change. *Regional Environmental Change, 19*(3), 807–818. https://doi.org/10.1007/s10113-018-1288-8

Termeer, C. J., Dewulf, A., & Biesbroek, G. R. (2017). Transformational change: Governance interventions for climate change adaptation from a continuous change perspective. *Journal of Environmental Planning and Management, 60*(4), 558–576. https://doi.org/10.1080/09640568.2016.1168288

Tong, S., Bambrick, H., Beggs, P. J., Chen, L., Hu, Y., Ma, W., Steffen, W., & Tan, J. (2022). Current and future threats to human health in the Anthropocene. *Environment International, 158*, 106892. https://doi.org/10.1016/j.envint.2021.106892

UNEP. (2005). *Overview of the Millenium ecosystem assessment*. United Nations Environment Programme. Retrieved October 3 from http://www.unep.org/maweb/en/About.aspx#14

UNEP. (2007). *Global environmental outlook 4: Environment for development* (978-92-807-2872-9). https://www.unep.org/resources/global-environment-outlook-4

UNEP. (2011). *Decoupling natural resource use and environmental impacts from economic growth*. https://www.resourcepanel.org/reports/decoupling-natural-resource-use-and-environmental-impacts-economic-growth

UNEP. (2012). *Keeping track of our changing environment: From Rio to Rio+20 (1992–2012)*. U. N. E. Programme. https://sustainabledevelopment.un.org/index.php?page=view&type=400&nr=321&menu=1515

UNEP. (2019). *Global environmental outlook 6: Healthy planet, healthy people*. https://wedocs.unep.org/bitstream/handle/20.500.11822/27539/GEO6_2019.pdf?sequence=1&isAllowed=y

United Nations (UN) Brundtland Report. (1987). 96th Plenary meeting. United Nations General Assembly, Report to the World Commission on the Environment and Development. https://www.are.admin.ch/are/en/home/media/publications/sustainable-development/brundtland-report.html

United Nations (UN). United Nations Environment Programme: Sport and environment. Retrieved from www.unep.ort/sport_env/

United Nations International Resource Panel. (2019). *Global resources outlook: Natural resources for the future we want*. https://www.resourcepanel.org/reports/global-resources-outlook

Wackernagel, M., & Rees, W. E. (1996). *Our ecological footprint: Reducing human impact on the earth*. New Society Publishers.

Weidema, B. P., Thrane, M., Christensen, P., Schmidt, J., & Løkke, S. (2008). Carbon footprint. *Journal of Industrial Ecology, 12*(1), 3–6. https://doi.org/10.1111/j.1530-9290.2008.00005.x

Winn, M. I., Kirchgeorg, M., Griffiths, A., Linnenluecke, M. K., & Gunther, E. (2011). Impacts from climate change on organizations: A conceptual foundation. *Business Strategy & Environment, 20*, 157–173.

Wise, R. M., Fazey, I., Smith, M. S., Park, S. E., Eakin, H. C., Van Garderen, E. A., & Campbell, B. (2014). Reconceptualising adaptation to climate change as part of pathways of change and response. *Global Environmental Change, 28,* 325–336. https://doi.org/10.1016/j.gloenvcha.2013.12.002

World Bank. (2018). *What a waste 2.0: A global snapshot of solid waste management to 2050* (Urban Development Series). W. B. Group. https://openknowledge.worldbank.org/entities/publication/d3f9d45e-115f-559b-b14f-28552410e90a

World Wildlife Fund (WWF). (2022). *Living planet report 2022: Building a naturepositive society.* W. W. Fund. https://wwflpr.awsassets.panda.org/downloads/lpr_2022_full_report.pdf

Wright, L. A., Kemp, S., & Williams, I. (2011). 'Carbon footprinting': Towards a universally accepted definition. *Carbon Management, 2*(1), 61–72. https://doi.org/10.4155/cmt.10.39

Zalasiewicz, J., Williams, M., Haywood, A., & Ellis, M. (2011). The anthropocene: A new epoch of geological time? *Philosophical Transactions of the Royal Society, 369,* 835–841. https://doi.org/10.1098/rsta.2010.0339

9

Environmental sustainability in sport, recreation, and tourism

"You ain't seen nothing yet"

Cheryl Mallen,
Justine Schwende,
Efthalie (Elia) Chatzigianni

We need space for sport, recreation, and tourism activities. Our natural environment of grass, hills, sky, and waterways provide wonderful opportunities for engagement. Much has been stated about the need to avoid the destruction of our natural resources. Examples of such destruction abound (Ahmet, 2021; Baloch et al., 2023). The tide is starting to turn, however, toward safeguarding such resources – environmental sustainability. This turnabout is due, in part, to a recognition that "Nature is the ultimate source of all economic value … No commerce or culture is possible without clean air and water; fertile topsoil; [and] a chemically stable atmosphere…" (Hershkowitz, 2014, n.p.).

The authors of this chapter purport that the song title "You Ain't Seen Nothing Yet" from the Canadian band Bachman Turner Overdrive is appropriate with respect to environmental activities in practice and research that will take place into the future in the event industry. Before we discuss the future, this chapter outlines calls for environmental sustainability and offers a plethora of practical examples illustrating a forward movement toward environmental sustainability, specifically in sport, recreation, and tourism event management. Next, examples from the body of research publications on the topic are outlined. A discussion leads to a presentation of key issues regarding environmental safeguards in event management. Suggestions from the

DOI: 10.4324/9781003391098-9

literature are presented concerning what is needed to move forward to reach our full potential in sport, recreation, and tourism event environmental sustainability – and then suggestions from the authors. Readers are encouraged to develop their own perspectives concerning the advancement of environmental sustainability.

As you read this chapter, keep in mind your answers to the following three questions:

1. Can an event manager be deemed to be doing their job well if they have not learned how to incorporate strategies that safeguard the natural environment during the implementation of an event?
2. What is an appropriate level of environmental impact one generation of sport, recreation, and tourism events should leave for the next generation?
3. Does enacting small/little environmental safeguards make a difference overall? In other words, does being "less bad" environmentally really count as a good thing?

Calls to enact environmental sustainability

Calls have been made around the world for the sport, recreation, and tourism event industries to promote and engage in environmental sustainability. For instance, the World Leisure Organization (n.d.) promotes environmental sustainability through research and the sharing of advancing knowledge. The United Nations World Tourism Organization (n.d.) has encouraged events that engage in climate action, including promoting a low carbon strategy, along with environmentally friendly procurement practices. Also, eco-tourism promotes environmentalism (Salahodjaev et al., 2022). Furthermore, the United Nations Department of Economic and Social Affairs (2022) stated that sport is an excellent avenue that can conduct and promote environmental sustainability as it offers a "broad social platform [that] makes it a strategic tool in influencing people's attitudes; its reach extends to almost all geographical areas and social backgrounds… [and], billions of individuals are involved … as spectators, practitioners, or facilitators" (para. 3). Stevenson (2020) proposes that recreational programs, including "small scale incremental, bottom-up, playful and pleasurable" (p. 1) activities can be a platform for teaching and encouraging sustainable behaviours within society. This means that all sport, recreation, and tourism events offer an opportunity to have influence from the grassroots to the international global community on how to engage in environmental sustainability. So, what has been accomplished to date?

Sport, recreation, and tourism environmental sustainability in practice

Examples of environmental sustainability have accelerated around the world of sport, recreation, and tourism event management. The practice of incorporating environmental sustainability into events has advanced in both practice and research journal publications and is multi-directional in focus. Examples of topics include: (a) events and network relationships, (b) awareness programs, (c) event actions toward carbon neutrality, and (d) event facilities that engage with environmental sustainability. An overview of these examples is now offered.

Events and network relationships that aid in environmental sustainability

Sport, recreation, and tourism events have benefited from links with strategies and programs offered by environmentally focused organizations. This means an environmental organization can offer guidance with respect to events and participation in environmental action. The assistance of an environmentally focused organization offers greater efficiencies than acting on one's own. Partnerships abound. Leeds United Football Club (England) partnered with Greenpeace, an environmental action group, and promoted a need for environmental safeguards for the rainforest and marine life (Hill, 2016). The United States based Natural Resources Defense Council (NRDC) is a not-for-profit advocacy group with a mission "to safeguard the earth – its people, its plants and animals, and the natural systems on which all life depends" (n.p.). The NRDC has built multiple relationships with professional sport leagues and teams to move toward environmental sustainability, such as with Major League Soccer (MLS), the National Basketball Association (NBA), and the United States Tennis Association (USTA). Meanwhile, the National Hockey League Players Association (NHLPA) linked up with the David Suzuki Foundation (Canada) for a "Carbon Neutral Challenge." Manchester United (England) joined forces with "Renewable Energy Group" to use renewable diesel at their facility, Old Trafford. Forest Green Rovers

Football (England) teamed up with the Sea Shepherd campaign to help stop plastics from entering the oceans. Additionally, the Phoenix Suns (NBA) partnered with a company called Footprint to raise awareness concerning the environmental impacts of plastics (McCormick, 2021). Additional examples include the National Association for Stock Car Auto Racing (NASCAR) that established linkages with Green Earth Technologies (GET), and the Minnesota Timberwolves (NBA) [who play out of Target Center] partnered with Juhl Wind Inc.

Despite what has been noted as "low communication of ES [environmental sustainability] practices by professional sport in the Asia-Pacific region compared to North America" (Wall-Tweedie & Nguyen, 2018, p. 741), there are still examples to be found. For example, the Indian Premier League (IPL – Cricket) joined with Schneider Electric for a carbon-neutral match, and the Coral Triangle Support Partnership supports recreational snorkeling and coral reef sustainability around Indonesia, Malaysia, the Philippines, Papua New Guinea, and the Solomon Islands. Also, West Indies Cricket linked with the Apex Group on the road to net zero carbon emissions.

Additionally, organizations have been formed that specifically focus on sport, recreation, or tourism environmental sustainability. Examples include Global Partnerships for Sustainable Tourism, Global Sustainable Tourism Council, Green Sport Alliance, International Ecotourism Society, Sport Ecology Group, Sports Environment Alliance, Sport for All and the Environment, and the World Leisure Organization.

Events and environmental awareness programs

Event staff, along with those working for event-related organizations, are promoting environmental awareness on their webpages and the diffusion of the message at events can influence participants at all levels of participation. For instance, the Africa Cup of Nations has used events to promote the protection of the forests and animal species on the African continent. The United States based National Intramural-Recreational Sports Association promotes environmental sustainability in collegiate recreation. Further, Green Sports Alliance (n.d.) stated that sports teams around the world promoted "Green Sports Day." Interestingly, hashtags have been used to promote environmental mindfulness, such as the Fédération Internationale de Natation (FINA) that promotes the topic with #WaterisOurWorld, the Indian Premier League (IPL) promoted #BeatPlasticPollution, and Fédération Internationale d'Escrime (FIE) promotes #FencingforourPlanet (Chatzigianni & Mallen, 2023). Meanwhile, the United Nations World Tourism Organization (n.d.) webpage headline promotes an awareness of sustainable tourism and the oneplanetnetwork.org webpage supports global tourism efforts for a reduction in the use of plastics. Martins, Pereira, Rosado, and Mascarenhas (2021) purport that environmental communication in tourism generates greater comprehension of the issue and spurs on action; while Tölkes (2018) indicates that managers need to keep working to ensure the messages generate positive change. Stewards of environmental sustainability can even illustrate their awareness by participating in the global phenomenon of "Plogging" (Gutiérrez, 2023, n.p.). This involves a global movement of awareness for a need to safeguard the natural environment and promotes clean natural spaces for participation. Outdoor participants, as they train by running, jogging, hiking, or traversing the outdoors, are encouraged to pick up and transport inorganic waste to an appropriate place.

From the grassroot level of events to national and international "jewel events," there are examples of promoting environmental awareness. Further, incorporating environmentalism within event planning and operations is expanding. We now explore examples relating to carbon emission reductions.

Event actions toward carbon neutrality to improve air quality

Events and their associated organizations are moving toward reducing their carbon emissions and achieving carbon neutrality or net-zero emissions. For instance, the United Nations Framework Convention for Climate Change (UNFCCC, n.d.) Sport for Climate Action Framework encourages sport organizations and their associated events to meet the target of net zero emission by 2040. By 2021, a total of 269 sport organizations from around the world had signed onto that pledge (Campbell, 2021, para. 4). Examples of signatories include the Nagoya Diamond Dolphins (Japanese Basketball League), Athletics Kenya, the Brazil Olympic Committee, and the Puerto Rico Soccer League. The trickle-down influence of these sport organizations and their push for carbon neutrality impact other levels of sport – right down to the grassroots level. Some sport organizations have even opted to beat the target noted above, as World Rugby released their 2030 plan for becoming net zero (WR, 2022). Events from the grassroots level and up are encouraged to participate. Additionally, the International Energy Agency (IEA) has pushed tourism organizations and their events to be net zero by 2050 (Scott & Gössling,

2021). Meanwhile, Race Tech Magazine (2020) has stated that Formula E is the first to have achieved a net zero event carbon footprint. This status was reached with "effective measurement of carbon output, prioritising reducing its footprint, and offsetting remaining unavoidable emissions" (para. 2).

Offsetting carbon emissions involves buying into environmental energy projects, such as paying into a tree planting program or bioenergy development program. A study by Chard and Mallen (2012) examined what the investment would be to offset the carbon emissions from travel in a community recreational hockey program. The total number of kilometres travelled by each team member for practices and games was calculated and the collective team emissions was determined with carbon calculators. There are many online carbon calculators such as www.planetair.ca or www.carbonzero.ca or https://climatecare-sme.co2analytics.com/. These sites take the total amount travelled and state the cost to offset the emissions and offer options for making payments to a company or project to bring your emissions to net zero. In this study it was determined that it would cost approximately $250.00 Canadian to offset the carbon emissions for each hockey team within the league – or just over $20.00 per player. Research by Cooper and McCullough (2021) outlined that the carbon impact per participant for a sport tourism event under study was 500 kg with travel making up eighty percent of the footprint. McCullough, Orr, and Watanabe (2019) indicated that event managers needed to measure the carbon impacts of their events and then work toward mitigating and managing such impacts. So, the question arises, should all events use the strategy of carbon offsets and ensure that they are carbon neutral? Meanwhile, Abraham (2020) is studying the important aspect of carbon disclosures.

Overall, the carbon issue is complex, as carbon offsetting does not reduce the travel that generates the carbon emissions in the first place. One must determine if offsetting is not as bad for the environment and if it makes enough of a difference to be a valuable event strategy. How much offsetting is acceptable compared to reductions in the carbon generating activities?

Another strategy to safeguard air quality involves a longitudinal study that was started in 2019 by World Athletics. This pilot project involved over 1,000 athletic tracks around the world that are used as event venues. Each was monitored for air quality. To do this, low-cost sensors or monitors were placed at the venue or on the competition route. For instance, at the World Athletics Half Marathon Championship in 2020, "more than 70,000 data points were collected for various pollutant gases concentrations, particle concentrations, and meteorological parameters" (Chatzigianni & Mallen, 2023, p. 11). The air quality monitors were placed at the starting line, and another was strapped onto a bicycle that was ridden behind the athletes. Over time, World Athletics plans to set the World Health Organization air quality standards as the baseline for major championships and sanctioned events. Air quality will be a hallmark requirement for hosting an event (WA., 2022). World Athletics is not only making a statement concerning moving toward better air quality for events – they are illustrating leadership on how to accomplish this endeavour. This leadership includes supporting the advancement of research data, making the resulting data transparent (albeit post-event), and working toward advancing policies concerning events and air quality with empirical support.

Questions arise, however, with any strategy you wish to pursue. If you were an event manager, would you monitor and post the air quality levels for the event? Should sport, recreation, and tourism participants/spectators everywhere know the air quality? Why? Why not? What are the issues and how can event managers overcome such issues?

Next, we focus on the site that is used to host events.

Event facilities and environmental sustainability

The selection of an event facility is an important consideration with respect to decreasing the environmental impact of an event. Facilities around the world are working to develop best practices that improve their pursuit of environmental safeguards. For instance, many event facilities have become carbon neutral by using renewable energy. Also, staff are finding waste efficiencies, as well as ways to safeguard water resources. Examples of each are now offered.

Event facilities and renewable energy

There are a growing number of examples that illustrate the use of renewable energy at event facilities. To begin, recreational centres have used renewable energy, including solar energy at TRAC Murwillumbah Recreational Aquatic Center (Australia) and Leduc Recreational Center (Canada). Sport venues around the world are installing solar arrays, such as at Antalya Arena (Turkey), Climate Pledge Arena (USA), Estádio Nacional de Brasília Mane Garriché (Brazil), Kaohsiung World Stadium (Taiwan), and TT Circuit

Assen (Netherlands). Interestingly, Amsterdam ArenA (Netherlands) generates energy from the movement of the venue elevators. New Tottenham Hotspur Stadium (England) is certified as utilizing 100% renewable energy.

Venues for festivals have also used renewable energy, including the *Bonnaroo Music and Arts Festival* (USA), in which solar arrays powered the kitchen and patrons were able to charge their cellular phones. The Johan Cruijff Arena (Netherlands) uses both wind and solar generated energy and has a back-up energy system involved reusing batteries after they have been discarded by electric vehicle use (Billington, 2018). Also, a festival called *Secret Solstice* (Iceland) is powered by geothermal energy. And intriguingly, Scotiabank Arena (Canada), along with downtown Toronto tourism hotels, get access to air conditioning from a Deep Lake Water Cooling (DLWC) strategy. Pipes are placed deep into Lake Ontario (one of the Great Lakes in North America) where the water is too cold to drink. This water is extracted, put through the facility pipes, and fans are used to spread the resulting cold air to cool the buildings during hot summer months (Corbley, 2021).

Event facilities generating waste mitigation and efficiencies

The United Nations Environment Program (2003) released the first edition of their waste and water efficiencies manual for tourism – and improving this performance has been promoted for over two decades. As a consequence of that document, event staff at sport, recreation, and tourism facilities are working to generate waste efficiencies. Additionally, eco-innovations in waste prevention are being developed through pilot studies by the *Urban Strategies for Waste Management in Tourism Cities* (Obersteiner et al., 2021). Sport and recreation facilities are adopting actions that include waste reduction and it is common to see recycling and composting bins at venues. Volunteers are also being trained in the proper disposal of waste. Programs exist, such as at Miller Park (USA) and the Air Canada Centre (Canada) in which unused food after events is donated to the local food bank. Additional efforts are ongoing; for example, the Union of European Football Associations (UEFA) developed and disseminated their circular economy guidelines concerning reducing, reusing, recycling, and recovering to decrease the impact of waste (Coliseum News, 2022).

Many sport, recreation, and tourism facility managers around the world are specifically working to eliminate single use plastics. The United Nations Environment Programme (UNEP) (2022) states that 80% of the plastics that currently flow into waterways, such as the oceans, can be reduced through action. Pressure to progress in this area stems from organizations such as the UNWTO (n.d.) along with the One Planet Network that are promoting sustainable consumption and production and the implementation of the Global Tourism Plastics Initiative. Efforts by the Miami Dolphins (NFL) were recently successful in eliminating over 800,000 plastic bottles and over 600,000 plastic cups from public use (McCormick, 2021). At Lincoln Financial Field (USA), when a stadium plastic seat breaks, it is turned into pellets and reformed into park benches (to divert the waste). Plastic waste is an issue for landfills and for our water resources – and a reduction in event plastic waste can help eliminate the potential for it to blow into streams, rivers, lakes, and end up in the oceans (Watkin, Mallen, & Hyatt, 2021).

Event facilities and water safeguards

Event managers around the world are working to ensure healthy water resources into the future. There has been a rise in water tourism that promotes the value and conservation of our global water resources (Folgado-Fernández et al., 2018), along with pressure for sport and recreation to further safeguard water supplies (Dingle, Dickson, & Stewart, 2022). Facilities that host events are working to reduce, reuse, and overall safeguard water resources. For instance, rainwater capture has reduced the use of potable water at Allianz Riviera (France), Melbourne Rectangular Stadium (Australia), Moses Mabhia Stadium (South Africa), and Toyota Center (USA). Harvested and filtered water has been used to wash down seating areas after games at Target Field (USA) and for landscaping irrigation at Amway Center (USA), all reducing the use of potable water. Further, stadiums such as the Estadio Azteca (Mexico) are working to ensure no toxic substances enter the water sources.

When it comes to making ice for skating, an updated strategy uses a reverse osmosis process that reduces chemicals added to the water at Air Canada Centre (Canada). Also, a Swedish technology process uses cool or ambient water and a 'degassing process' to remove the micro-bubbles from the water thereby making a harder & faster ice surface. This process does not need hot water and, thus, saves energy.

Interestingly, the species within water resources are also being protected, as Centurylink Field (USA) is guided by the Monterey Bay Aquarium to ensure their sale of seafood products are not on the endangered species list.

Events and other environmental strategies

There is a wide variety of additional environmental actions that events are using to move toward environmental sustainability. Scour your local events and develop a list of strategies that you uncover.

Overall, sport, recreation, and tourism environmental sustainability actions in practice are navigating what Jensen (2021) called the "sustainability puzzle" (p. 10). This puzzle is developed from the complexities that stem from dual pressures from (1) the increasing demands of events and (2) the simultaneous pressure to ensure environmental sustainability at events. Researchers have been working to discover how the puzzle is being pieced together.

Research in event sport, recreation, and tourism environmental sustainability

Journal manuscripts have described what has been happening in the event industry with respect to environmental sustainability. Researchers have assessed the overall body of research published concerning environmental sustainability in *sport* (Breitbart et al., 2022; Mallen, 2018; Mallen, Stevens & Adams, 2011; Cury, Kennelly & Howes, 2023; Trendafilova & McCullough, 2018), *recreation* (Marion, 2016; Sumanapala & Wolf, 2019), *sport tourism* (Jiménez-Garcia et al., 2020; Mascarenhas, Pereirs, Rosado, & Martins, 2021; Roe, Hrymak & Dimache, 2014), and *event tourism* (Wee, Mahdzar, Hamid, et al., 2017). Research publications continue to expand with attention on topics such as:

- barriers to environmental sustainability (Ross & Mercado, 2020)
- e-sport and environmental digital space considerations (Ross & Fissackerly, 2023; Robeers & VanDen Bulck, 2018)
- education in environmental sustainability (Graham, Trendafilova & Ziakas, 2018; Mercado & Grady, 2017; McCullough, Orr & Kellison, 2020; Orr, McCullough & Pelcher, 2020)
- vulnerability to climate (Orr & Inoue, 2019)
- understanding event environmental impacts (Tomino, Peric, & Wise, 2020; Dingle & Stewart, 2018); including the specific impacts of climate (Orr., Inoue, Seymour & Dingle, 2022; Scott & Gössling, 2022); and event carbon impacts (Collins & Cooper, 2017; Cooper, & McCullough, 2021;

Dolf & Teehan, 2015; Lenzen et al., 2018. Wicker, 2018, 2019; Zhang, Zhou, Zhou & Zhao, 2022), measuring environmental impacts (Boggia et al., 2018; McCullough, Orr, & Watanabe, 2019), impacts on the Olympics and FIFA (Ross & Orr, 2022), and the impacts of spectator transportation (Martins et al., 2022)
- sustainable business frameworks and models (Baloch et al., 2023; Orefice & Nyarko, 2020)
- water management and events (Phillips & Turner, 2014)
- waste management with a reduction in event food and beverage use of plastic (Watkin, Mallen & Hyatt, 2021).

Also, research publications have concentrated on environmental sustainability and specific leagues (Locke, 2019; Watanabe, Yan, Soebbing, & Fu, 2019), sports (Orr, 2020), a variety of events (Del Fiacco & Orr, 2019; Ross & Leopkey, 2017), and facilities used for events (Mallen, Adams, Stevens & Thompson, 2010). The history, current state, and future trends have been outlined (McCullough, Pfahl, & Nguyen, 2016; Trendafilova et al., 2014).

Researchers are also establishing centres that study environmental impacts and adaptation strategies on sport, recreation, and/or tourism. For example, an "Adaptation Lab" has been set up at La Trobe University (Australia), a "Centre for Sport and Sustainability" was established at the University of British Columbia (Canada), the "Centre for Sustainability, Tourism and Transport" is at Breda University of Applied Sciences (Netherlands), and the "Centre for Recreation and Tourism Research" operates out of the University of the Highlands and Islands (United Kingdom).

Many research manuscripts have outlined understandings and recommended strategies for moving forward toward environmental sustainability. Examples include the following:

- Carmichael (2022) outlined a need to expand the discussion on environmental sustainability. Meanwhile, Beckon and Coghlan (2022), stated that there is a need to build 'regenerative literacy' and this is supported by the position of Szathmári and Kocsis (2020) that the concept of sustainability is "future-oriented" (p. 13). Education of the next generation is, thus, a priority
- Chatzigianni and Mallen (2023) reported that networking is growing to aid the advance of understandings of the environmental issues and response options. Continuing this trend will hopefully mean moving away from a

fragmented learning environment to a coordinated event industry learning environment
- Ghobadian, Viney, and Holt (2002) indicated that when managers face multiple priorities, they tend to concentrate on the objectives that involve ensuring efficiency and effectiveness of their day-to-day activities, at the expense of any activity that requires long term efforts. To overcome this situation, congruence is required – or the alignment of the policy, support (including the required human, technical and financial support), and actions to further the successful implementation of environmental sustainability strategies
- Hutchins, Troon, Miller, and Lester (2023) stated that sport could be used to communicate points concerning climatic issues – such as droughts, change of seasons, etc. In particular, these researchers stated "that cricket is a significant site for the staging and perception of climate risks for worldwide audiences" (p. 1)
- Jensen (2021) supported the development of local sport event policy that offers inspiration for sustainability that is influenced by frameworks from the international sport body and the pre-established United Nations stated Sustainable Development Goals (SDGs)
- Mallen, Dingle, and McRoberts (2023) outlined current adaptation strategies being used in varsity sport for climatic impacts of heat stress. These researchers recommended enhanced educational training for all – including: athletic department management, athletes, coaches, trainers, therapists, and game officials to ensure all recognize the symptoms of heat stress. Further, a cell phone app was suggested for communicating in-the-moment-heat data that is transparent to all participants. Additionally, a 'buddy system' to aid in recognizing heat stress symptoms was suggested. More water stations and shade resources were also recommended. A particular concern was for game officials during times of extreme heat
- Monton (2020) promoted the development of research that fills in the knowledge gaps concerning environmental sustainability. Also, Monton promoted that governments needed to "enforce more sustainable operations" (p. 75) and be the "baseline and first line of defense in protecting our environment and sustaining our resources" (p. 75). Further, Morton proposed that an environmental coordinator be a key position for teams and organizations
- Orr, Murfree, and Stargel (2022) proposed being open to rescheduling events as a mitigation strategy for climate change

- O'Toole et al. (2019) proposed 25 adaptation options for recreational events for managing six specific areas, including: (i) protecting the infrastructure; (ii) preventing impacts from precipitation variability, (iii) managing impacts of changing use trends, (iv) communicating risks, (v) managing impacts on expected conditions; and (vi) making accommodations for conditions that can now be expected. Meanwhile, Butowslo (2021) promoted an approach for sustainable tourism and de Grosbois & Fennell (2021) offered adoption principles for ecotourism

Moving forward in event environmental sustainability

Environmental sustainability at sport, recreation, and tourism events is becoming a central focus and an increasing priority for practitioners and researchers. The examples outlined above confirm a statement by Chatzigianni and Mallen (2023) that there is a noted upward "trajectory of safeguarding the natural environment" (p. 9). This rise is predicted to continue and to provide a ripple effect in the event industry and beyond.

The authors of this chapter now promote their suggestions for moving forward to advance event environmental sustainability with a three-pronged approach, by (i) applying appreciative theory for a mindset that seeks solutions, (ii) embedding environmental action, and (iii) generate leadership to guide the way forward. Each prong in the approach will now be outlined.

Apply appreciative theory for a mindset that seeks solutions

An application of appreciative theory involves moving beyond complaining about the issue to enacting solutions – including seeking to resolve the environmental impacts when hosting events. The characteristics of this theory involve "a paradigm of thought and understanding that holds organizations to be affirmative systems created by humankind as solutions to problems" (Watkins & Cooperride, 2000, p. 6). This means one can develop a mindset for looking forward with positivity by understanding the problem(s) – and then not staying in a negative cycle – but moving forward toward developing and enacting solutions. This theory supports the concept that we can resolve environmental issues. An application of appreciative theory in event management means acting by spending one's time determining solution strategies, developing action plans, and implementing event environmental strategies that make a difference.

Embed environmental actions

It is the position of the authors of this chapter that, while event managers have the discretion or choice to act for environmental sustainability, event managers are encouraged to demand environmental sustainability for all events. This can be difficult as there is a paradox that arises with the simultaneous demands for event activities to be completed under time pressures, as well as the demands of completing the tasks in an environmentally friendly manner. The priorities of hosting the event can take precedent over any planned environmental action. We can, however, embed event environmental sustainability actions as a primary priority. This involves moving away from voluntary guidelines and optional proposed strategies to safeguarding the natural environment as part of any action. All actions are simply conducted in a manner that is moving toward environmental sustainability.

Generate leadership to guide the way forward

Leadership is critical in the movement to safeguard the natural environment during the hosting of events. This critical role is complex – but doable! There are plenty of leadership roles to be filled as the complexity stems from the multiple tentacles needed to guide the way forward. This means leadership for enacting environmental sustainability is not from one person but can be built into every all roles and responsibilities. The tentacles include, for example, leadership that can:

- *work to demand environmental sustainability as the standard means of operating events:* embed environmental actions with policy development. Currently, only guidelines (not policy) could be found that guide sport events
- *build empirical evidence:* work to collect data, complete analysis for measured results of implemented environmental strategies. Further, develop empirical evidence concerning an application of research results in practice. This evidence is needed to support policy advancements (i.e. the World Athletics air quality pilot project discussed above), as well as advancing understanding and the dissemination of best practices.

Research and pilot projects are needed to build such evidence and understandings on the successful strategies for implementation. Event researchers can follow the lead of those outside the events industry and apply the results from published manuscripts, such as Owen (2020) that examined literature from many industries and categorized "110 adaptation initiatives that have been implemented and shown some degree of effectiveness" (p. 1)

- *actively advance environmental sustainability educational strategies:* this includes the education of all event participants. Advancing best educational strategies is critical for success
- *ensure environmental actions are supported with human, financial, and technological resources*
- *build cooperation to harmonize actions:* the complexity of applying environmental sustainability makes it imperative that we coordinate efforts for efficient and effective action. This type of coordination is feasible with the harmonization of event initiatives to safeguard our resources as a world effort – as sport, recreation, and tourism events are happening around the globe. Individual event environmental activities can be blended into a cohesive and coordinated collective of actions for all segments of an event – such as accommodation, marketing, ticketing, transportation, etc. This means all segments of the event are in harmony with fully implemented environmental sustainability for any staged event. Advancing knowledge on how to generate cooperative bodies is the task of all involved
- *establish building blocks of environmental action:* use harmonized actions to build a platform of environmental success that keeps growing (eliminating work in silos). This moves individual events from silo activities to being integrated as an industry of environmental action (Mair & Smith, 2021). Benchmarks can be used to build the baseline of action at all events – and raise the baseline level over time. These benchmarks are not proposed to be built on standards (such as the International Standards Organization) that can be expensive and involve complex negotiations. Instead, these are industry established benchmarks that are free for all to use. The development of a website could make it easy for events to delineate advancements and benchmarks
- *support innovations:* for instance, additional innovations are needed to reach waste management capacity in sport, recreation, and tourism. One issue involves the current annual worldwide carbon fibre consumption – the principal item in racing cars and sport and recreation equipment

– and the need to find ways to manage this waste through recycling (Zahn et al., 2020). Innovations *can be* developed and supported to actively mitigate such issues

There is a role for you to lead the way forward!

Conclusions

Strategies for moving event environmental sustainability forward into the future were outlined – but you may have your own ideas of what these strategies should entail. This means event managers need to work toward a consensus on how to adapt the event industry to safeguard the natural environment. Currently, knowledge on how to adapt has not yet been achieved (Mallen, Dingle, McRoberts, 2023) in a manner that ensures success. There is much to do to pave the way forward.

WE CAN ... establish and implement environmental safeguards that will make a real difference in the next decade concerning the state of our natural resources held in trust for the next generation of sport, recreation, and tourism participants.

WE CAN ... work to achieve congruence for success in environmental sustainability. Such congruence involves ensuring the policy, support, and actions are aligned to further successful implementation of environmental sustainability strategies.

WE CAN ... build on the actions that have been taken to date and show the world that "you ain't seen nothing yet!"

DO YOUR PART ... to ensure successful environmental sustainability into the future within the management of sport, recreation, and tourism events.

Chapter questions

1. What answers did you provide for the questions asked throughout this chapter:
   - Can an event manager be deemed to be doing their job well if they have not learned how to incorporate strategies that safeguard the natural environment during the implementation of an event?
   - What is an appropriate level of environmental impact one generation of sport, recreation, and tourism events should make on the next

generation? (This includes impacts on the air, waterways, and the creatures that rely on our natural resources for life, along with our flora and fauna)?
- Does enacting environmental safeguards that are small/little make a difference overall? In other words, does being 'less bad' environmentally really count as a good thing?
- Should all events use the strategy of carbon offsets to be carbon neutral?
- If you were an event manager, would you monitor and post the air quality levels for the event? Should sport, recreation, and tourism participants/spectators know the air quality? Why? Why not? What are the issues and how can event managers overcome such issues?
2. What are you doing if you are "plogging?"
3. Describe appreciative theory and its application to environmental sustainability.
4. Discuss the proposed strategies for making progress in event environmental sustainability.
5. Develop an event policy for safeguarding either the air or the water at an event of your choice. What empirical evidence needs to be developed to support policy development? Who is responsible for instituting the policies at an event? What course of action does your policy require event managers to complete? What are the benefits/disadvantages of having/not having an environmental event policy?
6. What is your envisioned future for sport, recreation, and tourism event management that safeguards our natural resources?
7. Do you think it is possible that "you ain't seen nothing yet?" Is this a true statement of the future of events and environmental sustainability?

References

Abraham, B. (2020). Towards carbon neutral gaming: Report on the carbon disclosure in game development project. *Proceedings of DiGRA2020 Conference.* https://digraa.org/wp-content/uploads/2020/01/DiGRAA_2020_paper_35.pdf

Ahmet, A. (2021). Environmental sustainability and sports: An evaluation of sports-induced adverse effects on the environment. *Journal of Corporate Governance Insurance and Risk Management, 8*(1). https://doi.org/10.51410/jcgirm.8.1/2

Baloch, Q., Shah, S., Igbal, N., Sheeraz, M., Asadullah, M., Mahar, S., & Kan, A. (2023). Impact of tourism development upon environmental sustainability: A suggested framework for sustainable ecotourism. *Environmental Science and Pollution Research International*, 1–14. https://doi.org/10.1007/s11356-022=22496-w

Beckon, S., & Coghlan, A. (2022). Knowledge alone won't 'fix it': Building regenerative literacy. *Journal of Sustainable Tourism*. https://doi.org/10.1080/09669682.2022.2150860

Billington, J. (2018, July 4). Johan Cruijff ArenA switches on Europe's largest energy storage system created from EV batteries. *Stadia Magazine*. https://www.stadia-magazine.com/news/stadium-sustainability/johan-cruijff-arena.html

Boggia, A., Massei, G., Paolotti, L., Rocchi, L., & Schiavi, F. (2018). A model for measuring the environmental sustainability of events. *Journal of Environmental Management*, *206*, 836–845. https://doi.org/10.1016/j.jenvman.2017.11.057

Breitbarth, T., McCullough, B., Collins, A., Gerke, A., & Herold, D. (2022). Environmental matters in sport: Sustainable research in the academy. *European Sport Management Quarterly*, *23*(1), 5–12. https://doi.org/10.1080/16184742.2022.2159482

Butowslo, L. (2021). Sustainable tourism: A human-centred approach. *Sustainability*, *13*(4), 1835.

Campbell, M. (2021, October 14). *The sustainability report: Sport's pathway to net zero*. https://sustainabilityreport.com/2021/10/14/sports-pathway-to-net-zero/

Carmichael, A. (2022). Time for practice; sport and the environment. *Managing Sport and Leisure*, *27*(3), 189–198. https://doi.org/10.1080/23750472.2020.1757493

Chard, C., & Mallen, C. (2012). Examining the linkages between automobile use and carbon impacts of community-based ice hockey. *Sport Management Review, 15*, 476–484. https://doi.org/10.1016/j.smr.2012.02.002

Chatzigianni, E., & Mallen, C. (2023). Exploring congruence in global sport governance between environmental policy and practice. *Sustainability*, *15*(2), 1462. https://doi.org/10.3390/su15021462

Coliseum News. (2022, September 14). UEFA launches circular economy guidelines. https://www.coliseum-online.com/uefa-launches-circular-economy-guidelines/

Collins, A., & Cooper, C. (2017). Measuring and managing the environmental impacts of festivals: The contribution of the ecological footprint. *Journal of Sport Tourism*, *25*(1), 148–162. https://doi.org/10.1080/09669582.2016.1189922

Cooper, J., & McCullough, B. (2021). Bracketing sustainability: Carbon footprinting March Madness to rethink sustainable tourism approaches and measurements. *Journal of Cleaner Production*, *318*, 128475. https://doi.org/10.1016/j.jclepro.2021.128475

Corbley, A. (2021, November 26). *Toronto is replacing air conditioning with deep lake water to cool hundreds of buildings*. https://www.goodnewsnetwork.org/toronto-is-replacing-air-conditioners-with-deep-lake-water-to-cool-hundreds-of-buildings/

Cury, R., Kennelly, M., & Howes, M. (2023). Environmental sustainability in sport: A systematic literature review. *European Sport Management Quarterly*, *23*(1), 13–37. https://doi.org/10.1080/16184742.2022.2126511

de Grosbois, D., & Fennell, D. (2021). Sustainability and ecotourism principles adoption by leading ecolodges: Learning from best practices. *Tourism Recreation Research*, *47*(5–6), 483–498. https://doi.org/10.1080/02508281.2021.1875170

Del Fiacco, A., & Orr, M. (2019). A review and synthesis of environmentalism within the Olympic Movement. *International Journal of Event and Festival Management, 10*(1), 67–80. https://doi.org/10.1108/IJEFM-05-2018-0038

Dingle, G., Dickson, G., & Stewart, B. (2022). Major sport stadia, water resources and climate change: Impacts and adaptation. *European Sport Management Quarterly, 23*(1), 59–81. https://doi.org/10.1080/16184742.2022.2092169

Dingle, G. W., & Stewart, B. (2018). Playing the climate game: Climate change impacts, resilience, and adaptation in the climate-dependent sport sector. *Managing Sport and Leisure, 23*(4–6), 293–314. https://doi.org/10.1080/23750472.2018.1527715

Dolf, M., & Teehan, P. (2015). Reducing the carbon footprint of spectator and team travel at the University of British Columbia's varsity sports events. *Sport Management Review, 18*(2), 244–255. https://doi.org/10.1016/j.smr.2014.06.00

Folgado-Fernández, J., Di-Clementre, E., Hernández-Mogollón, J., & Campón-Cerro, A. (2018). Water tourism: A new strategy for the sustainable management of water-based ecosystems and landscapes in Extremadura (Spain). *Land, 8*(2), 1–18. https://doi.org/10.3390/land8010002

Ghobadian, A., Viney, H., & Holt, D. (2002). Seeking congruence in implementing corporate environmental strategy. *International Journal of Environmental Technology and Management, 1*(4). http://dx.doi.org/10.1504/IJETM.2001.000771

Gutiérres, J. (2023, January 15). Plogging: The curious sport that helps clean the plant. *Latin American Post*. https://latinamericanpost.com/43169-plogging-the-curious-sport-that-helps-clean-the-planet

Graham, J., Trendafilova, S., & Ziakas, V. (2018). Environmental sustainability and sport management education: Bridging the gaps. *Managing Sport and Leisure, 23*(4), 422–433. http://doi.org/10.1080/23750472.2018.1530069

Green Sports Alliance. (n.d.). *Our milestones*. https://greensportsalliance.org/about/

Hershkowitz, A. (2014, May 19). Conservation conversations. *The New Yorker*. https://www.newyorker.com/magazine/2014/05/26/the-mail-33

Hill, N. (2016). Leeds United announces 'unique' sponsorship deal with Greenpeace. https://bdaily.co.uk/articles/2016/06/13/leeds-united-announces-unique-sponsorship-deal-with-greenpeace

Hutchins, B., Troon, S., Miller, T., & Lester, L. (2023, March). Envisioning a green modernity? The future of cricket in an age of climate crises. *Sport in Society*, 1–15. http://doi.org/10.1080/17430437/2023.2190516

Jensen, C. T. (2021). Local sport event policies and sustainability: A puzzle approach. *Frontiers in Sport and Active Living, 3*. http://doi.org/10.3389/fspor.2021.667762

Jiménez-Garcia, M., Ruiz-Chico, J., & Peña-Sánchez, A. (2020). A bibliometric analysis of sport tourism and sustainability (2002–2019). *Sustainability, 12*, 2840. http://doi.org/10.3390/su12072840

Lenzen, M., Sun, Y. Y., Faturay, F., Ting, Y. P., Geschke, A., & Malik, A. (2018). The carbon footprint of global tourism. *Nature Climate Change, 8*(6), 522–528. https://doi.org/10.1038/s41558-018-0141-x

Locke, S. L. (2019). Estimating the impact of Major League Baseball games on local air pollution. *Contemporary Economic Policy, 37*(2), 236–244. http://doi.org/10.1111/coep.12404

Mair, J., & Smith, A. (2021). Events and sustainability: Why making events more sustainable is not enough. *Journal of Sustainable Tourism, 29*(11–12), 1739–1755. http://dx.doi.org/10.1080/09669582.2021.1942480

Mallen, C. (2018). Robustness of the sport and environmental sustainability literature: Where to go from here? In B. McCullough (Ed.), *Handbook on sport, sustainability, and the environment*. Routledge.

Mallen, C., Dingle, G., & McRoberts, S. (2023). Climate impacts in sport: Extreme heat as a climate hazard and adaptation options. *Managing Sport and Leisure*. http://doi.org/10.1080/23750472.2023.2166574

Mallen, C., Stevens, J., & Adams, L. (2011). A content analysis of environmental sustainability research in a sport-related journal sample. *Journal of Sport Management, 25*, 240–256. http://dx.doi.org/10.1123/jsm.25.3.240

Mallen, C., Adams, L., Stevens, J., & Thompson, L. (2010). Environmental sustainability in sport facility management: A Delphi study. *European Sport Management Quarterly, 10*(3), 367–389. http://dx.doi.org/10.1080/16184741003774521

Marion, J. (2016). A review and synthesis of recreation ecology research supporting carrying capacity and visitor use management decisionmaking. *Journal of Forestry, 114*(3), 339–351. https://doi.org/10.5849/jof.15-062

Martins, R., Pereira, E., Rosado, A., Marôco, J., McCullough, B., & Mascarenhas, M. (2022). Understanding spectator sustainable transportation intentions in international sport tourism events. *Journal of Sustainable Tourism, 30*(8), 1972–1991. http://dx.doi.org/10.1080/09669582.2021.1991936

Martins, R., Pereira, E., Rosado, A., & Mascarenhas, M. (2021). Exploring the relationship between sport demand's key players and environmental sustainability: Pointers from a systematic review. *Journal of Outdoor Recreation and Tourism, 35*, 100419. https://doi.org/10.1016/j.jort.2021.100419

Mascarenhas, M., Pereira, E., Rosado, A., & Martins, R. (2021). How has science highlighted sports tourism in recent investigation on sports' environmental sustainability? A systematic review. *Journal of Sport & Tourism, 25*(1), 42–65. https://doi.org/10.1080/14775085.2021.1883461

McCormick, B. (2021, September 13). Future venues: Greener, cleaner. *Sports Business Journal*. https://www.sportsbusinessjournal.com/Journal/Issues/2021/09/13/In-Depth/Concessions-and-facilities.aspx

McCullough, B., Orr, M., & Kellison, T. (2020). Sport ecology: Conceptualizing an emerging subdiscipline within sport management. *Journal of Sport Management, 34*(6), 509–520. https://doi.org/10.1123/jsm.2019-0294

McCullough, B., Orr, M., & Watanabe, N. (2019). Measuring externalities: The imperative next step to sustainability assessment in sport. *Journal of Sport Management, 34*(5), 393–402. https://doi.org/10.1123/jsm.2019-0254

McCullough, B. P., Pfahl, M. E., & Nguyen, S. N. (2016). The green waves of environmental sustainability in sport. *Sport in Society, 19*(7), 1040–1065. https://doi.org/10.1080/17430437.2015.1096251

Mercado, H. U., & Grady, J. (2017). Teaching environmental sustainability across the sport management curriculum. *Sport Management Education Journal, 11*(2), 120–127. https://doi.org/10.1123/smej.2016-0018

Morton, J. (2020). *Sustainability in sport? A case study*. M.A. thesis, Faculty of Environmental and Urban Change, York University, Toronto, Ontario, Canada.

Natural Resources Defense Council (NRDC). (n.d.). *About NRDC*. https://www.nrdc.org/about

Obersteiner, G., Gollnow, S., & Eriksson, M. (2021). Carbon footprint reduction potential of waste management strategies in tourism. *Environmental Development*, *39*, 100617. https://doi.org/10.1016/j.envdev.2021.100617

Orefice, C., & Nyarko, N. (2020). Sustainable value creation in event ecosystems – A business models perspective. *Journal of Sustainable Tourism*, *29*(11/12), 1–16. http://dx.doi.org/10.1080/09669582.2020.1843045

Orr, M. (2020). On the potential impacts of climate change on baseball and cross-country skiing. *Managing Sport and Leisure*, *25*(4), 307–320. http://dx.doi.org/10.1080/23750472.2020.1723436

Orr, M., & Inoue, Y. (2019). Sport versus climate: Introducing the climate vulnerability of sport organizations framework. *Sport Management Review*, *22*(4), 452–463. https://doi.org/10.1016/j.smr.2018.09.007

Orr, M., Inoue, Y., Seymour, R., & Dingle, G. (2022). Impacts of climate change on organized sport: A scoping review. *WIREs Climate Change*, *13*(3), 1–25. https://doi.org/10.1002/wcc.760

Orr, M., McCullough, B. P., & Pelcher, J. (2020). Leveraging sport as a venue and vehicle for transformative sustainability learning. *International Journal of Sustainability in Higher Education*, *21*(6), 1071–1086.

Orr, M., Murfree, J., & Stargel, L. (2022). (Re)scheduling as a climate mitigation and adaptation strategy. *Managing Sport and Leisure*. https://doi.org/10.1080/23750472.2022.2159501

O'Toole, D., Brandt, L., Janowiak, M. K., Schmitt, K., Shannon, P., Leopold, P., Handler, S., Ontl, T., & Swanston, C. (2019). Climate change adaptation strategies and approaches for outdoor recreation. *Sustainability*, *11*, 7030. https://doi.org/10.3390/su11247030

Owen, G. (2020). What makes climate change adaptations effective? A systemic review of the literature. *Global Environmental Change*, *62*, 1–13. http://doi.org/10.1016/j.gloenvcha.2020.102071

Phillips, P., & Turner, P. (2014). Water management in sport. *Sport Management Review*, *17*(3), 376–389. https://doi.org/10.1016/j.smr.2013.08.002

Race Tech Magazine. (2020, September 21). Formula E claims first sport to have net zero carbon footprint. https://www.racetechmag.com/2020/09/formula-e-claims-first-sport-to-have-net-zero-carbon-footprint/

Robeers, T., & Van Den Bulck, H. (2018). Towards an understanding of side-lining environmental sustainability in Formula E: Traditional values and the emergence of esports. *Athens Journal of Sports*, *5*(4), 331–335-. http://doi.org/10.30958/ajspo.5-4-7

Roe, R., Hrymak, V., & Dimanche, F. (2014). Assessing environmental sustainability in tourism and recreation areas: A risk-assessment-based model. *Journal of Sustainable Tourism*, *22*(2), 319–338. https://doi.org/10.1080/09669582.2013.815762

Ross, W., & Fisackerly, W. (2023, January). Do we need Esports ecology? Comparisons of environmental impacts between traditional and Esports. *Journal of Electronic Gaming and Esports*, *1*(1). https://doi.org/10.1123/jege.2022-0030

Ross, W. J., & Leopkey, B. (2017). The adoption and evolution of environmental practices in the Olympic Games. *Managing Sport and Leisure*, *22*(1), 1–18. https://doi.org/10.1080/23750472.2017.1326291

Ross, W., & Mercado, N. (2020). Barriers to managing environmental sustainability in sport and entertainment venues. *Sustainability*, *12*(24), Article 10477. https://doi.org/10.3390/su122410477

Ross, W., & Orr, M. (2022). Predicting climate impacts to the Olympic Games and FIFA Men's World Cups from 2022 to 2032. *Sport in Society*, *25*(4), 867–888. https://doi.org/10.1080/17430437.2021.1984426

Salahodjaev, R., Kongratbay, S., Rakhmanov, N., & Khabirov, D. (2022). Tourism renewable energy and CO2 emissions: Evidence from Europe and Central Asia. *Environment Development and Sustainability*, *24*, 13282–13293. https://link.springer.com/article/10.1007%2Fs10668-021-01993-x

Scott, D., & Gössling, S. (2021). Destination net-zero: What does the international energy agency roadmap mean for tourism? *Journal of Sustainable Tourism*, *30*(1), 14–31. https://doi.org/10.1080/09669582.2021.1962890

Scott, D., & Gössling, S. (2022). A review of research into tourism and climate change: Launching the annals of tourism research curated collection on tourism and climate change. *Annals of Tourism Research*, *95*, 103409. https://doi.org/10.1016/j.annals.2022.103409

Stevenson, N. (2020). The contribution of community events to social sustainability in local neighbourhoods. *Journal of Sustainable Tourism*, *29*(11/12), 1–16. https://doi.org/10.1080/09669582.2020.1808664

Sumanapala, D., & Wolf, I. (2019). Recreational Ecology: A review of research and gap analysis. *Environments*, *6*(7), 81. https://doi.org/10.3390/environments6070081

Szathámri, A., & Kocsis, K. (2020). Who cares about gladiators: An elite-sport-based concept of sustainable sport. *Sport in Society*. https://doi.org/10.1080/17430437.2020.1832470

Tölkes, C. (2018). Sustainability communication in tourism – A literature review. *Tourism Management Perspectives*, *27*, 10–21. https://doi.org/10.1016/j.tmp.2018.04.002

Tomino, A., Peric, M., & Wise, N. (2020). Assessing and considering the wider impacts of sport-tourism events: A research agenda review of sustainability and strategic planning elements. *Sustainability*, *12*, 4473. https://doi.org/10.3390/su12114473

Trendafilova, S., & McCullough, B. P. (2018). Environmental sustainability scholarship and the efforts of the sport sector: A rapid review of literature. *Cogent Social Sciences*, *4*(1), 1–15. https://doi.org/10.1080/23311886.2018.1467256

Trendafilova, S., McCullough, B., Pfahl, M., Nguyen, S. N., Casper, J., & Picariello, M. (2014). Environmental sustainability in sport: Current state and future trends. *Global Journal on Advances Pure and Applied Sciences*, *3*, 9–14.

United Nations Department of Economic and Social Affairs. (2022, February 2). *Addressing climate change through sport*. https://www.un.org/development/desa/dspd/2022/02/addressing-climate-change-through-sport/

United Nations Environment Programme (UNEP). (2003). A manual for water and waste management: What the tourism industry can do to improve its performance. https://wedocs.unep.org/bitstream/handle/20.500.11822/9432/-A%20Manual%20for%20Water%20and%20Waste%20Management_%20What%20the%20Tourism%20Industry%20Can%20Do%20to%20Improve%20Its%20Performance-2003648.pdf?sequence=2&amp%3BisAllowed=

United Nations Environment Programme (UNEP). (2022). *UNEP by the numbers*. https://www.unep.org/annualreport/

United Nations Framework Convention on Climate Change (UNFCCC). (n.d.). *Sports for climate action targets and requirements*. https://unfccc.int/climate-action/sectoral-engagement/sports-for-climate-action

United Nations World Tourism Organization (UNWTO). (n.d.). *Global Tourism plastics initiative*. https://www.unwto.org/sustainable-development/global-tourism-plastics-initiative#:~:text=Global%20Tourism%20Plastics%20Initiative%20The%20Global%20Tourism%20Plastics,the%20shift%20towards%20a%20circular%20economy%20of%20plastics

United Nations World Tourism Organization (UNWTO). (n.d.). *Events: Transforming tourism for climate action*. https://www.unwto.org/sustainable-development/events-oneplanet-stp

Wall-Tweedie, J., & Nguyen, S. (2018). Is the grass greener on the other side? A review of the Asia-Pacific sport industry environmental sustainability practices. *Journal of Business Ethics*, *152*(3), 741–7761. https://doi.org/10.1007/s10551-016-3320-6

Watanabe, N. M., Yan, G., Soebbing, B. P., & Fu, W. (2019). Air pollution and attendance in the Chinese Super League: Environmental economics and the demand for sport. *Journal of Sport Management*, *33*(4), 1–14. https://doi.org/10.1123/jsm.2018-0214

Watkin, G., Mallen, C., & Hyatt, C. (2021). Management perspectives: Implications of plastics free sport facilities' beverage service. *Journal of Management and Sustainability*, *11*(1), 1–14. http://dx.doi.org/10.5539/jms.v11n1p1

Watkins, J., & Cooperride, D. (2000). Appreciative inquiry: A transformative paradigm. *Journal of Organization Development Network*, *32*, 6–12.

Wee, H., Mahdzar, M., Hamid, Z., Shariff, F., Chang, F., Noor, W., & Ismail, H. (2017). Sustainable event tourism: Evidence of practices and outcomes among festival organizers. *Advanced Scientific Letters*, *23*(8), 7719–7722.

Wicker, P. (2018). The carbon footprint of active sport tourists: An empirical analysis of skiers and boarders. *Journal of Sport & Tourism*, *22*(2), 151–171. https://doi.org/10.1080/14775085.2017.1313706

Wicker, P. (2019). The carbon footprint of active sport participants. *Sport Management Review*, *22*(4), 513–526. https://doi.org/10.1016/j.smr.2018.07.001

World Athletics (W.A.). (2022). IAAF air quality project presented at United Nations Environment Assembly. https://worldathletics.org/news/press-release/air-quality-unea-unep

World Leisure. (n.d.). *Who we are.* https://www.worldleisure.org/about-us/

World Rugby (WR). (2022). *World Rugby and the environment: Environmental sustainability plan 2030.* https://www.world.rugby/organisation/sustainability/environment

Zahn, J., Chevali, V., Wang, H., & Wang, C.-H. (2020). Current status of carbon fibre and carbon fibre composites recycling. *Composites Part B: Engineering, 193,* 108053. https://doi.org/10.1016/j.compositesb.2020.108053

Zhang, C., Zhou, X., Zhou, B., & Zhao, Z. (2022, June). Impacts of a mega sporting event on local carbon emissions: A case of the 2014 Nanjing Youth Olympics. *China Economic Review, 73,* 101782. https://doi.org/10.1016/j.chieco.2022.101782

Event bidding
Cheryl Mallen

The process of bidding to procure a sport, recreation, or tourism event is presented in this chapter. Specifically, five key elements within the bid process are defined: a feasibility study, a candidature document, a bid questionnaire, a bid dossier/submission, and a bid tour. There is also a discussion on the critical factors outlined in the research literature concerning successful bidding. The chapter then presents and discusses the proposition that there is one key factor that is vital to successful event bidding.

What is a feasibility study?

The first key document in a bid process is the feasibility study. This document includes an assessment and opinion on the capability of a group to stage or host the particular event. An ability to host involves a determination as to the availability of the necessary resources required to host the event, as well as other elements that have been considered and used to determine if it is feasible to host the event. These elements can include, for example:

- event goals
- objectives
- intentions
- activities
- the event history
- the cultural context (such as the population growth in the area, the consumer power, and economic development)

DOI: 10.4324/9781003391098-10

- facility and equipment availability (such as parking, seating, accessibility, and spatial requirements, including space and the capability for simultaneous activity use)
- resource availability (including competent and experienced human resources)
- venue service access (such as scheduling, ticketing, media, crowd management and security services, the union regulations, zoning regulations for noise, along with health and fire codes)
- technical resources
- financial resource availability

Overall, a feasibility study outlines the assessment of the direction and availability of resources to meet the needs for hosting an event along with a determination as to whether pursuing the event bid is a practical and reasonable initiative. This means that a feasibility study outlines the plausibility of meeting the bid requirements with the resources available.

What is a candidature document?

The second key document in a bid process is the candidature document. This document is provided by the organization that is accepting the event bids. The candidature document outlines the critical path of deadlines and processes that must be followed for a bid submission to be eligible for consideration. Each deadline must be adhered to by each bid group in order to complete the bid process.

What is a bid questionnaire?

The third key document in the bid process is a bid questionnaire. This questionnaire is often contained within the candidature document and outlines the list of questions that must be answered in the bid submission. The bid questionnaire provides the format and frames the context for a bid dossier and must be followed precisely. This framework allows for easy comparisons with other bids being considered by the governing body or organization that is awarding the rights to host the event (Figure 10.1).

Theme	Sample bid questionnaire topic areas to be answered in a bid dossier
Theme 1: Olympic Games concept and legacy	The event vision, impact, legacy, motivation, and plans for sustainable development
Theme 2: Political and economic climate and structure	Guarantees provided, government structure, stability, per capita income, inflation rate, referendum results, and opinions concerning support
Theme 3: Legal aspects	Stipulation of authority, event exclusivity, trademark protection, and official languages
Theme 4: Customs and immigration formalities	Visa regulations, guarantee of entrance for those with Games accreditation, health and vaccination requirements, restrictions on media broadcasts, regulations on imported print media, guide dogs, and equipment
Theme 5: Environment and meteorology	Construction agreements and guarantees, protocols to protect the environment, geographical features, environmentally and culturally protected areas, collaborate efforts, plans and systems to manage the environment, the environmental impact, temperatures, humidity, precipitation, and wind directions and strength
Theme 6: Finance	Budget template outlining the financial details, including capital investment, cash flow, sponsorship and contributions, ticket sales, licensing, lotteries, disposal of assets, subsidies, and other hosting costs
Theme 7: Marketing	Guarantees of a marketing program, domestic sponsorship, ticketing, advertising, and advertising controls
Theme 8: Sports and venues	Venue descriptions, competition schedules, technical manuals for meeting competition standards, venue responsibilities and the tendering process and agreements, reporting, monitoring and management plans, workforce, and sport experience
Theme 9: Paralympic Games	Plans for financial, security, accommodations, transportation, sport venues, opening and closing ceremonies, finances, and accessibility and so on for hosting the Paralympic Games
Theme 10: Olympic village	Concept, location, venue design and construction, financing, including guarantees for construction, types of accommodation, distance from competition venues, control of commercial rights, accessibility, and post event use

Figure 10.1 Themes and topic areas requiring answers in the International Olympic Committee bid questionnaire

Theme 11: Medical services and doping control	Plans for meeting the world anti-doping code and the IOC anti-doping rules, guarantees of investment in anti-doping, medical service facilities, public health authorities, epidemiological issues in the region, and systems for managing Games medical expenses, including serving visiting foreign nationals
Theme 12: Security	Safety and peaceful hosting guarantees, international, national, regional and local government security involvement, analysis of risks concerning fire, crime, traffic, terrorism and so on, security organizations and intelligence services to be involved, and financial planning for security
Theme 13: Accommodation	Hotel room capacity, guarantees on room availability and room rate and other pricing control, construction guarantees, work timelines and finances, binding contracts, and accommodation tables with maps outlining sites and distances
Theme 14: Transportation	Traffic management guarantees, including public and private transport, control centres, distances, airport capability, parking and additional transport infrastructure, training and testing, timelines, and authorities
Theme 15: Technology	Guarantees of competent bodies offering communication services, systems and broadcast capabilities for print, radio, television and internet, and network support
Theme 16: Media operations	Provision of broadcast centres for print, radio, television, and internet outlets, construction, timelines, financing, media transport, and accommodation
Theme 17: Olympism and culture	Protocols, plans for ceremonies including opening, closing and awards ceremonies, provision of intent, location, seating capacity, financing, and facilities

Figure 10.1 (Continued)

What is a bid dossier?

The fourth key document in event bidding is a bid dossier or submission. This document follows the framework outlined in the bid questionnaire. The dossier outlines the overall plan, the particular strategies, supporting resources, and supplementary details of the bid. It will also contain testimonials of support, and all of these items serve to set the bid submission apart from the other bidding competitors. Each question listed within the bid questionnaire must be answered within the bid dossier, in precisely the order requested, and be numbered to directly correspond to the number assigned in the bid questionnaire.

Event bidding

One of the best examples of a candidature document and bid questionnaire is provided by the International Olympic Committee (IOC) and is available for viewing on its website (https://stillmed.olympic.org). One document to access from this site is the *2024 Candidature Procedure and Questionnaire* (IOC, 2015). This 137 page document outlines the candidature procedures for the 2024 Olympic Games, including the deadline dates, signatures required, the schedule of payments, guarantees required, the bid questionnaire, presentation layout, and requirements, along with an outline for the visit by the evaluation commission and the selection decision process.

There are multiple bid documents that can be used as resources in event bidding. A simple "Google" search can reveal the following, as well as others:		
Federation	Bid document	Web site
Fédératon Equestre Internationale	FEI Nations Cup™ Jumping Finals 2017 and 2018: Bid Application and Questionnaire	fie.org
International Triathlon Union	Multisport Festival Bid document 2017	triathlon.org
International Convention on Science and Medicine in Sport (ICSEMIS)	ICSEMIS 2016, Brazil, Candidate Procedure and Questionnaire	fims.org
International Floorball Federation (IFF)	IFF Event Organizer Bidding Questionnaire completed by the Singapore Floorball Association and/or by the Danish Floorball Federation	floorball.org
FISE World Series	Bid Documents for FISE World Series, BMS, Skateboard, Roller, Mountain Bike Slopestyle and Wakeboard (amateur and professional)	bidfise.com
European Commission	European Capitals of Culture 2020–2033, Guide for Cities Preparing to Bid	ec.europa.eu
International Olympic Committee (IOC)	IOC's Candidature Procedure and Questionnaire: Olympic Games 2024	olympic.org
Special Olympics	Bid Form to Organize and Conduct European or Invitational Single-Sport Competitions	media.specialolympics.org
Commonwealth Games Federation (CGF)	2022 Commonwealth Games Candidature: Report of the CGF Evaluation Commission, July 2015	thecgf.com

Figure 10.2 Resources – Online bid documents

To advance your common knowledge on the process of bidding, it is suggested that you select at least three events that are of interest to you and review their event candidature documents and bid questionnaires. Many of these documents can be located on the internet (Figure 10.2).

Specific examples include:

- the European Football Championship Final Tournament bid documents, which can be found at www.uefa.com. You will find bid documents on this site, including the bid regulations and reports on bid dossiers submitted for hosting events
- information on how to bid for the Universiades organized by the Fédération Internationale du Sport Universitaire (FISU), or the International University Sports Federation, can be found at www.fisu.net. Be sure to review the critical path of deadlines required for bids, as they begin years prior to the event.

Another website you may want to visit to find bid documents is: www.gamesbids.com.

You may also want to approach festivals, conferences, and conventions in your area to obtain their bid documents.

What is a bid tour?

A bid tour involves hosting the members of a bid evaluation commission that will make the selection of the winning bid. The opportunity to stage a bid tour generally means that the bid submission has been placed on the shortlist of potential groups that are eligible to host the event. The tour offers an opportunity to present the information outlined in the bid dossier, to tour and highlight the planned ceremonies and facilities, to demonstrate local community and business support for the bid, and to promote the reasons why your bid should win the competition to host the event.

A bid tour involves arranging for the needs of the bid evaluation commission members from the moment of their arrival until their departure. To meet this requirement, an event manager facilitates the adaptation of the event planning model phases to generate operational plans specifically for a bid tour.

To begin, the development phase of the planning model is instituted. This involves the facilitation of elements such as the organizational structure for governance of the tour, the policies and volunteer practices along with the determination of how corporate social responsibility can be incorporated within the tour. Next, the event operational planning phase involves the facilitation of the written logical, sequential, and detailed operational plans for the bid tour, including the arrangements for components such as transportation, accommodation, entertainment, tours of the facilities, and a presentation of the bid to the commission members. Contingency plans and a plan refining process should always be considered within the operational plans. Further, a bid tour involves the implementation, monitoring, and management phase, as the bid tour moves from the conceptual stage to reality. Finally, the evaluation phase must take into account the priorities of the bid commission members, as they will ultimately make the decision on the winning bid.

To understand the evaluation criteria used by bid evaluation committee members, a review of the literature has identified several factors that appear to be critical in winning the bid process. These critical factors are outlined below.

What are the critical factors in a successful bid?

The historical literature outlines several factors for successful event bidding; however, different studies describe an assortment of elements that lead you in many directions. We will review the key factors for success offered by researchers such as Emery (2002), Westerbeek et al. (2002), Persson (2000), and Hautbois et al. (2012). This text then puts forward the proposition that the natural environment is another key factor in bidding and that there is one further element that is vital to successful bidding.

To begin, Emery (2002, p. 323) suggested five essential factors for event bid success:

1. Relevant professional credibility;
2. Fully understanding the brief and the formal/informal decision-making process;
3. Not assuming that decision makers are experts, or that they use rational criteria for selection;

4. Customizing professional (in)tangible products and services and exceeding expectations;
5. Knowing your strengths and weaknesses relative to the competition.

Emery (2002) suggested that "credibility and capacity to deliver are fundamental to any application, but not normally the discriminating factor between success and failure" (p. 323). Emery emphasized the point that bid success was "dependent upon in-depth knowledge of networks, processes and people – in other words external political support at the very highest levels of government and the commercial sector" (p. 329). Therefore, the organizing team itself is an element that could make a difference in the pursuit of a winning bid. Emery suggested that an organizing team should be made up of members who have considerable experience with successful events.

Emery (2002) also stated that "the information process and protocol must never be underestimated" (p. 329). Some of the bid organizing team must have experience in the political aspects of bidding, as this area is an important element in the bid process. According to Emery, this means that a bid needs to be politically positioned for success. In addition, Emery suggested that an assumption concerning the use of rational and consistent criteria to select the winning bid may not be correct. An interpretation of this view is that the key factors for winning a bid may actually change depending on the members in a bid commission who are evaluating a submission. Each member's personal perspective on the priorities for the bid must be ascertained and then taken into account. Consequently, trying to anticipate the receptivity of a bid commission with several different members is a complex task that is underscored with uncertainty, but it is a necessary part of a successful bid process.

Another researcher, Persson (2000), suggested that a success factor for an Olympic Games bid involved "the fit between the bidder's and the IOC members' perceptions of the bid offers" (p. 27). This implies that the bid committee members must anticipate what the IOC will perceive as important in a bid. The IOC bid commission has several members, and the priorities of a bid are, therefore, subject to personal bias or agenda. Thus, both Persson and Emery assert that a key component to achieving success in a bid is gaining understandings of the priorities of the bid commission members and meeting those priorities through political positioning of the bid.

Persson (2000) further offered the suggestion that infrastructure was important to the success of a bid. Infrastructure, according to Persson, involves the capacity for the provision of appropriate accommodation, transportation, venues, finances, telecommunications, and technology, as well as a top-notch media centre.

Ingerson and Westerbeek (2000) found that experience in event hosting was a key element for success along with the scope of knowledge of the members on the bid team. This was based on the contention that the more experience a member has, the greater the opportunity they have previously had to develop relationships that may drive the success of the current bid and ultimately the event itself. As Westerbeek et al. (2002) have stated, "The ability to organize an event is evidenced by having a solid track record in organizing similar events" (p. 318). Thus, the theme arising from the literature continues to be that experience in hosting previous events is a key factor for future success in bidding.

Westerbeek et al. (2002) promoted stability as a key factor for bid success. Stability was defined as involving politics, but from a different perspective than being politically positioned for advantage with the bid commission. The political reference in this instance meant the stability of the country and the municipal politics of the city, along with the stability of the financial support for an event.

Meanwhile, Westerbeek et al. (2002) outlined eight factors that were important in the process of bidding. Although this research emphasized sport event bidding, these factors are also very applicable to recreation and tourism events. The eight factors outlined by Westerbeek et al. (2002) comprise:

1. *Ability to organize events.* This element involves multiple items such as the intra-organizational network established to manage an event, the technical expertise within the network, the equipment, and the overall financial support for the bid
2. *Political support.* This element involves support from the government for the event bid. This support is used to assist in gaining access to financial and human resources, as well as access to facilities
3. *Infrastructure.* This element involves providing convincing proof of the availability of excellent facilities and an ability to meet event component requirements to deliver the transportation, accommodation and so on to produce an event
4. *Existing facilities.* This element involves the current status of the major event facilities at the time of the bid submission
5. *Communication and exposure.* This element involves the host city's reputation as a destination and the available support system to handle the

technological communication system requirements for hosting and promoting the event
6. *Accountability.* This element involves proof of the event's reputation, presence and support in the event market, previous success in hosting events and excellent venues
7. *Bid team composition.* This element involves the talent mixture of the members involved in the development of the bid as important for increasing the favourable perception of the bid evaluators. The bid team members should be able to provide a high profile, build relationships, have the skill to manage the complexity of a bid and provide credibility concerning their expertise to host
8. *Relationship marketing.* This element involves the ability to gain access to the members of a bid evaluation team and to influence these members to promote a bid through the development of "friendship"

These eight factors for success in bidding outlined by Westerbeek et al. (2002) were listed in order of priority. This suggested that the most important factors in bidding was proof of one's ability to organize the network of personnel and the finances for an event.

Management effectiveness as indicated by Kerzner (1995) was dependent upon an ability to balance a number of items such as time constraints, cost and performance with the pressures of the environment, including political pressures. While Kerzner discussed project management, the link between the fields of project management and event management is apparent and represents one of the focal points in this text.

Hautbois et al. (2012) found that the bid environment was very complex. They suggested that it was both the involvement of public officials and athletes that made the difference for a winning bid. This research offered a conclusion that from "a political, symbolic and strategic point of view, [it is the] public officials ... [that] were central in the network of stakeholders" (p. 11). Yet it was deemed important to ensure that all groups or stakeholders involved were engaged in the bid process "as opposed to one single actor (i.e. mayor)" (p. 11). The participants were noted as being instrumental in ensuring that an event was designed for their needs.

A relatively new element gaining prominence in the literature and promoted in this text as an important factor in event bid success, is environmental sustainability. Over the last 10 years, environmentalism has moved onto the agenda. The authoritative United Nations Environmental Programme

(UNEP) Intergovernmental Panel on Climate Change (IPCC, 2007) has pulled together the world's leading researchers to study the issue that the world's natural resources – including forests, fisheries, water, soil and air – are at risk; this has created a social and environmental challenge. It has been noted that there is a need to shift to sustainable practices (Gadenne et al., 2009; Mitchell & Saren, 2008). This shift to sustainability has been used as one key factor in bid success. For example, the Fédération Internationale de Football Association (FIFA) released a legacy report on the environmental practices from the Germany World Cup (FIFA, 2006). This report illustrated the efforts made by event organizers to promote sustainable environmental practices. The International Federation of Motorcycling (IFM, 2006) produced a code for protecting the environment to be followed when producing events that is now instituted for all races. In addition, in 1999, the International Olympic Committee (IOC) established Agenda 21, a document designed to bring its members into a program that supports the environment (IOC, 2014). This Agenda was promoted on the IOC website as "putting sport at the service of humanity" (IOC, 2014, p. 1). In 2006, the IOC released an athlete code of conduct which stated that athletes were environmental role models (IOC, 2006). The IOC code of conduct presented six key principles: avoid wasting water; avoid wasting energy; travel as efficiently as possible; consume responsibly; dispose of waste properly; and support environmental conservation and education. The IOC expects event organizers and athletes to protect and promote the sustainability of the environment. Further, as major events can be a driver for tourism, the IOC code of conduct for environmental sustainability can also be extended to tourists and this element can also be outlined in bids.

There are, however, issues concerning bids that have included safeguarding the natural environment in the initial bid phase of an event. These bids have positioned the natural environment as a priority in the up-front bid phase, but it has then moved to a non-priority in the hosting phase. This means that the bid plans have not always translated into reality during the implementation, monitoring, and management phase of an event. Does this constitute lying in the bid process? Generally, no punishments have been enacted for events which have found themselves in this position. Negative media publicity that can ensue, however, is a type of punishment. Where do you stand on this issue? How would you resolve this issue during bidding and event implementation?

For decades now, the research literature has suggested that there are a number of critical factors for bid evaluation success. The suggestions are multi-directional, which increases the complexity of the bid and the uncertainty of bidding success. The complexity stems from the need for multiple groups that must come together to create a cohesive event bid.

Multiple areas of emphasis contained within a bid have created a complexity that could strain the cohesiveness of any given committee and thereby compromise the potential for success. In addition, there is political complexity. This means that while the guiding documents outline the bid requirements, intangibles such as underlying political requirements are not explicitly stated in a bid questionnaire. These intangibles need to be anticipated as they may be important in the final decision-making. This means that uncertainty is inherent in the bidding process. In the end, only one group is awarded the prize in a bid competition. Unfortunately, the rest have to bear the cost of competing in the process without receiving a reward.

To assist in working through the complexity and uncertainty of the bid process, the question is posed: Is there one critical factor that can be used to enhance the opportunity for a successful bid? The author of this chapter promotes the view that there is *one* critical factor in event bidding.

What is one critical factor for bid success?

This author presents the proposition that *communication* has been underplayed in the literature and should be positioned as *the one critical factor* in event bidding. Greenberg (2002) defined communication as "the process through which people send information to others and receive information from them" (p. 217). An application of this definition means that a bidding process "constitutes a communication process between the actors involved" (Persson, 2000, p. 139). Thus, event bidding is conducted within a social context and this vital communication element is the key factor in the process of winning an event bid.

Communication in event bidding is discussed in the literature, although the support is not emphatic that communication is the single key factor in successful bidding. The literature does indicate that "Event bidding is about communication to a degree, initially you have got to have communication, and you've got to be a really, really sharp communicator" (Hörte & Persson, 2000, p. 67). Westerbeek et al. (2002) included communication as one of the eight key factors in bidding; however, they indicated it was in a group of elements that were "more likely to be supporting rather than vital factors" (p.

317). Westerbeek et al. positioned communication as important in event bidding; however, they discussed communication from the perspective of providing contemporary technology for use in facilitating communication during the event. Also, communication underscores what Byun et al. (2020) discussed as the valuable development of bidding inter-organizational relationships that leads to what Bason and Grix (2023) indicated was coalition building.

This author, however, positions communication as the one key factor in successful bidding because the event context is teeming with opportunities to advance the success of a bid with the use of written, verbal, and visual communication. An ability to communicate underlies every task in the bid process and it can therefore be a deciding factor in the success of a bid dossier, a bid tour, and all other components in the bid process.

Communication is critical in a bid dossier. A dossier must clearly and succinctly express the intention to host and provide answers to a bid questionnaire. This document communicates the proposed plan for hosting an event. The level of planning detail communicated in the document can hinder or enhance the success of the articulated plans and can influence the interpretations concerning bid activities made by the bid commission members in their assessment. Depending on the event, a bid dossier may also require written communication in more than one language. An ability to clearly express the bid details and the subtle nuances of the bid in multiple languages is an opportunity to position the bid for success.

Communication is a critical factor in conducting a bid tour. A written operational plan for a bid tour outlines the activities to be conducted. In addition, verbal communication is used to help the network members implementing the bid tour plans clearly understand the tasks. It is important to have all members on the bid committee promoting the same message(s) concerning the bid. Poor communication, or a lack of communication coordination within the bid tour, can impact the success of a bid tour, illustrating that communication is a critical factor.

Formal and informal verbal communication is a critical factor in a successful bid. Examples of formal verbal communication opportunities include structured meetings with the bid commission members to present the highlights of the bid; meetings with key stakeholders such as the sponsors or venue managers; and meetings used to build relationships with the grassroots supporters such as volunteers, small businesses, and organizations. Examples of informal verbal communication include casual conversations with the bid commission members evaluating the bid or with the grassroots supporters of a bid. Each formal and informal communication opportunity can facilitate the transfer of knowledge concerning the bid or bid tour to all members in the bid network and to the bid commission members. Poor formal and informal communication can, from this viewpoint, profoundly impact the success of an event bid undertaking.

Visual communication is also a critical factor in bid success. The inclusion of visual elements in presentations, such as the use of diagrams in the bid dossier, video presentations or a fireworks display in the bid tour, can enhance either the understandings of the bid detail or the enthusiasm for a bid. Visually communicating the bidder's message can have a significant impact on the success of a bid.

Communications technology is also a critical factor in bid success. The use of the latest technology which allows for excellent verbal, written, and visual communication can clearly demonstrate the host's ability to maximize the use of technology in the conduct of the event.

Communication is also an underlying critical factor in the majority of bid activities that go beyond the topics covered in this text. For example, the financial component of a bid relies on an ability to communicate facts and figures that will attest to the host's financial capacity to successfully host the event with no negative long-term impact on the community following the event. Marketing and sponsorship in event bidding rely heavily on the ability to convey enticingly the opportunity of being a partner in the event, as well as the marketing and sponsorship opportunities that might be secured. Written, verbal, and visual communications along with the communications technology are all critical factors in the success of marketing and sponsorship proposals.

The bid process involves communicating to groups such as the network members, the potential sponsors, and the bid commission members. Communication is the critical factor in event bidding and must be facilitated in a manner that enhances the overall bid effort. Your facilitation skills will be tested throughout the bid process. A focus on enhancing communication at all levels when facilitating an event bid is a critical factor for success.

Conclusions

This chapter focused on bidding for a major event. However, the principles of a proposal to your local recreation committee for a niche event are essentially the same. In order to get permission to host your event you will have to provide, to a lesser degree, all of the same elements. The availability of facilities, your expertise, support from others, etc., and your ability to communicate is critical to success in small as in large events.

This chapter defined a feasibility study, candidature document, bid questionnaire, bid dossier, and bid tour. The viewing of candidature documents, bid submissions, and bid questionnaires was encouraged to develop your common knowledge about the requirements of bidding. You can follow a variety of bids on the internet at www.gamesbids.com. The research literature discussion indicated that there is a complex array of critical factors for successful bids. It was also indicated that environmental sustainability is a new key factor in bidding – albeit not always one that is implemented. Importantly, this text proposes that communication is the most critical factor for success in event bidding. Overall, it is important for you to weigh the key factors to win a bid, to analyze the requirements, and then to apply the factors based on your own conclusions.

Chapter questions

1. Describe a feasibility study, a candidature document, a bid questionnaire, a bid dossier, and a bid tour.
2. List at least five key elements of successful bidding that were outlined in the literature.
3. Do you feel that concern for the natural environment should be part of the bid process? If so, how should the natural environment be safeguarded at events?
4. Do you agree with the author's assertion that communication is the one key factor in successful event bidding? If not, why? If yes, explain how you see communication being used in the process of facilitating an event bid.

References

Bason, T., & Grix, J. (2023). Every loser wins: Leveraging 'unsuccessful' Olympic bids for positive benefits. *European Sport Management Quarterly, 23*(1), 167–187. https://doi.org/10.1080/16184742.2020.1838590

Byun, J., Leopkey, B., & Ellis, D. (2020). Understanding joint bids for international large-scale sport events as strategic alliances. *Sport, Business and Management, 10*(1), 39–57. https://doi.org/10.1108/SBM-09-2018-0074

Emery, P. (2002). Bidding to host a major sports event: The local organizing committee perspective. *The International Journal of Public Sector Management, 15*(4), 316–335.

Fédération Internationale de Football Association (FIFA). (2006). *Green goal: Legacy report. The environmental concept for the 2006 FIFA World Cup.* Organizing Committee, 2006 FIFA World Cup. https://www.oeko.de/oekodoc/292/2006-011-en.pdf

Gadenne, D. L., Kennedy, J., & McKeiver, C. (2009). An empirical study of environmental awareness and practices in SMEs. *Journal of Business Ethics, 84*(1), 45–63. https://doi.org/10.1007/s10551-008-9672-9

Greenberg, J. (2002). *Managing behavior in organizations.* Prentice Hall.

Hautbois, C., Parent, M., & Séguin, B. (2012). How to win a bid for major sport events? A stakeholder analysis of the 2018 Olympic Winter games French bid. *Sport Management Review, 15*(3), 263–275. https://doi.org/10.1016/j.smr.2012.01.002

Hörte, S. Å., & Persson, C. (2000). How Salt Lake City and its rival bidders campaigned for the 2002 Olympic Winter Games. *Event Management, 6*(2), 65–83.

International Federation of Motorcycling (IFM). (2006). *Environmental code.* IFM.

Ingerson, L., & Westerbeek, H. (2000). Determining key success criteria for attracting hallmark sporting events. *Pacific Tourism Review, 3*(4), 239–253.

Intergovernmental Panel on Climate Change (IPCC). (2007). *Global environment outlook 4: Summary for decision makers.* https://www.unep.org/resources/report/global-environment-outlook-4-summary-decision-makers-0

International Olympic Committee (IOC). (2006). *IOC guide on sport, environment and sustainable development.* IOC. https://library.olympics.com/Default/doc/SYRACUSE/40054/ioc-guide-on-sport-environment-and-sustainable-development-publ-by-the-international-olympic-committ?_lg=en-GB

International Olympic Committee (IOC). (2014). *Factsheet: The environmental and sustainable development – Update January 2014.* IOC. https://stillmed.olympic.org/Documents/Reference_documents_Factsheets/Environment_and_substainable_developement.pdf

International Olympic Committee (IOC). (2015, September 16). *Candidature questionnaire Olympic Games 2024.* https://stillmed.olympic.org/Documents/Host_city_elections/Candidature_Questionnaire_Olympic_Games_2024.pdf

Kerzner, H. (1995). *Project management: A systems approach to planning, scheduling, and controlling* (5th ed.). Van Nostrand Reinhold.

Mitchell, I. K., & Saren, M. (2008). The living product: Using the creative nature of metaphors for sustainable marketing. *Business Strategy and the Environment, 17*(6), 398–410.

Persson, C. (2000). The International Olympic Committee and site decisions: The case of the 2002 Winter Olympics. *Event Management, 6*(3), 135–153.

Westerbeek, H., Turner, P., & Ingerson, L. (2002). Key success factors in bidding for hallmark sporting events. *International Marketing Review, 19*(3), 303–322. http://dx.doi.org/10.1108/02651330210430712

11 Politics in event bidding and hosting

Trish Chant-Sehl

This chapter focuses on the underlying political aspects of event bidding and hosting. Managing and mitigating the political aspects within events is a key skill for an event manager. It would be ideal to tell you how to manage each type of political situation. Due to the complexity of places, people, and scenarios, however, this is not possible. To become a skilled political manager of events, you must develop knowledge and experience concerning where to expect political manoeuvres, how they could come into play, and then how to devise personalized management strategies based on personal knowledge and experience. To develop the foundational knowledge necessary for this skill, this chapter defines "politics." Further, a discussion applies this definition to bidding and event hosting experiences, explains the role that politics plays through the event continuum in three distinct phases including bidding, transition, review, and event hosting, examines scenarios, and offers some insightful ways in which the political effect can be mitigated. A case study in event bidding is included to guide the reader toward the development of personal insights concerning politics. Finally, a series of questions are posted to encourage the reader to contemplate how they might choose to navigate the complex world of politics in event bidding and hosting.

What is meant by the "politics of events?"

One does not have to look far to discover numerous definitions for "politics." Many definitions include a connection to government and/or government policy. The Merriam-Webster dictionary (n.d.) defined politics as "3a:

political affairs or business; especially competition between competing interest groups or individuals for power and leadership"; and "5a: the total complex of relations between people living in society" (n.p.). Further, it has been stated that:

> Politics has existed as long as humans have faced scarcity, have had different beliefs and preferences, and have had to resolve these differences while allocating scarce resources. It will continue to exist so long as these human conditions persist – that is, forever. Politics are fundamental to the human condition ... Politics exists wherever people interact with one another to make decisions that affect them collectively.
>
> (OpenStax, 2022, n.p.)

In addition, McGillivray, and Turner (2018) stated that "major event bids are deeply politicized activities, clearly motivated by a desire to pursue a range of agendas" (p. 32).

These perspectives on politics guide the discussion within this chapter. Therefore, "politics" is understood as encompassing both the competing relationships and interests between individuals and groups, as well as the political environment, as it relates to the event organization and/or government's interest.

Although this chapter will focus primarily on politics in bidding for major international sport events, it is important to not overlook that a majority of recreational and tourism events are local or regional in scope. For example, each year there are numerous local championships in a variety of different sports, as well as regional and invitational events, along with tourism events held around the world. Despite the generally smaller scale of more community-based events, politics will still be involved. Within large-scale and in small-scale events, there are relationships and power dynamics within municipal governments and local sport communities that cannot be overlooked. Often the politics of local bidding is more evident as the players involved are known to each other and the community at large, and they will need to continue to coexist in the local sport ecosystem in the future. Ultimately, the bidding process for smaller local and regional events is similar to bidding for major events insofar as it is complex, nuanced, and requires a level of political sophistication.

Politics in the decision to bid or not to bid

The world of event bidding is fraught with political agendas from the very beginning of the process. This is not surprising given that bids are human initiatives. It is almost impossible to discern a time throughout the bid process when politics are not involved. From the moment that the idea to bid for a specific event is conceived, politics play a role. The impetus for many bids is often to achieve political agendas. For example, South Africa's desire to host the 2006 FIFA World Cup (unsuccessfully but then successfully hosted in 2010) was:

> ... not just for benefits of capital accumulation or the development of civic social capital, but also to actively engage in an outward facing process of nation-building. For a post-Apartheid South Africa, the FIFA World Cup represented an opportunity to reposition itself on the world stage and announce its return to the league of acceptable nations once more following decades as a pariah state due to its apartheid policy"
> (McGillivray & Turner, 2018, pp. 17–18).

As the world of international event bidding becomes more sophisticated, and costly, it is incumbent upon interested bidders to spend time and energy on assessing the "win-ability" (the likelihood of their bid being successful) of a bid prior to formally launching a bid for a specific event. There are a number of items to consider when assessing a bid's win-ability, many of which are political in nature. For example:

> Is there a competitor who is already being seen as the likely next host?
> Has your area or region recently hosted the same event, or an event of similar size and scale?
> Do you have the full support of the necessary levels of government or organizational bodies?
> Is there a regional rotation at play for the event?
> Have other interested cities previously bid for the same event and feel that it is their turn to host?
> Is there an influential champion for your bid, and more importantly, for a competitor's bid?
> Who can influence the decision-making process?

These questions are important to ask and answer before making a final determination on whether to proceed with launching a formal bid. It is worth noting, however, that despite doing the due diligence on win-ability, the outcome of a bid process is never certain, and political influences play a part in this uncertainty.

If the bidders' assessment of the win-ability of their initiative is favourable, then it is time to proceed with completing the necessary bid requirements, as well as preparing for the inevitable politics that will now arise. It is imperative that the bidders accept the role that politics play throughout the entire process and enter the bid environment knowing that they must understand, navigate, and mitigate the political aspects of bidding and hosting events. Consider strategies you could complete to improve your knowledge and ability to manage politics in event management. This is an unending exercise that can impact your future success.

Also keep in mind that, interestingly, unsuccessful bids have generated worthwhile benefits, such as providing advantages for politicians (Chalip & Fairley, 2020) and helping a political generation of coalitions support national interests (Bason & Grix, 2020). Further, some cities have found tourism advantages from an unsuccessful bid – and yet this has not been the case for all bid groups (Sant et al., 2020). The ability to use a bid for political gains offers a paradox and it has been stated, thus, that "politicians generally favor hosting mega sport events despite the discouraging evidence of financial benefits or direct economic gain" (de Nooij & van den Berg, 2017, n.p.). This paradox provides a reason to bid despite negative assessments concerning the potential bid results and legacy as, generally, "politicians [can] still manage to infer positive gains from hosting" (de Nooij & van den Berg, 2017, n.p.).

Politics in the event bid phase – the committee

Before delving further into the politics involved within the bidding process, it is important to identify the governance structure for an event, from the international, national and the small-scale local events. Large scale events have formalized bid formats; however, smaller scale events can have many governance structural options that range from no formal bid protocols to well established processes that mirror some international bid processes. For example, for some national events, there may be a regional rotation through which it is known each year which region will host, but not which specific community or city. At the local and regional level, there may not be a formal bid process but rather expressions of interest by different leagues or communities. In these situations, the decision may be made by a staff representative, a committee or perhaps a Board of Directors.

In this chapter we are assuming that a national governing authority has endorsed a competitive bid process for their respective international event. Perhaps the easiest place to start when discussing the role of politics in this scenario is with the bid committee itself.

If you recall, the earlier definition of politics was "competition between competing interest groups or individuals" which situates politics within a bid committee. The determination of both who and what is represented on a bid committee is not an easy decision – and is open to political manoeuvring from those interested on serving on this committee. According to McGillivray and Turner (2018), "the formulation of bidding teams often occurs without significant public scrutiny" (p. 38).

Large events are seen as exciting to be a part of, as well as being thought of as potential "once in a lifetime opportunities." For these reasons, and many others, there are many people and organizations who want to be represented on a bid committee to serve and/or to ensure their opinions and interests are given due consideration. Often, the specific event program is not pre-determined and, thus, organizations see the bid phase as a significant opportunity to influence the inclusion of their focus within the program. Being represented on a bid committee is then considered an excellent means by which to achieve this objective. What criteria would you use to make committee member selections?

In Shaw's (2008) book entitled *Five Ring Circus: Myths and Realities of the Olympic Games*, he provides an excellent example of the politics involved in committee membership. The example Shaw focuses on is the Vancouver 2010 Bid Society membership. He identifies the influential role of the Chair, Jack Poole, who was a very successful and prominent real estate tycoon, who used his power and connections to garner support for the bid effort. In addition, Shaw (2008) notes that the Bid Society was comprised of a "who's who of developers, business interests and politicians" (p. 6).

This example indicates that bid committee membership has been rife with political scenarios over the decades. Overall, when establishing a bid committee, it is important to remember that the goal of bidding is to win the right to host the event. This may seem like a simple point, but it is one that is often overlooked when community and event leaders and/or government representatives try to influence the committee membership. Pulling together a bid is a major undertaking and one that is usually done within a tight timeframe. In short, there is a significant amount of work to be done. It is important that each bid committee member be able to deliver value to the bid process.

This value includes the criteria of being able to provide guidance and oversight, completing the work requirements, as well as securing support both financially and publicly. To mitigate some of the politics of membership on a bid committee, another criterion is to meet the necessary options for strategically placing individuals and groups to be engaged with the bid process without being named to the formal bid committee. The volume of work to be completed for a bid necessitates the development of sub-committees associated with a bid. Of key importance, however, is to weigh the placement of members that can complete the tasks and ensure the cooperation of sub-committees above the political appointments.

Politics in the event bid phase – the proposal

Despite the prescriptive nature of a national or international bid dossier, there are still many important decisions that a bid committee needs to make, and which are open to political manoeuvring. One particular item is selection of venues/facilities. International events are often seen as a way in which a community can benefit from new facilities, including sport, recreational, and tourism venues. The construction of new venues requires many questions to be answered. For instance:

> *Where should the new facility be built?*
> *Who should own and operate the facility?*
> *Who will pay for ongoing facility maintenance?*
> *Who will have access to the facility?*
> *What type of amenities should be included in the new facility?*
> *Can locating facilities in a specific area of the city help further a political or community interest?*

It is easy to see how politics can come into play when attempting to answer the questions posed here. A recent example to illustrate this point is the

2012 Olympic Games in London, England. It was noted that during the bid process that:

> the BOA [British Olympic Association] refused to give up... has already won the support of the Mayor of London, Ken Livingstone, provided the bid fulfilled his vision for transforming the desperately deprived East End and increased investment in the capital.
>
> (Lee, 2006, p. 7)

Further, a proposal for event facility construction can involve local workers as well as others from around the world, and the political issue of human rights can arise. McGillivray, Edwards, Brittain, Bocarro, and Koenigstorfer (2018) argue that this issue requires those involved in bidding to adhere "to internationally recognized standards, such as the Universal Declaration of Human Rights and the United Nations Guiding Principles on Business and Human Rights" (p. 175). Support for mitigating this political issue comes from Heerdt (2018) who promotes major sport events being contractually required to provide safeguards for human rights. An analysis by Heerdt, however, revealed that guidance and enforceability is still arising when this strategy has been used. In addition to human rights concerns, large sport events are increasingly focused on sustainability which contemplates "...the achievement of positive impacts on the people, planet, and profit, with a holistic contribution to meet the economic, socio-cultural, and environmental needs of all the involved stakeholders in the event, including the host community" (Cavagnaro & Postma, 2012, as cited in Meza Talavera et al., 2019, p. 2). Host nations may have differing standards, practices, and accountabilities when it comes to sustainability; however, governing bodies are moving to mandating sustainability practices within their processes (Meza Talavera et al., 2019). Different standards can be seen in the human rights positions of the United States, the home of the Professional Golf Association (PGA), with respect to their merger with Saudi-backed LIV Golf.

The bid committee is thus, open to political manoeuvring concerning social issues and not just concerned with the best construction of facilities for the staging of the event.

If facilities do not need to be constructed, the use of existing venues still poses some opportunities for political manoeuvring. For example, when existing facilities are used, decisions need to be made concerning elements, such as:

> *Which facilities will receive upgrades and/or renovations as part of their participation in the event?*
> *What level of service is the facility owner expected to provide for the event?*
> *Will the facility owner be compensated accordingly for the services?*
> *Who is responsible for accommodating displaced users during the event?*

These questions are important to consider during the bid phase to ensure that political issues are mitigated and that facility owners/operators have reasonable expectations of their participation within a bid, and ultimately as an event host and then legacy operator.

Facility decisions are not the only ones where politics come into play during the proposal phase. Decisions around delegate accommodations require careful consideration and political savvy. For instance:

> *Which hotel should be named as the "host hotel?"*
> *Who has priority access to the limited rooms available at the premier hotels?*
> *Who is negotiating a fair price point for event-time guests?*

In instances where an event has a cultural or festival component, there are many additional questions to answer, such as:

> *Which cultural communities will be involved in the event?*
> *Who will speak at the opening ceremonies and/or formal dinners?*
> *Where will cultural and festival sites be located?*

In large and international sport or tourism events that attract significant sponsorship dollars and television audiences, the politics involved are even more demanding. In this case, questions include:

> *Who can be an event sponsor?*
> *Which broadcast entity should be a partner?*
> *Is the bidding city in a lucrative or emerging market?*

Political manoeuvring in determining the answers to these questions requires careful attention. Also, when it comes to wider community support for a bid, social media has aided "in enabling resistant movements to form and articulate messages" (McGillivray et al., 2019, p. 69).

Politics in the event bid phase – the decision-makers

In event bidding, perhaps the most likely example of politics stems from the decision-making process, in which people are responsible for making final decisions concerning the event. The Salt Lake City scandal surrounding the selection process for the 2002 Winter Olympic Games shone light on the political games of corruption and bribery inherent in the IOC bid process at the time. Significant reform has taken place within the IOC, and the bidding process is now more structured and transparent; however, the final decision still rests with individual IOC members. That is to say, the human element cannot be overlooked when it comes to decision-making within a bid process. The Commonwealth Games Federation (CGF), Fédération Internationale de Football Association (FIFA) and the Pan American Sport Association (PASO) are three other examples of organizations that have their membership vote to determine a winning bid.

The IOC, as well as the CGF, FIFA and PASO, have documented bid guidelines and protocols that must be adhered to by all bid candidates. There are, however, many opportunities for politics to come into play with both the voting delegates and bid committee members. In some instances, the politicking will fall outside the scope of the rules and could be subject to disciplinary action by the governing body. In other scenarios, the politics at play are more subtle. A region or group of nations may plan to bid for the subsequent event and thus have a vested interest in where the current bid will be situated. Their votes may then have little to do with the quality of the bids, and more to do with geography and planning for their own future.

Another example of the politics within bidding is with the bid decision process itself – which is typically secretive in nature. Whether a bid is local or international in scope, if individuals are required to vote for one bid over another then politics will come into play. Enthusiastic and hard-working bid teams will do their best to develop and present an excellent bid package to the voting delegates. Each bid committee will do their best to convince the voters to choose their bid over their competitors. In the secret ballot voting scenario, there is no negative consequence for the voting delegate if they pledge their support to all candidates, as it is never known who votes for which bid. This makes the bidding environment vulnerable to politically motivated activities such as voting delegates asking for special favours, or bid committee representatives promising more than they can deliver.

In John Furlong's (2011) book *Patriot Hearts – Inside the Olympics that Changed a Country*, the former CEO of the 2010 Vancouver Olympic and Paralympic Winter Games shared personal stories of his time with the Vancouver Bid Team and the Host Organizing Committee. He supported the concept of potential politics in the voting strategy when he indicated his thoughts concerning his city's win for the rights to host. The fact that he mentioned this scenario means that it was a political point of potential importance. His statement was as follows:

> I was surprised at how close the final vote was. Three votes. We were behind after round one but grabbed all of Austria's 16 votes to sneak by the Koreans 56-53. Scary close. Only a couple of other decisions in IOC history had been closer than ours – both those determined by one vote. There would be a lot of talk about the role geopolitics played in our victory. How European countries wanted the 2012 Summer Games, so were not going to vote for a European city to win the 2010 Games
>
> (p. 75).

It does not need to be a large event for this type of politics to come into play. Small and medium sized events also manoeuvre through the politics of some of the decision-makers.

Politics in the event bid transition and review phase

Eventually, decision day will arrive, and one bid will be selected as the next host city for the event. After months and sometimes years of hard work, the bid process is complete. Now what? Depending on the outcome of the specific bid, the next steps are very different. Next steps for unsuccessful bids include financial reconciliation, closing the bid office, file storage and documentation, filing of any necessary legal paperwork, bid committee post-mortem, and writing a final report. Given the time, money, and resources put into bidding for events, it is not surprising to see politics at play even after a bid has been lost. There can be a tendency for blame and second-guessing of decisions that were made during the bid process. How would you manage these types of political situations? It is important that the bid team takes time to evaluate the bid process and document areas in need of improvement and general thoughts on why the bid was not successful. This type of analysis and documentation will be an asset for future bid committees. This falls within the transfer of knowledge concept and should be common practice for all bid processes – win or lose.

For those bid committees fortunate enough to win the bid competition and be named as the next host city, the next steps and the politicking can be daunting. Transitioning from a bid committee to a host organizing committee can be very stressful given that few people have had an opportunity to be involved in such a complex undertaking. For larger, international events, the bid committee is usually well structured with full time staff, office space, formalized policies and procedures, as well as financial and legal accountabilities. Small and medium size events, though, do not generally get away from having to deal with bid transition politics.

The bid committee is now no longer needed and a host organizing committee is required to take its place. While the bid committee is winding down, and the transition team is planning for the future host committee, there is an expectation that work continues with planning for the event. This is a key challenge as there is no shortage of politics at play concerning who is leading the process. Interested candidates may campaign strongly, and publicly, for their preferred position within the new host organizing committee structure. Individuals who may have been colleagues on the bid committee may now be adversaries in the competition for a specific position on the organizing committee. Leaders within key stakeholder groups, including governments, who have significant interests in the success of an event, may try to wield their influence over the decision-making process.

The composition of the new organizing committee is not the only forum where politics play a role in the transition and planning phase of an event. Perhaps one of the most politically charged tasks within any event planning process is the final determination of the venue plan. Although bid dossiers are required to include full details on all venues, once a bid is won, the host committee has an opportunity to revisit the original plans.

Despite best efforts at planning during the bid phase, there will inevitably be changes once a bid has been won. These changes happen for reasons, such as a change in government officials or priorities, revisited cost estimates, a change in the program, issues with land acquisition, or pressure from the public or other special interest groups.

Changes in government will happen and neither bid committees nor host committees can control this transition. The change could have a positive effect on the event in the form of available office space or personnel secondments. Or, it could have a negative effect, such as a demand to change the venue location. For example, a new ward councillor may not support a bid plan for the construction of a new building in their ward and may publicly campaign for a move to a different site within a city. This type of discussion opens the door for political jockeying as other ward councillors, landowners, neighbourhood associations, and businesses begin to lobby the organizing committee for their preferred site. Further, there are compounding effects on the event plans as delays in site selection can result in increased construction costs due to shortened timelines and a later than anticipated opening of the venue, resulting in less time for testing the venue and its systems for the event.

What additional political scenarios can you envision for the event transition phase for an event in which you may be involved?

Host organizing committees will be faced with significant change throughout the planning process, some of which will be political in nature. The key for any committee is how they choose to deal with the politics. This will be discussed again later in this chapter.

Politics in the event hosting phase

This chapter has discussed the politics evident throughout the bid phase and the transition phase of planning an event. Given the amount of time spent on these activities, it is not surprising that politics plays a more significant role in the lead up to hosting an event than during the actual event hosting period. Events can last for one day or longer. Tourism events can last up to thirty days or longer; regardless, the hosting timeframe is dramatically smaller than the time taken to bid and to plan. As a result, there are fewer opportunities for politics to come into play. The event production time period, however, is not exempt from political manoeuvring.

One area where politics often come into play is with the very important persons (VIPs) attending the event. These VIPs could be government officials, international sport delegates, sponsors, media, or other organizational representatives. Some events will have established protocols for VIP management, while others will not. Regardless, VIPs may have unrealistic expectations of the event organizers and can use their influence and strong connections to try to get what they want. The event management team needs to pay careful attention to how they handle this group of individuals. VIPs may engage in politics by trying to use their influence to obtain free tickets to the event, or merchandise, or to participate in ceremonies. Ensuring a sense of fairness for all VIPs is an important task for the event management team.

In addition to recognized VIP's, there may be individuals that believe they should be recognized as VIPs, and therefore should be entitled to special treatment. These types of requests may seem like minor headaches, however, how an organizer deals with them can have an impact on the success of an event, as their sharing of negative perceptions with the public and others can have significant impact. It is important for event organizers to anticipate these types of scenarios during the planning process, and to have planned messaging in place prior to being confronted with the reality.

Another example of how politics can come into play at events involves the ceremony performers. Organizations and advocates may use the performers as a vehicle to lobby for additional funding. For instance, if a performer gains a high level of success, government funders may use the publicity as a demonstration of their government's commitment and support of the program or a group may use it to promote their next bid and hosting initiative. Ceremonies also offer attractive platforms for political manoeuvring by special interest groups and cultural communities given the high visibility of these activities.

Overcoming politics in event bidding

This chapter has examined how politics plays a role in bidding and hosting of events. A range of examples have been provided within the three distinct phases – bidding, transition and planning, and event hosting. Understanding the role that politics can play in bidding and hosting is important and learning how to be successful is critical. It is naïve to believe that event bidding and hosting can occur without politics coming into play, given the working definition we have been using of politics as "the total complex of relations between people living in society" (Politics. n.d.).

It is proposed, then, that eliminating politics from the bidding and hosting process is impossible. Important, thus, is the skill necessary to effectively deal with the politics.

A key factor in managing event politics – consistent communication messaging

Consistent communication is the first tenet for successfully dealing with the politics involved in the bidding and hosting experience. One of the reasons why people and organizations engage in politics is because this type of activity can yield their desired result … even if it is not in the original bid or event plans. Often, this success is because of a lack of consistency within the messaging, or in understanding what the committee or organization is trying to achieve. This provides opportunities for political manoeuvring by outside groups or individuals who exploit the inconsistency in communication.

Bid committees and event hosts need to spend time developing their vision for the event, and the strategy by which they plan to fulfil the vision. They must spend time as a team ensuring that all members of their respective organizations understand what they are trying to achieve, and how they plan to get there. This requires consistent communication within the entire bid team, as well as the external stakeholders. Communication needs to not only be consistent over time, but also must be honest, open, transparent, and two-way to allow for feedback and questioning.

A key factor in managing event politics – establishing core values

The second tenet for successfully dealing with the politics of bidding and hosting is the establishment of core values. One of the first steps that a small or large event bid or host committee should undertake is to identify what their core values are and commit to having their values guide their decision-making and their actions. Examples of these values include promoting and encouraging diverse participation; a commitment to developing competencies, leadership, and personal development; contributing positively to the tourism, sport, and recreation industries; to develop and advance mutually beneficial partnerships; and to behave ethically and with integrity. It is often difficult, however, to abide by the values when it is close to bid decision day, and a political manoeuvre or the promise of a vote in return for a favour is presented.

Politics in event bidding and hosting

The leadership of an event bid must clearly articulate the importance of their organization's values and ensure that they will lead by example in demonstrating their values in each and every decision. The values must be more than a poster on the wall in the lunchroom, and all team members must ensure that their behaviours are reflective of the values in their everyday work. A good question to ask when in a difficult situation is: Would you be comfortable if this decision or action was posted online? This is an effective way to remind oneself of the importance of being true to the values that are important to you and your team. It is much easier to deal with the politics involved in the bidding and hosting process when you have a strong set of values to help navigate your way through the murky waters of political manoeuvring.

The only way to develop management skills for politics in event bidding and hosting is to develop understandings of the types of political manoeuvres that can come in to play and to practice considering potential responses. Figure 11.1 offers a case study for you to read (consider doing so in small groups), and to consider different potential responses, to determine the impact of each response on a bid and, ultimately, on the hosting of the event.

Read the scenario below and consider the questions posed at the end.

ABC Bid Committee had been working tirelessly for twenty-two months to secure the rights to host the 48th International Multisport Games. They have submitted their bid book to the international governing body and are now planning to host the Bid Evaluation Committee for an on-site visit and tours. Three weeks before the Evaluation Committee visit, the legacy tenant for the planned premier capital facility publicly declares that they will not compete in the new facility unless it is relocated from the previously agreed upon location (which is included in the bid book) to a site with better parking and visibility. The premier facility is a key part of the bid from a community legacy perspective as it would provide much-needed reactional space in a disadvantaged part of the city.

Case Study Questions

1. *Describe the politics at play in the above scenario.*
2. *If you were the Bid Committee CEO, what would you do in response to the legacy tenant's public declaration?*
3. *Who are the key stakeholders you would you reach out to following this announcement?*
4. *What steps should have been taken to prevent before finalizing the bid to avoid this scenario?*
5. *Based on the information outlined in this chapter, do you feel that politics in event bidding and hosting can have a positive impact on the process?*

Figure 11.1 Case study in event bid politics

Conclusions

This chapter examined the role of politics in both event bidding and hosting. The notion of politics has been defined and broken into three phases for discussion. First, the bidding phase was explored and included the initial assessment on whether or not to bid for a specific event, the bid committee competition, development of the bid proposal, and the decision-makers involved in determining the successful bid. Second, the transition and planning phase between bidding and hosting were discussed, followed by the event hosting period. Finally, two key tenets were offered for dealing with the politics of bidding and hosting. The first factor promoted communication as the key element in successful bidding. The second factor was the establishment of core values. Overall, the discussion in this chapter underscores that it is crucial that event managers develop their understandings and abilities to become skilful event political managers.

Chapter questions

1. Select a major event that has been hosted within the past two years and record the event name, year, host city/nation, and a brief definition of the event. Identify four political challenges that could have arisen during the bid phase, how you would eliminate or mitigate them once they had presented themselves, and if you believe anything could have been done to avoid them becoming issues. Please consider both global and local factors when identifying the challenges.
2. Consider the same event selected in question 1. You have now been selected as the Host City. List one possible political scenario that could arise during the first-year post-bid award in each of the following areas: sport program; venues; board of directors membership; and ceremonies.

References

Bason, T., & Grix, J. (2020). Every loser wins: Leveraging 'unsuccessful' Olympic bids for positive benefits. *European Sport Management Quarterly, 23*(1), 167–187. https://doi.org/10.1080/16184742.2020.1838590

Chalip, L., & Fairley, S. (2020). Thinking strategically about sport events. *Sport and Tourism, 23*(4), 155–158. https://doi.org/10.1080/14775085.2020.1732047

de Nooij, M., & van den Berg, M. (2017). The bidding paradox: Why politicians favor hosting mega sports events despite the bleak economic prospects. *Journal of Sport and Social Issues*, *42*(1). https://doi.org/10.1177/0193723517748552

Furlong, J. (2011). *Patriot hearts – Inside the Olympics that changed a country*. Douglas & McIntyre Publishers.

Heerdt, D. (2018). Tapping the potential of human rights provisions in mega-sporting events' bidding and hosting agreements. *The International Sports Law Journal, 17*, 170–185. https://doi.org/10.1007/s40318-018-0129-8

Lee, M. (2006). *The race for the 2012 Olympics: The inside story of how London won the bid*. Virgin Books.

McGillivray, D., Lauermann, J., & Turner, D. (2019). Event bidding and new media activism. *Leisure Studies*, *40*(1), 69081. https://doi.org/10.1080/02614367.2019.1698648

McGillivray, D., Edwards, M., Brittain, I., Bocarro, J., & Koenigstorfer, J. (2018). A conceptual model and research agenda for bidding, planning and delivering major sport events that lever human rights. *Leisure Studies*, *38*(2), 175–190. http://dx.doi.org/10.1080/02614367.2018.1556724

McGillivray, D., & Turner, D. (2018). *Event bidding*. Routledge Taylor & Francis Group.

Merriam-Webster Dictionary. *Politics*. https://www.merriam-webster.com/dictionary/political

.Meza Talavera, A., Al-Ghamdi, S. G., & Koç, M. (2019). Sustainability in mega-events: Beyond Qatar 2022. *Sustainability*, *11*(22), 6407. https://doi.org/10.3390/su11226407

OpenStax. (2022). *Introduction to political science*. OpenStax. https://openstax.org/details/books/introduction-political-science

Sant, S.-L., Misener, L., & Mason, D. (2020). Leveraging sport events for tourism gain in host cities: A regime perspective. *Journal of Sport Tourism, 4*, 203–223. https://doi.org/10.1080/14775085.2019.1711444

Shaw, C. (2008). *Five ring circus: Myths and realities of the Olympic Games*. New Society Publishers.

12 Facilitating quality in event management
Craig Hyatt and Chris Chard

How do you define "quality" with respect to an event manager and their role as a facilitator? In this chapter, we will examine how various theorists have defined quality over time. The theoretical concepts of quality will then be applied to the role of the event manager facilitating the staging of an event. The challenge of defining quality for the role of the event manager will be discussed, and quality statements to guide an event manager will be developed.

Every event manager wants to produce a *quality* event. While this seems a simple and straightforward concept, you must remember that most events have multiple sets of stakeholders such as the participant performers, staff and volunteers, sponsors, and media, along with spectators and/or tourists. Each set of stakeholders can emphasize different criteria when analysing the quality of the event; defining quality is thus complex.

Can an event manager meet all requirements for quality?

Each of the event stakeholders can have different needs when it comes to quality requirements. For example, performers may indicate that quality is based on the equipment, staging, and amenities in the locker room. To the volunteers, a quality event may involve obtaining experience that advances their personal skills and provides them with event clothing. The sponsors may indicate that quality involves having unlimited product sampling opportunities or being able to mingle with clients in a hospitality area. The spectators may want short lines for quick access into the venue, for food and beverages, and excellent sight lines from their seats. Within each of these stakeholder groups, quality is a relative concept. Each person involved in an event will have a personally determined idea as to what quality means. This fact challenges event managers as they need to develop a definition of quality based on their role – generating operational plans and facilitating event production. In order for an event manager to know if they have produced a quality event, understanding definitions of quality is a good place to start.

What is quality?

For decades, both academic theorists and industry practitioners have attempted to define quality. During the first half of the twentieth century, the service industry was not as prevalent as it is today (especially in the sport, recreation, and tourism industries), and the manufacturing and purchasing of durable goods had advanced to be a prominent concern. Here, quality was discussed predominantly in terms of the fabrication of hard goods. During the second half of the last century, there was a gradual shift in our economy's focus from manufacturing to services. The rise of the service industry, including event management, meant a change in how quality was conceptualized. We will consider these two perspectives briefly.

Quality is defined as ruggedness and longevity in the manufacturing industry

Initially, quality was thought of in terms of ruggedness and longevity and was often expressed in terms of meeting measurable specifications for the size and strength of manufactured parts. This meant that quality was the responsibility of the inspectors who assessed the completed goods prior to them leaving the factory – quality controllers. This type of quality process enabled mistakes to be caught and fixed without the consumers ever knowing they once existed.

Definitions for quality in the service industry

Unlike manufactured goods, services are simultaneously produced and consumed, making it very difficult to catch and fix service mistakes without the consumer's knowledge. In this environment, services often require the knowledgeable input of the consumer to ensure a quality outcome. This means that quality is no longer expressed just in terms of physical specifications; it is now conceived in terms of meeting the expectations of the consumer.

Expanded meanings of quality

Reeves and Bednar (1994), in their study of the evolution of the meaning of quality, concluded that the essence of all the various definitions of quality resulted in only four basic categories: *quality is conformance to specifications*; *quality is excellence*; *quality is value*; and *quality is meeting and/or exceeding customers' expectations*. Further, Yoshida and James (2011) promoted three additional definitions of quality including: *aesthetic quality*; *functional quality*; and *technical quality*. Each of these seven definitions of quality will now be discussed (Figure 12.1).

Quality is conformance to specifications

Quality can be defined as the "conformance to requirements or specifications" (Salvi & Kerkar, 2020, p. 26); this perspective provides product or service providers, as well as their consumers, with a standard that can be

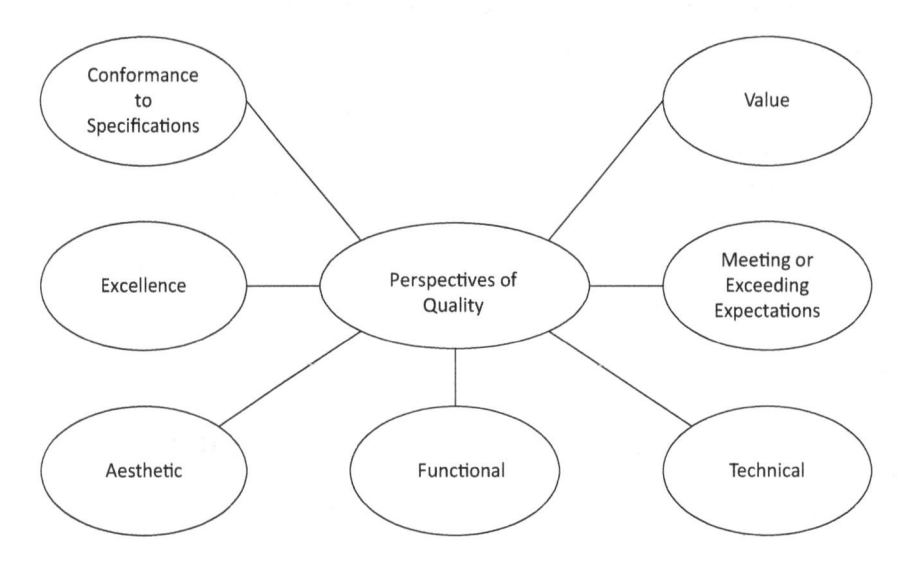

Figure 12.1 Meanings of quality

agreed upon. If a product/service's quality is called into question, the specifications are examined. Here, if the product/service meets the specifications, it is deemed to be of quality; if it does not meet the specifications, it is not.

Quality is excellence

Nguyen et al. (2020) note that a "conventional concept of quality is excellence," and that "a quality product is one that has been perfected" (p. 1049). If an alternative is found to be of higher quality, or superior in perceived excellence, yours may no longer be thought of as quality. When Henry Ford introduced his Model T Ford as a "universal car," he said it must have certain attributes (Ford & Crowther, 1922). This first attribute concerned the quality of materials used:

> Quality in material to give service in use. Vanadium steel is the strongest, toughest, and most lasting of steels. It forms the foundation and super-structure of the cars. It is the highest quality steel in this respect in the world, regardless of price.
>
> (p. 68)

While Ford and Crowther did not define quality as excellence explicitly, it is obvious from his description that excellence was the determining factor of quality. Ford indicated quality steel was the best steel available at any price. Here, quality as excellence means being distinguished as exceptional for a product or service.

Quality is value

It has been noted that there exists a "multidimensionality of the value construct" (Jones et al., 2023). Indeed, price and convenience (Rust et al., 2004), and elements such as physical environment and prestige (Jones et al., 2023), have all been identified as having influence on perceived value. Thus, quality conceived as value implies consumers of less-than-perfect products or services can still perceive them to be of quality if they are positioned financially as providing value. In other words, if you "get what you pay for," then quality transactions involve providing value instead of absolute excellence.

Quality is meeting and/or exceeding customers' expectations

Quality has been conceived of as meeting and/or exceeding customers' expectations. Here, when delivered appropriately, "quality can be interpreted as the expected level of excellence ... [and] to meet the quality of service as expected by the customers, the company must provide excellent service and excellence" (Fatonah, 2019, p. 72). To be sure, in this context, we have all heard the motto "under-promise, over-deliver." In a manufacturing environment, if the expectation for a set of golf clubs is to last four or five seasons, each summer spent golfing with the same clubs beyond this duration may be seen as a bonus – exceeding expectations. However, when it comes to defining expectations for a service, relativity plays a role. For example, in their study of live sport events, Jones et al. (2023) identified comfortable seating as an important variable for facility managers to deliver; however, "comfortable" may mean different things to different people. Indeed, exceeding expectations for those consumers who find a metal bench comfortable would seem to be quite easy; for those consumers looking for plush, spacious reclining chairs, this would appear to be a significant challenge.

Zeithaml et al. (1990) noted that "service quality, as perceived by customers, can be defined as the extent of discrepancy between customers' expectations or desires and their perceptions" (p. 19). This definition is of some use when considering the expectations of event attendees. It acknowledges that each patron is unique and may have unique needs or wants that they wish to fulfil by attending your event. It also notes that the onus is on the attendee to decide if their expectations were fulfilled.

Aesthetic quality

Aesthetic quality focuses on the "interactions between the consumer and the aesthetically pleasing characteristics of the service environment" (Yoshida & James, 2011, p. 21). This type of quality concentrates on the *atmosphere* generated at a sport, recreation, or tourism event. This atmosphere encompasses conditions that elicit excitement, participation, and/or an appreciation of the appearance. Aesthetic quality can be generated with high standards in seating and services, the inclusion of participatory activities, such as athlete signing sessions, consumer tours that allow groups of individuals to walk across a stage, or an event location that is of remarkable natural beauty. Aesthetic quality can be expressed in themes that are displayed in designs and decorations to enhance the atmosphere of an event. The crowd experience is an important and foundational characteristic of aesthetic quality. To be sure however, as highlighted previously, differing opinions exist on these elements of the service delivery making managerial decisions impactful for organizational success. For example, large crowds have been noted to enhance fans' experiences (Uhrich & Benkenstein, 2012); however, more is not always better! Indeed, Jones et al. (2023) found that a packed arena can negatively impact fan experiences.

Functional quality

This next type of quality is based on the "interactions between the customer and functional services" (Yoshida & James, 2011, p. 21). Functional quality, thus, is derived from products and services delivering what they are "supposed to deliver." For example, a bicycle with wheels that will not turn does not deliver functional quality. Similarly, from an event perspective, staff, and volunteer *services*, including *attitudes* and *behaviours*, are a part of the functional quality – an usher who will not direct attendees to their seats does not deliver functional quality. The staff/volunteer function must also be supported with elements such as easy access to the seats, the provision of excellent seating space, as well as crowd density, that is conducive to easy movements. When functional quality exists, the benefits derived by consumers can be substantial; for example, Theodorakis et al. (2019) studied sport consumers (runners) and found that an event's functional service quality was correlated with experiential happiness and even opinions on perceived quality of life.

Technical quality

Finally, technical quality is described by Yoshida and James (2011) as consisting of customers' "overall perceptions of the quality of a core product characterized by features and performance" (p. 16). Specifically, in the context of sport, features, and performance refer to "the activity designed to entertain sports tourists" (Zarei & Ramkissoon, 2021, p. 5). This has some overlap with sections described previously, which makes sense in a dynamic world versus compartmentalizing through static academic frameworks. Here, considering sport, recreation, and tourism events, features can include the time (day/night), season (summer/winter), location (rural/urban), and price (Vassilliadis et al., 2021) of the event.

Craig Hyatt and Chris Chard

A lack of guidance for quality in event management

Current definitions of quality fall short when it comes to event management. Let's briefly re-examine the basic definitions of quality to explore their shortcomings when they are applied to the role of an event manager. To begin, let's consider the definition of "quality as conformance to specifications" in the context of event management. This definition applies when there are, for example, predetermined specifications in a contract for a stage and lighting or for equipment. However, there are no predetermined, agreed-upon specifications for services. Can you imagine getting everyone involved in an event to agree on what, specifically, constitutes an "entertaining" event? What about, how long concession lines should be if an event involves tens of thousands of people? Should service still be able to be provided within a minute or two as some may expect? The specifications for these types of services are not perceived in the same manner by all stakeholders, as they are not predetermined in writing. There is the opportunity for stakeholders to apply their personal idea of specifications. However, even if all of the stakeholders could agree on specifications for many service elements, including entertainment outcomes, the event manager does not have control over all the elements.

When "quality is defined as excellence," there are factors that hinder an event manager from meeting this standard. For instance, resources (financial, human, natural) may not be available to make every component of the event the best it can be. As a result, compromises must be made if, for example, the budget is restrictive. Does this mean that any event that is forced to compromise due to budgetary restrictions should not be staged as it will not be a quality event? If it is staged, with certain conciliations, can an event manager ever meet the standard of quality?

When "quality is defined as value," the notion is that the consumer incurred a financial cost for attending the event. In some cases, however, events are free to spectators. Does this mean that a non-paying customer cannot be disappointed? In such cases, can event managers deliver subpar services because "the event is free?" The answer is clearly no! Even if a spectator incurs no financial cost to watch an event, that person still invested their time and experienced opportunity costs by forgoing other opportunities. These consumers need to know that it is worth the time it takes to attend an event and that quality will be delivered.

Facilitating quality in event management

When "quality is defined as meeting and/or exceeding customers' expectations," not all customer expectations are realistic. Everyone knows that the old adage 'you can't please all of the people all of the time' is something event managers should never forget. For instance, if an event manager facilitates easy parking and venue access, quality food provision, clean restrooms, excellent sight lines, and exciting performers, but the consumer was hoping there would be free childcare, then the evaluation of the event as meeting expectations is based on different categories. Can a food and beverage service offer enough varied cuisine to meet the tastes of all stakeholders? Not every credit card will be accepted at the box office. If the expectations for an event are personally established, is it realistic to believe an event manager can meet and/or exceed all of the expectations for every stakeholder group? It is our contention that some expectations may be unreasonably high. If an event manager used the definition of quality as meeting and/or exceeding expectations to guide their work, could they ever be successful? Would there not always be some of the many stakeholders unhappy? Does this mean the event manager did not produce a quality event?

When quality is defined based on the 'aesthetic quality,' an event manager must create conditions within the operational plan that elicit excitement, participation in, and/or an appreciation of the environment. This can be as simple as decorating a venue. However, generally, an event manager does not have control over this aspect of an event; in medium to large events, generally someone skilled in designing the artistry of the event is hired. The event manager does, however, ensure the operational plans for instituting the event and other areas of aesthetic quality are well planned and executed. Some of these other areas include the need, for example, for high quality seating, but event managers may not have control over ensuring a high level of these types of services at the facilities. The crowd experience, however, is the foundational characteristic of aesthetic quality.

Event managers do have influence in terms of "functional quality." This type of quality means that they must design training for staff and volunteers that includes service level expectations. This can include expected staff and volunteer attitudes and behaviours of the highest level. Some aspects of functional quality, however, are beyond the managers' control. Seat access, seating space, and crowd density can be dictated by the size, age, and type of venue used for the event.

Event managers may be guided by a wish for "technical quality," but it is difficult to ensure this type of quality. Technical quality is based on the participants' behaviours displayed during the sport, recreation, or tourism event. The event manager may attempt to influence this type of quality by offering briefing sessions with the participants, however, the individuals' practical behaviour and the group behaviour between participants is difficult to control. These behaviours are guided by the rules established for each event. Frequent violations can influence the technical quality perceived by event attendees and other stakeholders.

While the definitions of quality in the literature offer good points, none are truly applicable to all types of events. This certainly does not mean that the quest for quality should be disregarded by the event manager. It simply means that every event manager needs to *create a unique quality statement that can guide their work.*

Issues in creating quality statements and defining quality in event management

Creating a guiding quality statement for event management is a difficult task. There are many issues that arise as an event manager attempts to define quality specifically for their role and their tasks. One of the parameters concerning quality statements is to concentrate on the items the event manager can control. You cannot promise a level of excellence if management literally cannot deliver at that level due to circumstances beyond their control. What follows is a list of issues that can directly affect whether or not stakeholders can have their reasonable expectations met. As you will see, many of these issues involve circumstances over which the event manager has little control.

Limited control over inputs influences quality

An event needs inputs. The event manager will need to order supplies from the venue and from outside suppliers. Depending on the nature of the event, you may have to order all items for a media conference to be held prior to the event. For instance, the order may include a platform and tables, along with tablecloths, microphones, chairs for the media, and so on. A technical check is held just prior to the media conference, and all is determined to be working well. However, during the media conference, one microphone has technical problems. Does this constitute an event that does not provide quality, or does the manner in which one handles the issue determine if the event is of quality? If you have a technician on hand to manage the issue or have preplanned the use of an extra microphone for such a case, will this contribute to making a quality event? The answer is obvious. As has been mentioned before, contingency planning is a paramount concern for an event manager.

Financial constraints influence quality

Most event managers must deal with some financial constraints. Here, event managers might not be able to afford the inputs necessary to meet the reasonable expectations of some stakeholders. For example, spectators may wish to purchase high-end items at your souvenir stand, such as embroidered sweatshirts. However, the cost to order these items is high, and given the time it takes for the garment supplier to fill a large custom order, you must place the order weeks in advance. It is prudent to give them a delivery date a few weeks before the actual event as insurance in case of delays. This might mean that you are paying for these sweatshirts before you have any of the cash flows that you would expect to generate during the actual event (same-day ticket sales, or sales at the concession stand, sales at the souvenir stand, etc.). Ideally, the event manager would have sponsors pay part of their sponsorship fees well in advance, and have a budget that takes these advanced cash flows into account. This will help ensure that there is sufficient cash flow long before the day the event opens in order to buy all the quality inputs required. If, however, in the weeks leading up to the event the actual revenue from sponsorship and advanced ticket sales falls short of the projected numbers forecast in the budget, there may not be enough funds available to purchase items such as embroidered sweatshirts. As a result, the event manager may be forced to buy cheaper items (such as silk-screened T-shirts made of a cotton-polyester blend) to stock the souvenir stand. As a consequence, the lack of premium items could create negative associations with quality for this part of the event in the eyes of some consumers.

How can the event manager avoid this type of negative perception? There are no easy answers. Issues of finance and cash flow plague many businesses and organizations. If financial survival depends on selling sponsorships and tickets in advance of the event, then you, the event manager, must educate the sales staff that sales success in the months and weeks before the event is crucial. As for the bigger picture, all students interested in event management may wish to consider learning all they can about the sales process; the quality of your future event may depend on your ability to sell.

Issues in stakeholder expectations as quality perceptions

Keep in mind that you cannot meet and exceed expectations if you do not know the expectations in the first place. If using "meeting and exceeding expectations" as a parameter of quality, be sure to build in a system through which you can hear what the expectations are prior to the event – and then you can work to meet them. An understanding of expectations may come from the evaluation report, from an event held previously, from a survey of upcoming participants, and/or from a live feedback system during the event.

What happens when one stakeholder group has expectations that are in direct conflict with the expectations of another stakeholder group? Consider the potential tension between event performers and sponsors. The title sponsor may have a hospitality area near the action where they entertain existing or potential clients, or host employees that are being rewarded for achieving excellence in their field. As part of a great experience for their guests, the sponsor may wish performers to be available for autographs, photos, and chatting with the guests. The performers, on the other hand, might want to focus on their tasks and may consider time in the hospitality area to be a distraction. As such, they may wish to have no obligation to interact with sponsors or guests. Even when contracted to do so, they may provide only a minimal level of service. How is an event manager expected to facilitate a positive outcome from these two contradictory expectations? By promising the elements she or he can control and making it clear that they cannot deliver certain elements that are outside their control, an event manager can potentially modify a stakeholder's reasonable expectations and facilitate a satisfactory outcome for all parties.

A pre-event survey may be needed to determine the expectations prior to the event so you are not guessing concerning these expectations. If you ask someone their event expectations, however, are you now obligated to meet their opinion on what should happen concerning the event? Their expectation(s) could be beyond your event human, technical, and financial resources, can include contradictory opinion or be outside an event manager's control – the use of meeting and exceeding expectations as a determination of quality of an event is, thus, a complex activity. As you have asked a particular individual or group for their expectations of the event, this may generate an expectation that all articulated statements will be met. An event manager may want to reduce the complexity of this statement of quality and focus on the opinion of specific groups with respect to their expectations. This can, for example, be narrowed to include the event board of directors and the event participants. Further, parameters can be provided when asking for perspectives, such as outlining that there is a requirement to stay within the budget.

Contingency plans influence quality

No event manager needs to be told that things can go wrong. Managers need to plan ahead to identify potential bumps in the road; this planning is vital and necessitates the development of contingency plans. For example, an experienced event manager might anticipate that the food wholesaler may not deliver the exact product that was ordered. In such a case, a contingency plan may empower the director of concessions to call an alternative wholesaler to arrange the delivery of the necessary product. This is straightforward and ensures a quality product. However, not all contingency plans can be implemented in such a straightforward manner. Consider an outdoor event that cannot be held in inclement weather, such as a fireworks show. A simple contingency plan for a fireworks show is to advertise both the specific date (weather permitting) on which the event will be held, and the rain date should the show be cancelled due to bad weather. The problem lies in the unpredictability of bad weather. Imagine your fireworks show is slated to take place at 21:00 on a Saturday, with the following day listed as the rain date. Starting on the Wednesday prior to the event, the weather forecasts call for evening thunderstorms on Saturday. You can be sure that the phone will start ringing that Wednesday and throughout the remainder of the week with worried potential attendees asking if the event will be postponed. Maybe the folks who are calling live a few hours away and plan on leaving home mid-afternoon on Saturday to do some shopping and enjoy dinner before the fireworks. They do not want to spend many hours in the car and not see fireworks. While you understand their situation, you also know that even if the weather forecast is true, an evening thunderstorm might mean rain from 17:30 until 18:30, leaving plenty of time for things to dry out enough for the 21:00 show. Or it could mean rain starting at 23:00, long after the event is over. You also know that for every attendee who could easily attend the event on the rain date, there is one who cannot. Maybe hundreds of tourists have planned a weekend getaway around your event and have hotels booked for Saturday night only, having to return to their hometowns during the day on Sunday. If you postpone the fireworks a day or two in advance and it turns out that things are dry enough at 21:00 on Saturday that you could have had the show, the out-of-town tourists will probably conclude that their reasonable expectations were not met. If you wait until the night of the show and decide to postpone, the folks who drove in that day who just as easily could have rescheduled their day trip until the following day will probably conclude that their reasonable expectations were not met. As the event manager, what can you do?

Unfortunately, the nature of weather forecasting often means the event manager must rely on both the data provided and their gut instincts leading for decisions on the event. If, in the hours leading up to the event it still looks as if there is a reasonable chance that the event can go ahead as scheduled, the event manager may elect to proceed until the skies open just minutes before the start time. If, however, the noon weather forecast clearly shows a massive slow-moving weather system heading your way that meteorologists state will bring six straight hours of heavy rain starting at 19:00, the event manager may announce the postponement of the event at 13:00. In most cases involving inclement weather, the telephones at the event headquarters may ring nonstop before, during, and after the event with folks wanting to know if the event is still proceeding, wanting to know when the decision to cancel (or not) will be made, wanting to know why the decision to postpone the event was not made sooner, wanting to complain that their weekend plans were ruined by the poor decisions of the event staff, etc. The best an event manager can do is to train the staff handling the phones about what to say to the callers and how to say it. If all the staff are briefed on the reasons why decisions to proceed or to postpone are made, they have the opportunity to educate the callers. This education may enlighten the caller to the point where they conclude that their expectations for the event might not have been as reasonable as they thought. In such situations, the caller (who questioned the quality of the event when the phone call was first made) may not have that opinion by the time the phone call is over.

As noted above, although there are difficulties, an event manager is expected to be able to produce work that is of quality. Therefore, they must be able to define a quality statement to guide their work in the development and implementation of event operational plans.

Assignment 1: Evaluate sample quality statements

Below we offer three sample quality statements for three events. The first one is in a sport context, the second a tourism context, and the third a recreation context. While it is debatable whether these quality statements have too much or too little detail, they seem to meet the basic requirements of a quality statement: to define quality and to indicate how quality will be delivered and measured.

Read each event overview and the sample quality statement. Next, evaluate the quality statement as one that can guide an event manager in their work and be used as an evaluation framework to determine if their work is of quality.

Quality statement for Rally in the Valley

Imagine a recreational 3-on-3 basketball tournament that is held annually in a small city in your country. It is organized and managed by a local youth basketball organization, which has named it Rally in the Valley. The tournament is meant to both be a celebration of the game of basketball, and a fundraiser for the organization. Temporary outdoor courts are set-up throughout a park located in a residential neighbourhood near the city's downtown. Dozens of teams, grouped according to age, sex, and skill level, will play games all weekend until winners in each division are determined late on Sunday afternoon. What could a quality statement for Rally in the Valley look like? Here is an example:

> *Rally in the Valley is committed to meeting or exceeding the reasonable expectations of the event's stakeholders, including the players, spectators, sponsors, volunteers, media, and city government. Rally in the Valley management will actively encourage the input of all stakeholder groups for the purpose of mutually determining what constitutes "reasonable expectations." This process will include three key activities that support a quality event. First, a pre- and post-event survey that will be conducted and updated annually, as "reasonable expectations" may change from year to year as the event evolves. Second, a thorough training process to educate the volunteers will be implemented before the event that will empower them to handle routine stakeholder concerns during the event, so that reasonable expectations can be met in a timely manner. Third, communication is key and Rally in the Valley will ensure a system is in place that supports constant radio contact with the volunteers, should non-routine stakeholder concerns arise during the event. In such cases, staff and*

> volunteers will meet with any concerned stakeholder as soon as possible to rectify the concern. Additionally, after the event's completion, Rally in the Valley management will advance their communication activities by making themselves available to meet with concerned stakeholders to hear about and to rectify any issues regarding meeting their reasonable expectations.

Quality statement for Nantou Balloon Fest

Imagine a small town in the picturesque Taiwanese county of Nantou that annually hosts a five day long hot air balloon festival called Nantou Balloon Fest. Hundreds of hot air balloons take to the sky as a quarter of a million visitors converge on the festival grounds during the day and fill the local and regional hotels each night. Local vendors sell balloon-themed arts and crafts, while the food concessions offer a variety of both regional and international cuisine. A children's play area offers face painting, pony rides, a petting zoo, clowns, child-sized carnival rides, and plenty of balloon-themed hands-on activities. What would a quality statement for Nantou Balloon Fest look like? Here is an example below:

> The Nantou Balloon Fest is committed to providing our guests the opportunity to witness world-class hot air ballooning in a spectacular natural setting. We will provide safe, fun, family-friendly surroundings while celebrating the local culture that we offer to the world. The balloonists and visitors will be treated professionally and courteously, and all event staff and volunteers will make all reasonable attempts to satisfy their wants and needs. We are committed to continuously improving this event through our attention to detail. Excellent communication will be fostered as event staff and key volunteers will meet every morning to discuss any ongoing concerns to solve any issues that might impact the event's quality. A further determination of quality is that all efforts will be made to ensure environmental sustainability so this event will be a success for generations to come.

Quality statement for Rocking on the River

Imagine a small city on a river in South Africa. The city government, with the help of corporate sponsors, produces and finances a one-day, mid-summer

Facilitating quality in event management

float fest called Rocking on the River. Thousands of participants in bathing suits float 5km down the river using inner tubes and other floatation devices until they reach a stage on the downtown riverbank where a local band performs. Both the 5km float and the post-float entertainment are free. Food and drinks (both soft drinks and alcoholic drinks) are available for sale. The event produces a very festive atmosphere. What would a quality statement for Rocking on the River look like?

> *Rocking on the River will provide a quality experience to our river floaters, other attendees, sponsors, musicians, media members, residents, and all event staff and volunteers. We will make every attempt to meet or exceed their reasonable expectations. We will both embrace a festive atmosphere while encouraging responsible behaviour so that everyone has a safe experience. Our staff and volunteers will be well-trained and empowered to provide solutions promptly when questions and concerns are brought to their attention. Both during and after the event, attempts will be made to survey the stakeholders to gather data to see if our event met expectations. Staff and key volunteers will meet once this data has been analyzed to determine ways to improve this event in the future. It is our goal to produce a first-class event that stakeholders will want to be involved in for years to come.*

Assignment 2: Generate your quality statement for the work of an event manager

Every event manager who wishes to provide a quality product or service should address the issue by *generating their personal written statement on what quality is based upon* for each event. This quality statement should address the specific definition of quality, and how quality will be applied to the event manager and their generation of event operational plans. In this assignment, you are not looking to meet or exceed the expectations of others involved in the event – only your own expectations of your work as a facilitator in generating operational plans, managing staff and volunteers and event implementation.

To be sure, there is no "one way" to create a quality statement for evaluating your own work. A quick internet search reveals a large number of organizations attempting to create quality statements. The quality statement can be as short as two sentences and as long as multiple pages. If a statement is too short, there is a chance that it will be so vague as to be meaningless. If it is too long, it might not be practical enough to serve as a useful guide.

Think of an event that you see yourself managing soon or in the future. Take some time right now to create a quality statement for this event with a focus on quality in the work that you will complete as an event manager. Consider what the literature offers when defining quality and what elements you can use from this literature. Consider also that the event may currently have a mission statement, vision statement, and a statement of values. Your quality statement should be congruent with these other event statements. The difference is that in this case, *the quality statement you are developing must guide your work as a facilitator* and needs to be available as a realistic platform through which to articulate your expectations and determine a framework for quality event management, to allow you to evaluate your work throughout and at the end of an event. This implies that you cannot use the meeting and exceeding of the expectations of others in this assignment. Your quality statement needs to seamlessly integrate the facilitation activities that you are personally responsible for as an event manager. This statement guides your work and is used as an evaluation tool post event.

Conclusions

No event manager wants to put in countless hours dedicating their time and energy to end up staging an event that lacks quality. All the careful planning leading up to the event must be done with quality in mind. Because of the unique components of each event, managers must define quality in a way that makes sense for their situation. To better ensure that their conceptualization of quality is met, they must also institute policies in a quality statement that are meaningful and easy to implement. Managers should also be mindful that other issues (such as conflicting stakeholder expectations, limited control over inputs, financial constraints, and contingency planning) can create challenges for anyone wishing to facilitate a quality event. Event management is a complex and challenging field; a personally established statement of quality to guide the facilitation of an event is a key element in succeeding in this industry.

Chapter questions

1. Describe the characteristics of the seven different definitions of quality (including conformance to specifications, excellence, value, meeting or exceeding customers' expectations, aesthetics, functional, and technical quality) and show how these definitions can guide event managers.
2. Discuss how stakeholder perceptions, limited control, financial constraints, and contingency plans affect an event manager striving for quality.
3. Consider a specific sport, recreation, or tourism event and generate a guiding quality statement for the event manager. Record the issues that arise as you attempt to create a definitive guiding quality statement.
4. Consider the same event as above (#3) and list three or four items that you think would be expected by different stakeholder groups (such as the participant performers or athletes, the staff and volunteers, the sponsors, and the media, along with spectators and/or tourists) to consider the event of a high quality.
5. Discuss why quality can be an elusive concept in event management and how knowledge of quality can aid you in your work as an event manager.
6. With the complexity discussed above concerning quality as meeting and exceeding expectations, can this aspect be truly used in a quality statement devised to evaluate an event quality and the quality of the work completed by an event manager?
7. Using various definitions of quality, complete Assignment 1 above and evaluate the sample quality statements.
8. Complete Assignment 2 above and generate a statement of quality that can be used to guide your work as an event manager generating event operational plans, along with facilitating staff and volunteers, and overseeing event implementation.

References

Fatonah, S. (2019). The role of mediation of customer satisfaction in service quality relationship on hospital patient loyalty in Indonesia. *International Journal of Supply Chain Management, 8*(4), 72–78. https://core.ac.uk/download/pdf/230748112.pdf

Ford, H., & Crowther, S. (1922). *My life and work*. Doubleday Page.

Jones, C. W., Byon, K. K., Williams, A. S., & Pedersen, P. M. (2023). Live events and the sport customer: A sport spectator quality-value-behavior model. *Journal of Global Sport Management, 8*(1), 340–360. https://doi.org/10.1080/24704067.2020.1846908

Nguyen, Q., Nguyen, D. V., Chu, N. N. M., & Tran, V. H. (2020). Application of total quality management in developing quality assessment model: The case of Vietnamese higher education. *The Journal of Asian Finance, Economics and Business, 7*(11), 1049–1057. https://koreascience.kr/article/JAKO202032462597233.page

Reeves, C. A., & Bednar, D. A. (1994). Defining quality: Alternatives and implications. *Academy of Management Review, 19*(3), 419–445. http://doi.org/10.2307/258934

Rust, R. T., Lemon, K. N., & Zeithaml, V. A. (2004). Return on marketing: Using customer equity to focus marketing strategy. *Journal of Marketing, 68*(1), 109–127. https://doi.org/10.1509/jmkg.68.1.109.24030

Salvi, S. S., & Kerkar, S. S. (2020). Quality assurance and quality control for project effectiveness in construction and management. *International Journal of Engineering Research & Technology (IJERT), 9*(2), 26–29. https://doi.org/10.17577/IJERTV9IS020028

Theodorakis, N. D., Kaplanidou, K., Alexandris, K., & Papadimitriou, D. (2019). From sport event quality to quality of life: The role of satisfaction and purchase happiness. *Journal of Convention & Event Tourism, 20*(3), 241–260. https://doi.org/10.1080/15470148.2019.1637805

Uhrich, S., & Benkenstein, M. (2012). Physical and social atmospheric effects in hedonic service consumption: Customers' roles at sporting events. *The Service Industries Journal, 32*(11), 1741–1757. https://doi.org/10.1080/02642069.2011.556190

Vassiliadis, C. A., Mombeuil, C., & Fotiadis, A. K. (2021). Identifying service product features associated with visitor satisfaction and revisit intention: A focus on sports events. *Journal of Destination Marketing & Management, 19*, 100558. https://doi.org/10.1016/j.jdmm.2021.100558

Yoshida, M., & James, J. (2011). Service quality at sporting events: Is aesthetic quality a missing dimension? *Sport Management Review, 14*, 13–24. http://doi.org/10.1016/j.smr.2009.06.002

Zarei, A., & Ramkissoon, H. (2021). Sport tourists preferred event attributes and motives: A case of Sepak Takraw, Malaysia. *Journal of Hospitality and Tourism Research, 45*(7). http://dx.doi.org/10.1177/1096348020913091

Zeithaml, V. A., Parasuraman, A., & Berry, L. L. (1990). *Delivering quality service: Balancing customer perceptions and expectations*. The Free Press.

Conclusions
Lorne J. Adams

Event management – it sounds finite. It sounds like a discrete point in time. Indeed, it has a beginning and an end point, but event management is certainly not static. It is best to view events as dynamic, complex, and ever-changing entities. No two events are the same; what worked in one situation may not necessarily work in a similar but different situation. That is why this text does not provide you with a series of prescribed checklists that you can simply mark off as you go along. While checklists are helpful, they are static and do not, cannot, take into account new events and contingencies that you will have to deal with.

There is an old baseball adage that "you can't steal second with your foot on first." If you remain there you will be safe, and to take steps toward second base increases your discomfort and your risk of a potential negative outcome. However, taking a lead can potentially help you accomplish a goal and also help your team succeed.

We feel you have successfully made it safely to first. You have some experiences and are in a programme that can help you achieve your goals. It's time to step off first, to take a risk, to learn new things, to try new things, examine new approaches and explore the many paths of becoming an event manager.

We have spent some time introducing you to some theories that support the notions of change, contingency, and complexity. We suggest that you do further reading in that area. A sound theoretical framework will provide you with an anticipatory mindset that will help you deal with deviation and with inevitable unforeseen issues. In fact, a message that we have delivered is the need for anticipation in the short term and anticipation in the long term. As a critical element in the dynamic system of event management, you should now understand that anything you do has the potential to affect many other things. Some of those outcomes will be positive, others will create unforeseen outcomes.

We have also stressed the importance of setting goals and writing them with clarity. Goals need to be communicated clearly to everyone involved. The less clarity, the greater the chance for misinterpretation, and we want everyone to be on the same page and heading in the same direction. You will note throughout the text how often the need for clear goals is expressed both directly and indirectly.

Further, we have spent a good deal of time talking about planning and committing that planning into a written format. We have pointed out the need to plan using the three horizons, that includes a focus on the current situation, and positioning the event for 3–5 years and 6–10 years into the future. You should also be aware that planning exists on a continuum, with overplanning and underplanning as polar opposites. The more uncertain we are, the greater the tendency to overplan. The concrete act of planning can become a trap; it can become an end in itself. Immersing yourself in the process feels good; it feels like you are actively involved in problem solving, and it produces a highly detailed, visible product – the plan of the event. The more certain we are about an event, perhaps through having done it a number of times, the greater the tendency to underplan. You know what to do because you've been there before, or "this is the way it has always been done." Unfortunately, this approach leads to many assumptions about, for instance, who is responsible for what, or what needs to be done. Because the plan is unstated, the chance for oversight or misinterpretation increases dramatically.

Somewhere between these polar extremes is the amount of planning that is right, not only for the event but also for the people involved. Where is that magic place that is not too much and not too little? Unfortunately, there is no way of prescribing where that might be. It is, as we have already mentioned, in those indeterminate zones (Schön, 1983) that go beyond simply what you have been taught. Experience will help you find that place. As an emerging professional, take the opportunity to volunteer at different events and to do as many different jobs as you can. As you begin to see events from different perspectives, you will see how written plans affect your particular function. You will then be developing "event sense" in the same way experiences in the lived world help you develop common sense. You will learn that there are very few absolutes either in life or in event management. There are lots of

Conclusions

examples of "sometimes," "in many cases," "in general," "based on my experience." While the running of an event could be seen as the most exciting piece of the process, we have pointed out that this phase too is not without its issues and problems. In Chapter 7, Greco pointed to some of the issues that can arise, but also provided a number of best practices from experts in the field. These experiences and insights can help you form your own ways of resolving problems unique to your own situation.

We have also pointed out the need to analyse events. It is essential to analyse errors, where they might have come from, what processes were in place that set the stage for their occurrence, and so forth. At some point in time, you will accept your own fallibility – that sometimes errors are a direct result of our own action or inaction, that we tend to court disaster in our own unique ways through prior experience, bias, or ability. Error, however, is only a small part of the overarching need for evaluation. Once again, though, evaluation needs to be placed in context. For what purpose, to what end is evaluation being conducted? What is or should be evaluated? These questions have been posed in previous pages, and we have tried to give you a reasonable starting point to answer them.

We have borrowed a line from a popular song, "You ain't seen nothing yet," as a title for a chapter on environmental sustainability within this text. While it may at first seem like a strange thing to do, we believe that the sentiment of the line rings true when it comes to how we think about and what we do for the environment. The chapter is rife with examples of organizations and associations that have not only thought about environmental stability but have mandates that environmental sustainability be an integral part of hosting events from grassroots levels to the world's premier events. Environmental sustainability has moved on from being a catchphrase through which one could pay lip service to the concept but essentially not change one's behaviour. Environmental sustainability is now targeted, measurable, and an essential component of event management. This enhanced concern and action leads us to believe we are merely on the threshold of what can be done and, in truth, "You ain't seen nothing yet!"

We live in a dynamic, changing world and we now recognize that what we do in the name of event management can have long-lasting and permanent effects on our most valuable resource – the environment we live in. It is essential that we consider carefully what these impacts might be and how they might be mitigated. As Dingle indicated, our resilience and ability to adapt to a changing environment will be an essential skill as an event manager. The section on environmental sustainability should provide you with a sense of the reach that events can have, and also how you might manage some of the responsibilities that ensue.

Event management is a human initiative with many interested stakeholders, both within and outside the event management team. Not everyone has the same agenda and indeed, there may even be some opposition to what you are trying to accomplish. Trying to navigate your way through and around some of these political issues will challenge you as an event manager. As we have pointed out, even small local events are not immune to the potential effects of political manoeuvring. On a much larger scale, using events for political gain has become a geopolitical tool. The sense is that by focusing on all the potential positive outcomes from hosting large international events, basic issues such as human rights garner less attention from international scrutiny. Certainly the hosting of the World Cup of Soccer in Qatar and the emergence of the Saudi Arabian LIV golf tour have highlighted the attempt to mask human rights issues. While some of the "politics" can be anticipated readily, some other political concerns can be far less obvious and require an anticipatory mindset or that you "read" the situation properly. It is a skill set that will be developed over time as you increase your base of knowledge and experience.

As an event manager, you will be confronted with many challenges and choices that need to be made to ensure a quality event and a quality experience for all parties involved. You are therefore expected to act in an ethical manner – not a small task. We have provided some frameworks to help you develop this advanced skill. Once again, careful thought and a sense of the "big picture" will help you navigate your way through an, at times, difficult process.

Finally, you will note that many of the examples we have used pertain to big events, such as the Olympic Games or other major attractions. These examples clearly provide information about the multi-level detail and advanced preparation required to successfully host these spectacles. It would be a mistake, however, to conclude that events on a much smaller scale require little thought and would not benefit from the processes described in this text. From a charity dance to a banquet or a small golf tournament, the process is the same – only the scale differs. We are confident that what you have been provided with will equip you to be a successful event manager.

Many different authors have tried to bring their experience to bear and to condense a vast amount of knowledge into manageable and useful sketches

Conclusions

that will help you develop the tools to be a successful event manager. None of the chapters in this text are intended to be conclusive. We have recommended throughout the text that you continue to read in the various areas – to develop common knowledge that will help you develop advanced knowledge. Some of the chapters will seem like they are speaking directly to you; they will resonate with your experience, skills, and present abilities. Some of the chapters you will struggle with. They will take you outside the comfort zone of your present skills and abilities. This is the place you want to be. It is where the greatest development will take place. Spend time with them until you are comfortable, and then seek out the next place of discomfort. We have mentioned in several places that events will grow and evolve – so will you. If the previous pages have been or can be an agent in that evolution, we have done our job.

Index

3 C's of effective decision-making 148
3 P's of sustainability 188
5 P's of evaluation 160
5 P's of implementation 140

adaptation: incremental 38, 180, 191, 200; transformative 10–11, 179–80, 192, 245

best practices 14, 20, 24, 115–16, 121–2, 129, 135, 205, 212, 277
bidding: bid dossier 223–7, 235–7, 244, 249; bid questionnaire 223–8, 234–5, 237; bid tour 228–9, 231, 235–7; candidature document 223–4, 227–8, 234, 237; critical factors 223, 229, 233, 236–7; feasibility study 223–4, 237

carbon 185; calculator 204; cycle 177; emissions 202–4; fibre 213; footprint 175, 183, 190–1, 196, 204; impact 204, 208; neutrality 201–5, 215; offsets 204–15; output 204; pricing 180; strategy 200
collaborative individualism 8
communication 3, 9, 28–35, 37, 40, 42, 46, 49–50, 64, 67, 72, 80–1, 85, 116, 118–24, 152–3, 161, 171, 185, 202, 203, 234–7, 251–2, 254, 269–70; lines 28; process 28, 50, 133; requirements 24, 27, 29–34, 87–8; skill 57; style/structure 3, 19, 28, 81; system 12, 16, 45, 51–2, 78–80, 143–4, 147, 231–2
conflict: affective 147–9, 162; cognitive 148–9, 163

contingency; issues 37–8, 43, 51, 53–5, 64, 76–81, 84; plans 78–9, 86, 88, 141–2, 144, 229, 265–7, 272–3, 275
control: perceived 145; scope 145

decisions: nonprogrammed 144; programmed 79, 144

ecological footprint 175, 183, 186–7
environmental sustainability 1, 3, 21, 29, 49–50, 64, 175, 177, 180–1, 183–4, 188–92, 199–203, 205, 208–15, 232–3, 237; awareness *see* 'carbon'; life cycle assessment 175, 183–5, 187; resilience 82, 178–80, 191, 277; triple bottom line 175, 183–4; triple top line 175, 183–4; vulnerability 128, 178–9, 183, 192, 208; waste management 177, 181–2, 184–5, 189–91, 203, 205–7, 209, 213–14, 233; Water management 177, 181–2, 185–6, 188, 190, 199, 202, 205–7, 209, 215, 233
evaluation: context evaluation 166; empowerment approach 165; formative 172; goal-based approach 163; goal-free approach 163–4, 167; input evaluation 166; process evaluation 166; product evaluation 166; professional judgment approach 166–7; responsive approach 164; summative 172; swot analysis 167–8; system approach 165; the Three Horizons 171–2
event components: accommodation 1, 17, 35, 38, 45–6, 51, 67, 69, 81–3, 186, 190–1, 213, 225–6,

Index

229, 231, 246; accreditation 1, 17, 35, 45, 48, 67, 80, 82–3, 87, 161, 225; ceremonies (opening, closing, awards) 1, 17, 35, 67, 82–3, 96, 102, 226, 228, 246, 251, 254; communications 19, 30, 35, 40, 67, 120, 161, 189, 231, 235–6; competition management 9, 11, 35, 37–8, 168, 179, 204, 225, 228, 230, 249; diversity and inclusion 19, 28, 70, 147; drug testing/doping control 35, 48, 236; finance/ economics 19, 116–17, 119, 121, 123, 127, 157, 160, 166, 168, 170–1, 178, 183–4, 188–91, 199, 223–6, 230, 232, 242, 265, 270; food beverage management/service 1, 17, 35, 45, 49, 52, 67, 81–2, 84, 87–8, 185, 206–8, 256, 262–3, 267, 270–1; hospitality 35, 67, 83, 105–14, 256, 266; human resource management 1, 19, 35, 37, 58, 120, 122, 134, 156, 189, 224, 231; Legal (transactions/contracts) 19, 45, 48, 50–1, 64, 135, 175, 188–9, 225–6, 248–9; marketing 7, 19, 82, 156, 171–2, 189, 213, 225, 232, 236; media 1, 16–17, 19, 30, 35, 60, 63, 67, 74, 81–2, 85, 87–8, 117, 123–4, 126–7, 168, 225–6, 231, 233, 247, 251, 256, 264, 269, 271, 273; medical services 1, 35, 53, 78, 80, 88, 226; merchandising 35, 251; officials (for competition) 1, 35, 69, 124, 210; protocol management 35, 47–8, 54, 61, 80, 118–19, 121, 124–6, 230, 242, 247, 251; public relations 1, 17, 19, 123; sales 19, 171–2, 191, 225, 265; security/safety 1, 17, 35–6, 67, 78, 80, 82, 87–8, 92–5, 98–9, 101–2, 161, 224–6; spectator services 36, 67, 205, 208, 215, 256, 262, 265, 269, 273; sponsorship 19, 127, 156, 168, 225, 236, 246, 265; ticketing 1, 17, 36, 161, 213, 224–5; transportation & parking 1, 17, 36, 45, 48, 50–1, 53, 67, 74, 76–8, 81–4, 87, 97–104, 126, 161, 177, 183, 185, 203, 209, 213, 224–6, 229, 231, 253, 263

facilitation 24–7, 30–4, 42–3, 45, 55, 64, 147, 148, 149, 151–2, 229, 236, 272
feasibility study 223–4, 237
flexibility effect 2–4, 15, 19–21, 32

game-within-the-game (GWG) *see* 'politics'
goals 27–8, 30, 45–6, 50, 56–7, 59, 61–2, 64, 71–2, 116, 124, 137, 139, 143, 145, 152, 157–8, 161–3, 165–9, 183–4, 210, 223, 275–6
governance - event structure/principles 29, 34–6, 39–43, 47, 56–7, 120, 122, 134, 162, 211, 233, 236, 245

innovation and entrepreneurship 4, 8–9, 19, 206, 213–14

knowledge: advancement knowledge 2, 12–15, 17–19, 22, 43, 74, 79, 121, 129, 141, 143, 175, 200, 213, 230, 279; base/background 8, 13, 33–4, 68, 155, 157, 172, 278; common knowledge 2, 12–18, 22, 43, 74, 79, 228, 237, 279; development 1, 4, 12, 19–20, 27, 30, 239; differentiation 3, 5, 15, 21; enbrained knowledge 15, 22; encultured knowledge 14, 17, 22; management/issues 24, 115–16, 118, 120, 122, 129–30, 135, 146–7; rating your event knowledge 15–20; sharing/transfer 24–5, 32–4, 36, 39, 116, 121; Tacit 140–1, 152

network/strategic alliances 1, 19, 28, 33, 40, 42, 46–7, 60, 67–76, 83–4, 86, 88, 122, 137–8, 144–7, 149–51, 156, 201, 209, 226, 230–2, 235–7

objectives 29, 45–6, 50, 56, 59, 61, 64, 71, 124, 128, 137, 139, 141, 146, 157–8, 161–8, 210, 223

perspicacity 2–4, 11–12, 14–15, 20–1, 34
plogging 202, 215
policy 16, 19, 36, 39–52, 55, 61–2, 64–5, 125–7, 129, 181, 210, 212, 214–15, 239, 241; congruence in policy 49, 64, 210, 214
politics/political games/game-with-the-game 19, 84–6, 115, 117, 124–7, 231, 239–44, 246–54, 278
production meeting 84, 120, 137–9, 149, 151–2

relationships: building relationships 33, 79, 201, 231–2, 235; group

Index

relationships 26, 30–1, 54, 117–18, 165, 240; managing relationships 128–9; network relations 201; organizational relationships 42, 48–9, 234; public relationships 1, 17–19; relational dynamics 49, 52–4, 188; relational politics 240, 251; relationship issues 122–3, 129–30, 135; relationship marketing 231; reporting relationships 35; sharing 116; symbiotic relationships 62–3

scope control 145

theory: agency theory 69, 71–2, 89; appreciative theory 211, 215; complexity theory 36, 39, 41–3, 69–70, 89, 162, 169; contingency theory 36–9, 41–3, 69–70, 76, 89, 169; coordination theory 116, 129–30; dissipative structures 37–8, 42–3, 69–71; facilitation theory 25–6; institutional theory 170; process theory 169; relational coordination theory 116, 129; resource dependency theory 170; systems theory 36–7, 41–3, 141, 169; theory of change 169; theory of marginal gains 69, 72, 88
Three Horizons 171–3, 276

value(s) 8, 13, 26, 28–30, 47, 49, 56, 61, 63–4, 85, 126, 134, 139–40, 156, 158–9, 164, 166, 172, 176, 180, 184–6, 199, 207, 244, 252–4, 258–9, 262, 271–2

weaving 74–5, 88

Taylor & Francis Group
an informa business

Taylor & Francis eBooks

www.taylorfrancis.com

A single destination for eBooks from Taylor & Francis with increased functionality and an improved user experience to meet the needs of our customers.

90,000+ eBooks of award-winning academic content in Humanities, Social Science, Science, Technology, Engineering, and Medical written by a global network of editors and authors.

TAYLOR & FRANCIS EBOOKS OFFERS:

- A streamlined experience for our library customers
- A single point of discovery for all of our eBook content
- Improved search and discovery of content at both book and chapter level

REQUEST A FREE TRIAL

support@taylorfrancis.com

Routledge Taylor & Francis Group
CRC Press Taylor & Francis Group